A LOT OF LOOSE ENDS

A vet in Africa

ROLAND MINOR

A LOT OF LOOSE ENDS

A vet in Africa

MEMOIRS

Cirencester

Published by Memoirs

MEMOIRS
PUBLISHING

25 Market Place, Cirencester, Gloucestershire, GL7 2NX
info@memoirsbooks.co.uk www.memoirspublishing.com

ISBN 978-1-909304-72-7

Printed in England

PREFACE

Popular imagination may well be excused for thinking that most veterinary activity in Africa is related to wildlife, thanks to the numerous books and television documentaries. This, in fact, is far from the truth. Most veterinary work is related to the control and eradication of livestock diseases — an endeavour which has occupied much of my career.

Life is precarious for many of the pastoralist and agro-pastoralist groups which live in the marginal, low-rainfall areas which cover a great part of the African continent. Food and water are essential requirements for survival. In some years crop production may be adequate, but in many years the rains come late or last for too short a period for a good harvest. At worst, there may be total crop failure. In such an event pastoralists have to rely totally on their herds and flocks for their survival.

With such uncertainties afflicting the lives of millions of people in marginal areas, the prevention of animal diseases removes one hazard from their insecure lives. And although it does not remove the hazard of their animals' deaths from thirst and starvation, their better health boosts their chances of survival.

There is another disadvantage in this day and age which afflicts the lives of pastoral people. Many of them are obliged by their search for water and grazing to lead peripatetic lives. This seriously limits their access to modern educational facilities. As a consequence they have little political power and are disparaged by their educated, urban compatriots, with the result that their grazing lands are alienated for game parks, large scale agricultural projects and other purposes. And yet the same pastoral people are the most efficient users of the lands in which they live and, despite the very low levels of investment in their areas, make a substantial contribution to the gross national products of their countries. A comparatively small investment in disease control is therefore money well spent.

CONTENTS

ACKNOWLEDGEMENTS

My old sailing companion Barry Mitchell may have much to answer for. Over a number of years he has constantly pressed me to commit my memories to paper.

Equally answerable, were she still alive, would be the late Cynthia Salvadori. Cynthia was an acknowledged anthropologist and historian with experience of some of the pastoral peoples of Kenya, southern Ethiopia and southern Sudan and an encyclopaedic knowledge, so her assistance was most helpful and her urgent enthusiasm to read the next chapter acted as a goad, compelling me to get on with the task. As each chapter came off the printer she suggested various changes and improvements.

I am also grateful to a number of friends, colleagues and others for their assistance including David and Carol Anderson, Gitta Ashworth, David Dyson, Tim Fison, Graham Greener, Jeremy Howat, Else Iversen, Frederick Kayanja, Moetapele Letshwenyo, the late Bosco Lopeyok, Jino Meri, Paul Rossiter, Maurice Rumboll, Michael Soltys, Errol Trzebinski, Stuart Watson and Roger Windsor. Their assistance has been essential because inevitably in writing any memoir there are questions of fact that need verification and there is also a grave danger in re-telling an old story of embellishing it and in the re-telling over many years the embellishments become the 'true story' so I was reassured to have confirmation in a number of instances that the original accounts of many events had not been forgotten.

Any errors of fact or opinion are in no way the fault of any of the above but entirely mine.

LIST OF ACRONYMS

ADC - Assistant District Commissioner
AHA - Animal Health Assistant
AHRC - Animal Health Research Centre (Entebbe)
BMC - Botswana Meat Commission
BVI - Botswana Vaccine Institute
CBPP - Contagious Bovine Pleuropneumonia
CFT - Complement Fixation Test
CID - Criminal Investigation Department
CTVM - Centre for Tropical Veterinary Medicine (Edinburgh)
DANIDA - Danish International Development Agency
DC - District Commissioner
DEFRA - Department of the Environment, Food and Rural Development, U.K.
DVO - District Veterinary Officer
DZ - Debre Zeit (a town in Ethiopia)
EATRO - East African Trypanosomiasis Research Organization
EAVRO - East African Veterinary Research Organization
ECF - East Coast fever
EEC - European Economic Community
FAO - Food & Agriculture Organization of the United Nations (Rome)
FMD - Foot-and-mouth disease
IRA - Irish Republican Army
JAVMA - Journal of the American Veterinary Medical Association
KBF - Karamoja Buggerance Factor
MAFF - Ministry of Agriculture, Fisheries and Food (UK)
MBU - Mosquito Biology Unit
OIE - Office International des Epizooties
PARC - Pan African Rinderpest Campaign
PDU - Project Development Unit (Southern Sudan)
PMO - Provincial Medical Officer
PVO - Provincial Veterinary Officer
RMS - Royal Mail Ship
RSPCA - Royal Society for the Prevention of Cruelty to Animals.
TA - Technical Assistant
TCV - Tissue Culture Vaccine; for protection against rinderpest
USAID - United States Agency for International Development
VSO - British Voluntary Service Organization, a volunteer therein
WFP - World Food Programme

This book is dedicated to the many Africans who have assisted me
in my work and in particular to

Ahmed Hamza Fundi
and
Kadhi Athman Abubakr

in grateful recognition of their loyal support
and friendship over four decades.

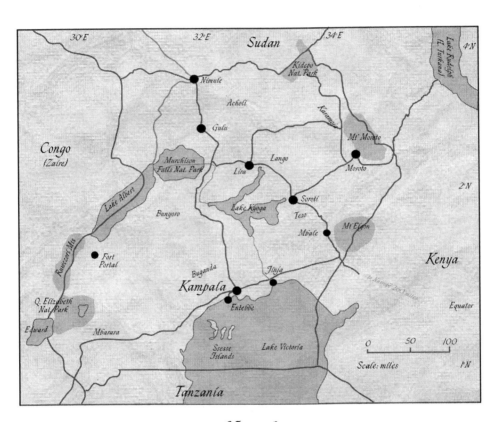

Uganda

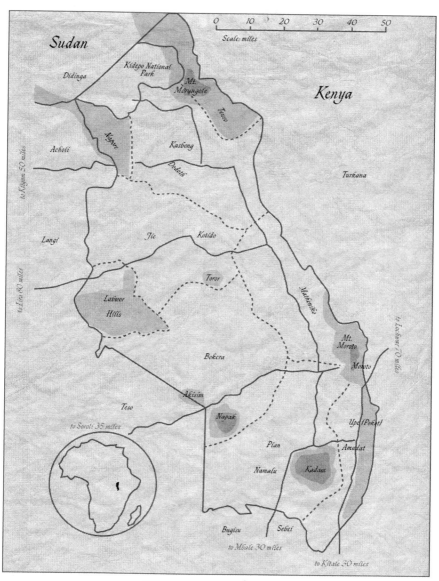

Karamoja District

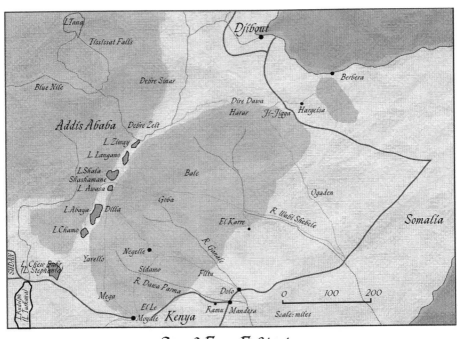

South East Ethiopia

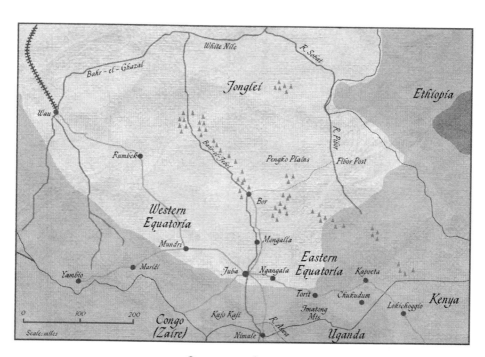

Southern Sudan

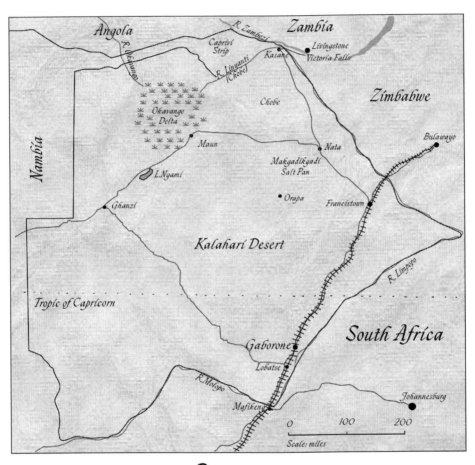

Botswana

CHAPTER 1

An Argentine boyhood

It is generally considered that a story should have a beginning, a middle and an end, even if sometimes these become disordered chronologically. This story has not reached its end, for if it had I would not be writing it. I have no recollection of the beginning, but I have been told that I first saw the light of day in the German Hospital in Buenos Aires a few days after the New Year of 1939, though the phrase 'light of day' is not quite accurate because, according to my birth certificate, it was 2.55 a.m.

My arrival was unexpected. It was not that my parents were ignorant of the facts of life or had been unaware of my mother's increasing girth. In fact my birth was preceded by the arrival of an identical twin brother ten minutes earlier. I was the runner up, a fact of which I was frequently reminded in later years, particularly by my grandmothers. Paradoxically I was legally older than my brother, for by Argentine law, derived, I am told, from the Napoleonic Code, the second-born of twins is the older. The logic behind this somewhat anomalous law is that the second-born is higher up the uterus and therefore was conceived first. It is certainly anomalous in the case of identical twins, who are conceived simultaneously. However, neither of my grandmothers cared much for Argentine law.

My father was not pleased on finding he was the father of twins. As we were some weeks premature and covered with downy hair, his first comment on seeing us was that he was now convinced of the Darwinian theory of evolution, a comment for which he was rebuked by the ward sister.

The name Philip had long been chosen for the first-born son to commemorate my father's father, who had been killed fighting with the Durham Light Infantry in France in 1918. It was therefore left to my mother to choose a name for the second born. She chose Raymond to please her father, but when my father reached the Registry Office in Buenos Aires he could only remember that the name started with an R, so he called me Roland which has been my name ever since. There had been a Roland Minor in the family, killed in France in 1916, but as my father was only four years old at the time he had been unaware of his existence. That Roland had been an only son, so that side of the family, who were never told of my father's error, were delighted that I should be called after him. This was of some benefit to me later in life.

My father's error has been of benefit in another way, since I can blame my frequent inability to remember names on a possible genetic disorder I acquired from him.

We were not the first set of twins in the family. My paternal grandfather, Philip, had been a twin and a great-grandfather on my mother's side had also been a twin. That great-grandfather, father of my mother's father, was Walter Raleigh Gilbert Hickey. With such a name, with a father who had been in the army and two uncles who became generals, he probably had little choice but to make a career in the army.[1] Accordingly, he entered the Woolwich

---

[1] The two uncles were Major-General Sir Walter Raleigh Gilbert and Major-General Lord Robert Kerr, the youngest son of the 5th Marquess of Lothian.

Military Academy, from which he passed out first and was presented with the sword of honour by the Prince Consort. He then joined the Royal Engineers and was sent to India. There he transferred to the East India Railway Company, which probably paid better than the army. He fathered seven children and died of jaundice in Calcutta in 1872, when my grandfather, the youngest, was only two, leaving a widow to continue in genteel poverty in Berkshire until she died in 1902.

Walter Raleigh Gilbert Hickey's father, William Hickey, my great-great-grandfather, was an Irishman from Dublin. He had obtained a commission in the 41st Regiment of Foot in 1813 at the age of 19, but was put on half pay in 1817, as many of his contemporaries had been after the end of the Napoleonic Wars. In 1819 he married Frances Isabella Gilbert, the daughter of a clergyman from a well-known West of England family. Following his marriage, he went to India, where he was appointed Adjutant of the Calcutta Native Militia but resigned from military service after a few years and went into business and died of cholera in Calcutta in 1841. Among other appointments, he was secretary to the Board of Superintendence for improving the breed of native cattle. Since I only became aware of this in recent years, I could not knowingly have been influenced by it in my choice of career.

On the other hand my paternal family, the Minors, apart from the brief military careers of two of them in World War I, were not a military family. The first reliable record I have of any ancestor is of a Walter Myners who was baptised in Baswick, Staffordshire, and died there in 1640. He was described as a husbandman.[2] He was followed by several generations of yeoman farmers with widespread holdings in Staffordshire and Shropshire.

[2] The College of Arms has evidence that the Mynors or Miners had lived in Uttoxeter, Staffordshire, prior to the 17th century with a pedigree stretching back to Roger de Myners who lived in the reign of King John.

By the middle of the 19th century the family had abandoned farming and my great-grandfather had become a solicitor in Manchester. His son, my grandfather Philip, in time became an architect. According to family history, this profession was considered so effete that he was urged to move away from Manchester, whereupon he set up his plate in Darlington, County Durham.

It was my great-uncle, Harold Henman, who was the cause of my maternal grand-parents emigrating to Argentina. After fighting in the Boer War he had been reluctant to return to England and had taken ship to Buenos Aires from Cape Town to try his luck there. The British expatriate community in Argentina was large and much involved in ranching, railways and shipping. So numerous were they that not only did they establish numerous sporting clubs and other facilities such as schools and a hospital around Buenos Aires but they had their own exclusive telephone directory.

Finding Argentina agreeable, my great-uncle Harold persuaded his sister (my grandmother) and her husband to join him in business. In this my grandfather had hoped that his mother's brother, who had been the first Anglican bishop of the Falkland Islands and South America,[3] would give him an entry into British society in Argentina, he but soon found that the merchants of Mammon were uninterested in his episcopal links.

In 1911 my mother Carol was born, the second of five sisters. Harold's wife, my great-aunt Eve, was reputedly a great snob, as was my grandfather. She took a house in Bexhill in the 1920s while her five children were being educated in England. A story is told of her thinking in 1926 that it was time to buy a car, so she went to a local garage, looked over the cars in stock and decided on the one she

---

[3] Waite Hockin Stirling; bishop 1869-1900

liked. Then she proceeded to sit in the back seat and looked out of the window. She liked what she saw and then shifted to the other side where she also liked what she saw, whereupon she got out and told the garage proprietor she would take the car.

'But don't you want to try it?' he asked.

'I have, and I like it,' she replied imperiously.

'But don't you want to drive it?' enquired the garage proprietor.

'I don't know how' she said, even more imperiously.

So her daughter, Betty, who was then aged 17, was sent to have driving lessons and returned two days later to collect the car. Neither my great-uncle nor great-aunt ever learned to drive.

My father had specialized in botany at university, but he graduated at the time of the Great Depression and was unable to find a job. Apparently only one suitable job was advertised, that of a curator in the Raffles Botanical Gardens in Singapore, for which there were 400 applicants. When he found he was one of the 399 unlucky ones he decided to take up schoolmastering. In this he was luckier, and in 1935 he got a job teaching at St George's College, a school modelled on the British public school system, in Quilmes on the outskirts of Buenos Aires. It was there he met my mother, and they were married in 1937.

Of course I have no memory of my first few years. According to my mother she could only distinguish her two sons by weighing us. I was usually the heavier. However, if she was disturbed by a caller when feeding us, she would identify the unfed one later by weighing us again and feeding the lighter one.

The possibility of an identity switch doesn't seem remote in the early part of our lives, but was unlikely to have occurred after we became aware of our own identities. My father could never tell the physical difference between us, and I suspect he never made the effort. When we visited our Hickey grandparents, who lived about 10 miles away, my grandfather would tie a blue ribbon on Philip and a pink one on me. At the time it did not matter, but when my grandmother knitted blue and pink socks for us when we were six, I resented it when Philip was given first choice; it seemed I was getting the runner-up's consolation prize.

Aside from their inability to tell us apart, there was another issue which concerned my parents. We didn't start speaking intelligibly until we were almost four. Before that, Philip and I had spoken to each other in a strange language which only we understood. According to my mother, we would laugh together at some joke they totally missed. My parents employed a very lovable Argentine housemaid called Elsa and when we did start to speak we were virtually bilingual.

The first memory I now recall was of the morning my middle brother was born in late 1942, when I was just two months short of my fourth birthday. My parents, unknown to us, had departed for the hospital in the middle of the night and left us in the care of the neighbours. At breakfast we were given an amazing new experience; we had cornflakes and not porridge as usual. It seems such a trivial experience and yet I have a very clear memory of it, whereas I have no recollection of my baby brother coming home. He was named Basil after my father's brother, who had been killed in Libya a few weeks previously.

Small children have no experience other than their own to use as a yardstick by which to compare their upbringing. Argentine law required all children to undertake the primary school syllabus and take a state exam at the end of each academic year before moving on to the next grade. So from the age of six a teacher was engaged to teach us the Argentine syllabus. I remember being taught that '*las Islas Malvinas son Argentinas.*' This differed from the opinion of my parents who considered the Falkland Islands as being British, so I told my father. He urged me to accept that they were Argentine if I wanted to pass the examinations. I was shocked, as I had always been told not to fib. It was my first experience of political cynicism.

With Basil's birth we moved to a bigger house in Quilmes – it was a single storey, colonial style building with a central patio and a hitching rail for horses along the road front. Its greatest asset was a large garden, divided into a kitchen garden and a more formal floral garden. It also had numerous trees to climb, including one which produced lemons on one side and oranges on another, as well as other trees producing kumquats, tangerines, plums, apricots and apples. On the flat roof a network of aerials was set up by my father so that he could listen in to German shipping radio messages, for he had some knowledge of German and had been persuaded by the British embassy that he could be more usefully employed in intelligence work than volunteer for the Royal Air Force as had been his original intention.

Quilmes is some ten miles east of Buenos Aires on the south bank of the River Plate. After the bombing of Pilsen in 1944, the town had the distinction of having the largest brewery in the world. The name still sends out widespread echoes for the brewery sponsors Boca Juniors, one of the top Argentine football teams. Quilmes should have a place in British history because in 1806, during the Napoleonic Wars, a British military expedition under

General Beresford had landed on the beach at Quilmes and attempted to wrest the Viceroyalty of the River Plate from the Spanish crown. After the attack had been repulsed, General Beresford withdrew to Montevideo on the opposite bank of the river before making a second attempt to take Buenos Aires in 1807, with similar lack of success. This has conveniently been erased from the British record, but it is well remembered in the Argentine one. Beresford proved equally inept in the subsequent Peninsula Wars.

When I was eight my father became the headmaster of St George's College preparatory school. From our pleasant colonial house the family, which had now been enlarged by the birth of my sister Susan, had to move to the headmaster's house, which was a wing of the large school building. Philip and I were enrolled in the prep school. It was not a happy time, for the school was a boarding one so we were boarded in our own home.

Like other boys we had to call our father 'Sir' in school, and in my mind this put a space between father and son which even in later life was never closed. My father also had a difficult time, for we were usually at the top of our form, which must have been somewhat embarrassing when he met other parents, for they might have suspected favouritism was involved. In fact it was the reverse, and I often felt I was being rather harshly punished for some misdeed for which other boys would only get a mild reprimand. Unsurprisingly, Philip and I were bullied for being swots and for being the headmaster's sons.

Over the next few years several careers came to my mind, engine driver, sailor and missionary being among them. All had a common factor: they would ensure I would get away from my unhappy school situation.

It wasn't all school, of course. My father, brought up in the north of England, felt he would be driven mad by the flatness of the pampas, so most summers the family travelled by overnight train to Córdoba in central Argentina, where my father shared ownership of a small estate in the hills near Alta Gracia. It was called the Canyon Guzmán, because of a deep ravine in the hills in which were numerous clear pools in which we could swim. But when Philip and I were twelve we all went to stay on an *estancia*, a cattle ranch managed by a distant relative of my mother. Leader Leonard was the brother of the husband of my mother's cousin, Betty. His was a large, commanding presence, and he was known by the peons on the estancia as Don Tedoro.

Estancia El Refugio was about 250 miles west of Buenos Aires in the province of Santa Fé. Estancias were and possibly still are measured in leagues, each league being three miles square; El Refugio covered four leagues, in other words 36 square miles or roughly 23,000 acres. On it were 8000 cattle, 400 horses, most of which were unbroken, and several thousand sheep.

The main business of the ranch was to fatten stock bred further north in Paraguay and brought down the River Paraná by boat. Then every fortnight or so a hundred or two head were sent by train, for the trans-Andean railway passed through the estancia, to the great abattoirs in Buenos Aires. In addition to the main fattening business the estancia had two foundation herds of beef cattle, Sussex and Hereford, and was running a breeding experiment using zebu bulls to develop a line of cattle resistant to heat stress.

The estancia was split into about forty large paddocks, divided by barbed wire fences, with windmills at strategic places to pump water for the stock. At that time, shortly after the war, vehicles were in short supply and horses were the main means of transport. Don Tedoro always rode a fine chestnut horse and every peon had three or four horses which he had broken in from the estancia's herd.[4]

I revelled in the life, fascinated by the details of cattle breeding, as well as the excitement of chasing rhea (the ostrich-like birds of the pampas) on horseback or hunting foxes, skunk and opossums with border terriers (though there was a drawback to hunting skunk; the terriers would inevitably stink afterwards and had to be kept out of the house for several days thereafter). It was then I knew that I wanted to be a vet. It was not because of any sentimental affection for animals - my interest then and still is in the productivity of farm animals which I know are likely to be sent for slaughter at some time.

But what I needed now was a doctor. On the Easter Sunday after returning from El Refugio I developed an acute abdominal pain. My mother was unsympathetic and blamed me for eating too many chocolate Easter eggs. A few hours later Philip developed similar pains and got an equally unsympathetic response. But the next day the family doctor was called. He was perplexed by the shared symptoms and after two more days we were taken to the British Hospital in Buenos Aires. The surgeon was similarly perplexed. He told my father he suspected one of us to have appendicitis and the other to be mimicking the symptoms, so he confined us to separate wards so that we could not collude.

The symptoms - for both of us - worsened and after two more days the decision to operate could not be delayed. It turned out

---

[4] Many horses, including the well-known polo ponies, in Argentina are descended from horses introduced by Don Pedro de Mendoza when he established the first Spanish settlement on the River Plate in 1536. Because of Indian hostility the site which he named Nuestra Señora de Buen Ayre was abandoned in 1541 and the horses escaped to breed freely on the pampas.

that we both had appendicitis. I was also found to have tubercular lesions in my abdomen. Almost certainly the disease was contracted from milk from cows with the bovine variant of tuberculosis. I wasn't told I was infected, but some months later I was readmitted to the hospital, where I underwent a series of injections at six-hour intervals with streptomycin, a very new drug at the time, over a period of three weeks. I have never felt so much like a pin cushion.

It had always been my parents' wish that their children should have an English education, and by 1948 they had five of us, for by this time my youngest brother, Hugh, had been born. The British-owned railways had been mortgaged during the war for much-needed food and it was also a time when anti-British sentiment had been stirred up by the fascist Peronist government, so that many British people were upping and leaving Argentina, among them all the members of my mother's family. The decision to leave was made easier following a serious diplomatic row caused by an incident in the school in 1950. It was the Year of the Liberator - the centenary of the death of General San Martín, the liberator of Chile and Argentina from Spanish rule in the second decade of the 19th century. All institutions were obliged to celebrate the event in some way.

In the absence of the headmaster of the upper school, who was on leave in Britain, father commissioned a bronze bust of the general. It wasn't ready in time for the unveiling, so a plaster replica was used for the occasion, though few knew that it was only a replica. One who did was a bachelor master called Simpson, and on a rainy night he brought the bust in from the wet. Unfortunately he was so drunk that he dropped it on the floor, where it smashed to pieces. As soon as father discovered the culprit he dismissed him and instructed him to go to Montevideo immediately for the sake of his own safety. A huge row ensued and father took the blame for getting Simpson out of the country. The government called it an act of desecration. Our home was shot at by rabid Perónista youths and father had to be accompanied by a private detective whenever he left the school grounds, in case he was kidnapped by secret police and 'disappeared', which was until recently a frequent Argentine arrangement. Plans were also made for my mother and us children to sail to Montevideo, though they were subsequently abandoned.

What I didn't know at the time was the extent of the political and diplomatic consequences. I discovered this later when reading contemporary British newspaper accounts. My mother's family had a link through a previous Member of Parliament for Bedford with Christopher Soames, who was then standing as Conservative candidate for the Bedford constituency. Soames was Winston Churchill's son-in-law and Churchill was then Leader of the Opposition. As any opposition leader might, Churchill used the incident to attack the Labour government for its failure to protect British citizens adequately, a failure which is still very evident in the 21st century. Even King George VI was drawn in, for he was persuaded to invite the Argentine ambassador to luncheon in an attempt to cool the situation. In the end it all blew over, but it was this incident that finally persuaded my father to leave Argentina, in 1952.

CHAPTER 2

An English education

We sailed from Buenos Aires in the Royal Mail ship Alcantara early in 1952, calling at Montevideo and several ports on the Brazilian coast before crossing the Atlantic to Europe. All of us children had our pockets stuffed with soaps when we boarded and salted hams hung from the water pipes in our cabins destined as gifts to my mother's family, for post-war food rationing was still in force in Britain at that time. Just outside the port of Montevideo the superstructure of the German heavy cruiser *Admiral Graf Spee* could be seen above the waterline, where she had been scuttled after being irreparably damaged in the battle of the River Plate. At the entrance to Rio my father showed me the masts of another ship, the RMS *Miranda*, on which we had been scheduled to sail from Buenos Aires to England in September 1939. Apparently the British embassy in Buenos Aires had warned my father against sailing. It was as well that he took the advice seriously, for the *Miranda* was sunk by a German torpedo two days after war was declared.

It was a cold, grey January afternoon when the Alcantara berthed in Southampton. Quite a crowd of family members, all of whom I had known in Argentina, had collected there in expectation of the hams and other goodies we had brought with us. My paternal grandmother always spent her winters in

Bournemouth and it was to that town that we went for a few weeks while my father commuted to London in urgent search of a new job. Poor Philip had developed a knee problem soon after sailing from Lisbon, and was referred to the Royal Victoria Hospital in Boscombe near Bournemouth immediately after we landed. He remained there for many weeks. Some months later I developed a similar problem, and for the next two years we were both dogged by disorders in both knees and had to hobble around with crutches, a serious inconvenience for teenage boys. It was only many years later that an orthopaedic colleague told me the problem was almost certainly of tubercular origin.

Despite these recurrent problems, which involved hospitalization and subsequent out-patient physiotherapy to get us walking properly again, we still had to go to school. My father had wanted us to go to Haileybury, the public school in Hertfordshire which he had attended, but it seems the Master of that establishment had a different opinion, so we were sent to school in Bedford. There were family reasons for this. My Hickey grandmother's parents had farmed in Bedfordshire and she had been at the girls' high school there, while several of her brothers, including Harold Henman, had been at the boys' school. What is more, my great-grandmother's sister had married a brewer called Charles Wells, whose son had been an MP for the town and was chairman of the school's board of governors. That, my mother thought, influenced the headmaster to take a more favourable view of us than had the Master of Haileybury.

The best stratagem for a new boy at a public school was, and may still be, to make himself invisible, though visibility on the playing field was tolerated and even encouraged. Swotting was not a social asset and was best done secretly, if at all. But there was no way I could make myself invisible stomping about on crutches, with my own personal *doppelgänger* and a quasi-colonial accent with quasi-colonial manners to match. I was frequently reminded that wogs begin in Calais and Buenos Aires was, and is, a great deal more remote than Calais. I was a square peg in a round hole, though five years in the English public school system did have the effect of smoothing some of the rougher corners to give me a fair semblance to a round peg.

Philip and I had always been good at mathematics.[5] The combination of English and Argentine syllabuses with their use of pounds, shillings and pence, inches, feet and yards in the English curriculum and the metric system in the Argentine one meant that we arrived at Bedford with a better grounding in mathematics than our contemporaries. At an early stage Philip decided to specialize in mathematics with a career in engineering in mind. One of the great disadvantages in having a twin is that there is an immediate benchmark with which to make comparisons whether it is to compare physical heights or performance at school. It created an unhealthy rivalry between myself and my brother. My frequent absences from school because of illness certainly put me at a disadvantage, so I made it plain to my father that I didn't want to be in the same boarding house as Philip, nor did I want to read mathematics in the sixth form. I am glad to say that both my father and the school authorities agreed with my wishes. Although I had always had an interest in history, in the sixth form I chose to read biology, more specifically zoology and botany. This, of course, fitted in with my intention to become a veterinary surgeon.

---

[5] For a time we were taught geometry and trigonometry in Argentina by a Mr William Proudlock who many years later I discovered was the original for Somerset Maugham's character Robert Crosbie in his famous short story 'The Letter;' a story of lust and murder in the Malay States.

Other people had other plans for me. The school's headmaster, Clarence Seaman, who had been a great classical scholar at Oxford, thought I was ideally suited to becoming a schoolmaster. He was a kindly man and taught me Latin. When I asked him what subjects he thought I could teach, he suggested the classics. I was aghast, as I got no joy from translating accounts of Caesar's military expeditions in Gaul or Ovid's loveless poetry - though I thought it imprudent to tell him so. I could not for the life of me think why anybody would want to spend time learning a dead language unless one intended to find employment in the Vatican, and by then I had long abandoned any idea of becoming a missionary.

In the event the only examination I failed at ordinary level after two years at Bedford was Latin. This was a blow, since Latin then was necessary to matriculate into most British universities. It was another hereditary disposition in addition to being unable to remember names, since both my father and his brother had also failed Latin in their attempts to matriculate. Mr Seaman's response was to tell me that he had taught me all the Latin I needed and it was up to me to get it right.

In retrospect, he could not have given me better advice. Until that time I had just taken in information and stored it to be repeated as necessary in examinations. Now for the first time I had to put information in order and establish the logic behind it. At the next opportunity, five months later, I passed. I now appreciate that grounding in Latin, not because it is of any great advantage in medicine (knowledge of Greek would be more pertinent) but because it has helped me considerably in the use of the English language and, later in life, to learn Swedish and Swahili.

My mother also tried to dissuade me from becoming a veterinary surgeon. In her mind it was neither an honourable nor a learned profession but more akin to quackery. She also thought I might become a good schoolmaster. This proposition was put to me over a family meal at home one night.

'But why don't you want to be a schoolmaster?' my mother asked irritably. 'Because the pay is poor' I replied.

My father, at the other end of the table and himself a schoolmaster, was quick to say that that was a very good reason. At least he was on my side.

When I look back to my schooldays I think how very ordinary many of my teachers were. But there were exceptions. Mr Seaman, of course, was one. In my second year, although I was often absent, I had a splendid form master, Mr MacKay, or Harry Mac as he was affectionately called. Harry Mac was a larger than life person with some notable eccentricities and a great sense of humour. He taught us both French and history. One of the oddities of his classroom was that he had a piano in it. All the rules of French grammar were turned into 'dotty ditties' and put to the music of Bizet's opera, Carmen. Sadly I can only remember one ditty:

> *If what is interrogative and subject of the verb*
> *Qu'est-ce qui? qu'est-ce qui? qu'est-ce qui?*
> *qu'est-ce qui? is the word.*

He also had a cane, much bound with Sellotape after numerous breaks from many years of use. If a howler was committed, the offender's neighbour was thrown the cane with which to beat the miscreant while he sang the appropriate ditty to remind himself of his error. This caused great hilarity at his expense, but the point was made. No injury befell him, for the layers of Sellotape ensured that the cane was no more than a broken reed.

Harry Mac's pupils had considerable success in formal examinations, for as an invigilator he would amble up the aisles of students, look over the shoulders of his own set to see what they were writing, and amble away humming some aria or other from Carmen. Those who couldn't take the hint had only themselves to blame. He also got top marks for his students when he narrated a piece for *Dictée*. Here the cane came in useful, as its flexible qualities could indicate whether an acute or grave accent, a cedilla or circumflex was appropriate. The examining authorities may not have approved but, though I cannot claim any proficiency in French, I have retained an affection for the language which is wholly attributable to Harry Mac's teaching methods.

In due course it was time to go to university. My father had read Natural Sciences at Cambridge and it had always been assumed that Philip and I would go there also. As if for my convenience, a veterinary school had been opened in Cambridge shortly before I went up. Philip, being proficient at mathematics, had no difficulty in getting a place at Peterhouse, which had been my father's college. I flopped in chemistry. I had been poorly taught and thought of chemistry as an arcane branch of algebra where each side of an equation had to add up, but I had little idea of the experimental basis for the concept of ions, atoms or molecules. However I was given a second chance and was allowed to sit the organic chemistry examination, the so-called First MB Part 4, an essential element for a medical degree, three months later. Previously I had not done any organic chemistry, so it was a whole new field. Nevertheless I managed to bluff my way through and was accepted by Peterhouse.

Peterhouse is the oldest, smallest and, reputedly, best-fed college in the university. The fellows were said to be the most consistently well-fed gentlemen in England and the chef allegedly was paid a better stipend than the fellows. Undergraduates also fared very well. In common with other centres of learning the college had a fine cellar. This was no luxury; as everyone knows, or should know, that *in vino veritas*, and the pursuit of truth is the basis of all scholarship.

Being a small college, it had the great advantage that one's friends came from a fairly wide social spectrum with different interests and different fields of study, be it medicine, law, engineering, history or classics, which I discovered was not always the case in the larger colleges. But there was a somewhat ugly tendency, in those first few weeks, to quiz other freshmen about their schools or regiments (at that time conscription for military service was just ending and half the intake in 1957 had served in the armed forces). The best one could say for the practice was that it was an attempt to find a common basis on which to hold a conversation with a total stranger; at worst it was an attempt to establish the other person's social status. Looking back I feel at fault that I should have tried to classify other freshmen, my intellectual equals and better, in such a way. Happily, by the end of my first term I had found a coterie of friends from across the board. And yet every year for the next six years I was at Peterhouse I heard similar interrogations of freshmen by freshmen. I think it was then that I became aware of the nuances of the English class system and its stress on speech and the way one held one's knife and fork.

The veterinary course at Cambridge was very much integrated into the medical course, and for the first three years of pre-clinical medicine both vets and medics attended the same lectures. But while the medics studied human anatomy, we future vets went to the animal dissection room, where we cut up dogs, ponies, sheep and chickens. We were also obliged to attend extra lectures on ruminant physiology with emphasis on ruminant digestion. The combination of the two disciplines, I believe, served both groups well. I am certainly glad that I had insights into some of the human medical conditions and, no doubt, some medics became aware of animal models which later in their lives they could use for the study of certain pathologies.

At that time medical students outnumbered veterinary students by a ratio of about 12 to 1, so our examiners, other than in veterinary anatomy, were usually medically orientated. I once tried to use this to my advantage. The examination in pharmacology was notoriously difficult; I certainly didn't want to sit it twice, so I put in long hours swotting up prior to the exam. Repeatedly we were told that the examiners wanted to find out what we knew, not what we didn't know. Sufficient hints were made that it was essential to have a full understanding of the cardiac glycosides - a group of sugars derived originally from foxgloves which have a stimulating effect on heart muscle. I took the hints seriously.

The *viva voce* was a formal exam in which we were obliged to wear suits and academic gowns. Four examiners sat across the table from me, two of them known to me as lecturers, while two were external examiners. As I had hoped, the first question related to the actions of the cardiac glycosides, so I fired off a reply with great confidence. But instead of pursuing this line of questioning to find out what more I knew, as I had been told were the examiners' intentions, and in which I felt secure, the subject was changed.

'What is the action of insulin?' 'What muscle relaxants can you name?' 'What are the causes of the release of histamine?' Every half minute the subject was changed; it was relentless. My confidence under questioning was waning. And then it came 'What is the action of oxytocin?' I had been left behind. Four pairs of eyes stared at me remorselessly across the table. I knew I should know, but at that moment in time my mind was a blank. The four pairs of eyes became more intimidating. I had to bluff. I admitted that I didn't know what its action was in humans but that it had minimal activity on the bovine uterine musculature; at least I remembered that it had some effect on uterine muscle, but couldn't remember what. 'Go on' said one of the external examiners. So I concocted a long story about work done by Eccles in Australia on bovine uterine muscle, hoping that none of them read papers by veterinary physiologists or pharmacologists in the Antipodes. 'You fascinate me,' said the external examiner, 'I'm the professor of veterinary physiology at Liverpool and I'm not aware of that work.' I had been rumbled and admitted it. But they let me pass. I assumed they thought I might make a good clinician with my aptitude to deceive without so much as a blush.

After three years of the pre-clinical course we moved to the vet school on the outskirts of the city. But clinical medicine still seemed far way. There was a great deal to learn about farm animal husbandry, management and nutrition, reproduction and housing and the physical means of restraining animals. There was also much animal pathology, including a huge list of animal diseases not covered in the pre-clinical pathology courses, to study. Parasitology was one element of these and of much greater importance than in human medicine. Since animals spend much of their time outdoors they are subjected to a large spectrum of external parasites, and their tendency to defecate on the same surface from which they eat exposes them to a galaxy of intestinal parasites far greater than afflict man. So only in the last five terms of the course were the subjects of medicine and surgery fully addressed.

There was another source from which we acquired knowledge of medicine and surgery. It was compulsory to spend at least six months of the final years working in private practice (time which now is termed extra-mural studies). This is a very valuable experience. Surgery in a university teaching establishment is done in state-of-the-art operating theatres with an anaesthetist, theatre sister and other assistants in attendance. Surgery on a farm has none of these advantages and, to keep costs down for the farmer, the surgeon is his own anaesthetist, assistant and general dogsbody.

Most of that six months was spent in a practice in Lewes in Sussex. The senior partner's particular interest was horses and he looked after a number of Jockey Club and National Hunt stables. The junior partner's interest was cattle, which coincided with my own interest. Much of the work was with dairy herds and involved the treatment of infertility, a not uncommon condition in high-yielding dairy cows. Infections of the udder were also common, a consequence of being stretched beyond normal limits and buffeted twice daily by unyielding milking machines. The treatment of small animals was considered a secondary occupation, and was in large part supplementary to the veterinary services offered to farming clients.

To extend my knowledge I also spent some time in a small animal practice in Brighton, a mixed practice in Southampton covering the New Forest and a Veterinary Investigation Centre in Cambridge. The work in the investigation centre was largely routine but was of great use to me later in places where diagnostic laboratories were either remote or non-existent. It also brought me face to face for the first time with the actual finances of veterinary work. I had been allowed to investigate an outbreak of a disease which was causing considerable mortality on a poultry farm in East Anglia. On post mortem the disease was easy to identify and treatment with sulphonamides usually resolved the problem in a short time. The trouble was that there were a quarter of a million birds in the flock, so the daily cost of treatment was very considerable.

The head of the laboratory, Tony Stevens, asked me if I felt confident to recommend such treatment. I did a quick mental calculation comparing the probable value of the flock and the cost of treatment and felt comfortable in replying yes. I was right to do so but glad that Stevens had tested me. Although it was not the sort of question one faced in examinations, it was one that vets confront frequently in their careers.

I have few recollections of my time in Hampshire except that it was cold -excruciatingly cold. It was the winter of 1962/63. The snow started falling on Boxing Day and didn't stop for eight weeks and more. Day after day the temperature stayed below 0° Fahrenheit, in other words -18°C. It didn't help that I was just recovering from an attack of glandular fever and didn't feel particularly strong. Under inches of snow there was no grazing available (not that there ever is in midwinter), so it seems incomprehensible that farmers put their animals out into the fields, but some did. Dairy cows expend considerable energy in the production of milk and even under normal conditions their energy demands are often greater than can be supplied in their diet. Under such circumstances the carbohydrate metabolism becomes disturbed and acetone and other ketones are produced as secondary products of such metabolism. The condition is known as acetonaemia and can often be detected by the smell of acetone in the animal's breath. In the acute form, the animal may behave in a bizarre fashion, eventually collapsing and unable to stand again. Treatment is by intravenous administration of glucose solutions.

In the extreme cold of that winter the energy demands to maintain body temperature made the situation even worse, and large numbers of cows were going down in the fields. Getting to them wasn't easy as most roads were snow and ice bound; in fact I was involved in four road accidents in three days. None were serious, just a matter of sliding into a ditch or through somebody's fence. On one of these occasions I stepped out of the car into four feet of snow, which promptly filled up my Wellington boots; six hours later when I took off my boots the snow was still there. It hadn't thawed; that's how cold my feet and legs were.

But motor accidents weren't the only predicament. As a student I felt obliged to be as helpful as possible and, in the absence of any drip stands in the middle of a field, I became a mobile drip stand, obliged to hold bottles of glucose solution above my head while the solution slowly dripped into the cow's vein. Standing motionless, fingers and feet frozen, there was no way I could keep warm. I had often thought, since leaving Argentina eleven years earlier, of working in sunnier climes, and it was that winter that finally resolved my determination to specialize in tropical medicine.

When my time was over in Hampshire, I had completed the six months of practice that was required for attaining membership of the Royal College of Veterinary Surgeons. I had decided that I would use the Easter holiday before the final examinations in June for revision. But that wasn't to be. I had only been home for a few days at Easter when I got a phone call from the senior partner of the practice where I had spent most of my time. His partner had gone down with chickenpox and it was the busiest time of the year, with lambing and all the other springtime activities that pile up on farms after the end of winter. 'Could you come and help?' was his plea.

In earlier times veterinary students had been allowed to perform some activities unsupervised, but this was now frowned upon by the Royal College. The senior partner tried his hardest not to infringe the rules and attempted to ensure that he visited those farms where a diagnosis had to be made and that I only visited farms where follow-ups were necessary. But it wasn't always possible, and frequently after undertaking some job the farmer would ask me to have a quick look at a pig or other animal, and naturally I did not want to be disobliging.

On my first morning I went to one farm where I had to castrate about a dozen young bulls. I used a burdizzo, an instrument which when used judiciously clamps down on the spermatic blood vessels in the scrotum, thereby blocking the blood supply to the testes, which then atrophy. It has the advantage that there is no incision, so there are no complications from flies and extraneous dirt getting into the wound. My next visit was to a farm where the stock manager had used the burdizzo injudiciously, blocking all the blood vessels to the scrotum, which had resulted in gangrene of the scrotum and much of the underbelly and prepuce. The best I could do was to give the poor animal a large shot of penicillin and offer to return the next day. But for the next few days I could not help worrying if I had been equally incompetent in castrating some of the bulls, and I was much relieved that there were no complaints from the first farmer.

This was a very valuable experience. The veterinary course is a lengthy one, but at no time does a student have to take responsibility for any of his or her actions, which are always done under the supervision of a qualified veterinary surgeon. This was the first time I had to take responsibility, and I was very much aware of it. In later life I have had several students come and see practice with me, and all admitted a lack of confidence and a concern for the responsibilities they would be taking on.

The passing of the final exams, difficult as they may be, were of less concern. Without exception all veterinary students had got so far by passing all their previous examination hurdles (although in my case I had stumbled over Latin and chemistry) but they had never had to make decisions on diagnosis and treatment without supervision.

In some ways medical students, even though their responsibilities may be more awesome, have it a little easier. After qualifying, they spend some time as interns where they can refer to a more experienced colleague if they are uncertain about what action to take. The economics of farm practice seldom allow for much professional time to be allotted to any one case. As knowledgeable as they may ever be in theory, young veterinarians are let loose to practise medicine and surgery on animals the day after qualifying. Modern small animal practice may differ somewhat, since it is practised on dedicated premises where more that one veterinary surgeon may be available in times of uncertainty and where costs do not have to relate to the commercial value of an animal as in farm practice.

I learned another lesson in those weeks while helping out while the junior partner recovered from chickenpox, and that was the social role a vet can play. A little old lady lived alone with her dog a few hundred yards from the surgery's premises. Regular as clockwork, she would bring her dog to be examined. Fortunately the practice's secretary-cum-receptionist and theatre assistant briefed me beforehand: the little old lady was lonely and wanted someone to chat to. So I examined her dog, congratulated her on looking after him so well, mentioning that few other owners were so considerate to their pets, and charged her half a crown; the equivalent of 12½p in today's money, or 20 US cents.

CHAPTER 3

Uganda

Eventually in June 1963 I cleared the last hurdle and was able to designate myself a member of the Royal College of Veterinary Surgeons. I am not sure now that I ever entertained the thought of practising in Britain. Farm animal work was what interested me. Throughout my school years in England I had wanted to return to Argentina, but there was a strong disincentive; if I returned I would be liable to military service, because I had dual nationality, Argentine as well as British. Because of my knee problems I had been declared unfit for military service in Britain, but I could not be sure that the same would apply if I returned to Argentina. To avert confusion Argentine law only required that one of a pair of identical twins should be conscripted, but Philip showed no signs of wanting to be conscripted either.

The winter in Hampshire had served to strengthen my interest in tropical medicine and I had spent hours in the veterinary school library reading up on the subject instead of concentrating on the diseases of the temperate world, on which the examiners were far more likely to question me. Although I knew very little about black Africa it had for a long time fascinated me. When I was a boy my Hickey grandmother, an earnest and devout woman, had given me a biography of David Livingstone for Christmas which I read from cover to cover two or three times. I did not have any serious inclination to spread the Word, and it would seem Livingstone converted only one man, who lapsed soon after, but his travels in Africa and encounters with animals made a big impression on me.

One of my teachers, Dr Marian Soltys, a Polish bacteriologist, had worked at the East African Trypanosomiasis Research Organization[6] in Tororo in Uganda, close to the border with Kenya, and he urged me to look for a job in Uganda instead of Kenya because of the anticipation of disturbances in Kenya following the granting of independence from Britain which was scheduled for December 1963. Soltys was a fine teacher who had participated in the last cavalry charge against a Panzer tank division and subsequently escaped to Britain through Romania, Italy and France. In addition to his teaching role in Cambridge he was also a consultant for the Food and Agriculture Organization (FAO) and was involved in developing a curriculum for a veterinary faculty in the University of Khartoum, to which he travelled regularly. He had also suggested that I should take up a teaching appointment there but I really did not think I was suited to teach; I had almost no practical experience and would only be regurgitating my own lecture notes and, as students are no fools, I felt I would be found out very quickly. So Uganda it was.

I was booked to travel to Mombasa by sea early in September by the British government's Overseas Development Agency. Before that, in the intervening two and a half months after graduating, I made two quick trips to Sweden to court a girl I had known in Cambridge. She would say neither yea nor nay to my proposal, which was understandable as she knew nothing of Uganda.

---

[6] Diseases caused by parasites were described by adding the suffix –iasis to the name of the causative organism but the convention now, in common with bacterial diseases, is to add the suffix –osis to the name of the causative organism, hence the modern nomenclature for parasitic diseases includes trypanosomosis, theileriosis, fasciolosis, etc.

The SS *Kenya Castle* was a passenger cum cargo vessel. The three weeks it took to go by sea from Tilbury to Mombasa to some extent eased the culture shock which I later found accompanies air travel. On board were a large number of other new graduates on their way to do a Dip. Ed. at Makerere University in Kampala and thereafter to fill the many gaps in the staffing of secondary schools in the three East African countries. Other passengers included old hands from Kenya, tobacco farmers from Southern Rhodesia and assorted white administrators and teachers. They were good company and patiently told us neophytes the way of the world as it was lived in Africa, and with it some of their racial attitudes. One incident stands out. Several of us hired a taxi to take us up the Rock in Gibraltar. As I spoke Spanish I was delegated to negotiate with the Spanish-speaking taxi driver.

'Ask him what is the ratio of Europeans to Spaniards in Gibraltar' one of my colleagues suggested when we were half way up the Rock. The taxi driver knew enough English to take affront. 'We are all Europeans here,' he said testily. It reminded me of the taunt in school that wogs begin in Calais.

Port Said was our first meeting with the East. Bum boats surrounded the ship as we entered the canal area with djalabiya-dressed men offering 'very nice feelthy pictures' and other works of art for sale. While the ship steamed through the canal a number of us took the opportunity to take a trip to Cairo. It was late evening when we got there, so we were propelled by our dragoman to visit a night club to watch sinuous belly dancers and long-haired whirling dervishes and to drink very bad champagne.

After a few hours sleep he then took us in the dawn hour to the west side of the Nile to see the Great Pyramid at Giza built for the pharaoh Khufu (known as Cheops by the Greeks) in about 2560 BC. I was overwhelmed by this huge funerary monument, which even now is the most massive single building in existence, covering thirteen acres. It was a relief to go inside and climb a long passageway to the Great Hall and Cheops's funerary chamber beyond it and be spared the constant attention of all the beggars outside and in the streets of Cairo. Then, after a quick breakfast, we had no more than an hour to visit the Cairo Museum and stand in awe before the magnificent golden mask of Tutankhamen and other splendid artefacts before bussing to Suez to rejoin the ship.

There was nothing remarkable about Suez other than the fact it was hot - extremely hot. Flat desert surrounded the waterway on either side, yet as soon as we had debussed a hully-gully man appeared to entertain us. How he did it I do not know but he seemed able to extract a young chick from every sleeve and pocket of his audience, muttering 'hully-gully, hully-gully' throughout his performance.

Aden was our next port of call. The ship spent just a few hours there one night, moored to a floating platform to bunker, but that gave us enough time to take a launch to Steamer Point with its numerous little duty-free shops.

Four days later the ship docked in Kilindini, the main port of Mombasa. Immediately the ship moored, Indian tailors flocked aboard to measure passengers up for shorts, shirts and other clothes which were delivered, neatly stitched and well fitting, in time to catch the boat train to Nairobi and Kampala the following night.

Passengers in the know who were destined for Lourenço Marques (now Maputo) and Durban, often left the ship while it discharged its cargo to stay in the Manor Hotel or the Mombasa Club, both noted for their old-time ambience and good food. The club overlooked Fort Jesus, built by the Portuguese in the late 16th century, and the Old Harbour - the original port of the city and then, in 1963, still frequented by dozens of dhows from the Red Sea, the Arabian Gulf, Cutch and Cambay when the northeast monsoon blew, bringing with them Persian rugs and wooden chests to exchange for ivory, rhino horn, ambergris and timber.

We had only a day to discover Mombasa before the boat train to Nairobi and Kampala departed. The train journey itself was a delightful introduction to the beauty of East Africa. After the first night, when it coursed through the dry plains of the Tsavo game park, we woke on the Athi River plains; a scene of green pastures populated with wildebeeste, Thompson's gazelles, ostrich, zebra and other plains animals.

At Nairobi the train shed some passengers and some sleeping coaches before the slow climb to the edge of the Rift Valley. Then it was down and down, gently snaking round the contours to reach the floor of the valley, where even more wildlife abounded along the shores of lakes - Naivasha, Elmenteita and Nakuru. At Nakuru more passengers were shed before the train started its ponderous climb up the western flank of the valley, wheels screaming on the tight bends, reaching the summit at over 9000 feet near Equator Station late in the evening. Some time in the night we crossed the border into Uganda and in the second dawn we woke as the train crossed the Nile bridge into the kingdom of Buganda. Three hours later and we had reached Kampala Station.

A middle-aged white man with a military-type moustache was

on the platform, busy inspecting the labels on items of luggage. I assumed he was looking for somebody in particular and had not expected a whole crowd of young people to get off the train simultaneously. Wanting to be helpful, I asked him if he was looking for anyone. 'Yes, Roland Minor.'

Sam Walshe became my mentor over the next few days. I had known a little about him previously, for his two sons had been my contemporaries at Bedford. Sadly, the older one, Noel, died while he was there, but Mike had been one of Philip's group of friends. I knew from them that their father was a veterinary surgeon, but I had no idea he was the deputy commissioner of veterinary services in Uganda. There are times when the old school tie is an asset.

Within two days Sam had arranged for me to get a loan to buy a car. On his advice I bought a Peugeot 403, the most popular work horse at the time for the rough conditions of East Africa. It cost me all of 16,100 shillings, or £805 in sterling terms. Sam and the veterinary commissioner, Hugh Newlands, briefed me on what I would be doing. A large number of expatriate veterinary officers had left the service at the time of independence the previous year and their Ugandan replacements were in training at the newly-created veterinary faculty at Kabete on the outskirts of Nairobi. As a result the veterinary department was seriously understaffed. I was therefore expected to visit dairy farms around Kampala in the mornings and run a small animal clinic in the afternoons. I was told it would be a temporary assignment until more veterinary surgeons could be recruited from Denmark and Germany. Then I would be posted as a veterinary officer to Moroto, the administrative headquarters of Karamoja district in the extreme northeast of the country.

The farm work was based on the kingdom of Buganda's veterinary office, to which I was seconded. Buganda had retained a considerable degree of autonomy during the period of the British protectorate of Uganda which had ended in 1962 and this autonomy continued for the first few years of independence. It was ruled by a hereditary sovereign called the Kabaka with his own government, headed by a chief minister, the Katikiro, assisted by a council of state, the Lukiko, made up of senior chiefs and other leading personalities in the kingdom. The Lukiko was housed in an imposing white building with a commanding copper spire on a hilltop facing the Kabaka's royal compound, the Lubiri. This covered a whole hill-top to the southwest of Kampala called Mengo and was surrounded by a stout brick wall three to four miles in circumference. Almost hidden in a clump of trees in the centre of this large compound was the Twekobe, the actual residence of the Kabaka. The veterinary office was one of several government offices in the royal compound and opposite it were the royal drummers, who drummed frenetically and, to my mind, somewhat monotonously whenever the Kabaka was in residence.

Kabaka Mutesa II was a great-grandson of that Mutesa to whom Speke had paid court in 1862 to get consent to traverse his kingdom to find the source of the Nile. Mutesa II was a handsome man of slight build who was often criticized by Britons in Kampala for his moral excesses. They had irreverently nicknamed him Banana Freddy. This seemed to me unnecessarily sanctimonious, for he had *droit de seigneur* over all the maidens in his kingdom, a privilege that many other men might have envied. Soon after my arrival I found that I had a special status in the kingdom, for only the Kabaka was thought man enough to father twins, so I acquired a special name, Kató. But whatever his failings, Mutesa was a man of impeccable good manners. Within the royal compound his subjects treated him as an almost divine figure to whom they abased themselves in full prostration.

The chief veterinary officer of the kingdom, a man called Kayanja, was greatly admired by all who knew him. Guessing that I might be embarrassed by abasing myself, he would pin a notice to my office door with the words 'Do not disturb, Meeting in progress' whenever he suspected the Kabaka might be in the vicinity. No man could have been more helpful. Kayanja assigned a veterinary assistant called Fred Mwanje to support me. Fred was about my age; I would not have called him handsome but he had a smile that spread right across his face and made him a very engaging person. I could not have done my work without him for he knew all the highways and byways to reach the dairy farms on our daily rounds. He also knew a lot more about tropical diseases than I did.

One of my first assignments was to visit a British dairy farmer, one of the sort that was convinced that he knew a great deal more than any African. His problem was a disease called East Coast fever, usually abbreviated to ECF, probably the greatest killer of cattle in the higher rainfall areas of eastern Africa. It is caused by a protozoal parasite, *Theileria parva*, which is spread by one particular tick, the brown ear tick. As with other protozoal diseases such as malaria, it had not yet been found possible to develop a satisfactory vaccine and at that time there was no drug to treat the disease, so control of the vector tick was imperative. The farm had no water supply of its own, so once a day the cattle were trekked down to Lake

Victoria to be watered. Since other cattle also watered there, there was plenty of opportunity to pick up infected ticks. However the farmer had a very confused idea of how the disease was transmitted so I, a white vet, was sent to try and put him wise. He and his wife were a strange, elderly couple, looking - and behaving - as if they were living in the early part of the twentieth century. I still wonder at Kayanja's generosity in being willing to help an arrogant white man who insisted that he knew better than any African vet.

All the other farms I visited were owned by Ugandan farmers. For most it was their first experience of handling 'exotic' cattle, meaning European breeds, which are a great deal more susceptible to ECF than the indigenous breeds. The departure of many expatriate farmers from Kenya on the eve of independence gave the Ugandans an opportunity to buy up some of their dairy animals. There was a bizarre consequence to this for these cows had names such as Daisy and Buttercup; names which had no meaning to Ugandan farmers.

Strict regulations were established before the Ugandans were given licences to buy exotic cattle: their farms had to be double fenced around their perimeters to minimize any invasion by ear ticks and all the animals had to be dipped or sprayed twice a week with tick-killing chemicals - acaricides. The fencing of land was a thorny problem, for there was a confusion of land laws and few people had legal title, while some land was communal; only in the townships did people have title to plots. There was, therefore, on occasion, considerable animosity from neighbours towards those who fenced off land for their exclusive use. This could result in the destruction of fences and, happily rarely, mutilation of the imported cattle. But the enthusiasm of the owners for their newly-acquired exotic cattle was heartening and I was soon very busy.

One of the characteristics of these farmers and Africans in general is their great courtesy; not for them the perfunctory 'good morning' of a westerner. This is well summed up by the Swahili maxim *haraka, haraka, haina baraka*, meaning roughly 'hurry, hurry is not a blessing.' Luganda greetings can be lengthy; first the host asks how one is, to which the guest replies '*Bulungi*' (fine), after which the host gives a sigh of satisfaction '*Eeeeh!*' Then it is the guest's turn to ask after the health of the host. This litany with its responses can continue for several minutes as the wellbeing of spouses, children and other relatives, homes, herds and other issues are enquired about. Additionally, it is the Baganda custom for women, even of advanced age, to overtly pay great deference to men, curtsying right down to the ground as in the west only a ballerina can. Almost always I would be offered tea or a soft drink at every farm I visited and again the women would curtsy as they offered the drink. I found this embarrassing, thinking the deference was being shown to me because I was a white man. In this I was wrong. It had nothing to do with being white. I learned to repay the compliment by offering my hand to raise them from their deep curtsy. I erred sometimes in showing my impatience at all these courtesies, but at the back of my mind was the knowledge that time was short and I was trying to do the work of two people.

In the afternoons and on Saturday mornings I ran the Kampala City Council's small animal clinic. It is not the purpose of any government veterinary department to provide services for people's pets, though they do have an obligation to control rabies, a much-

feared disease of animals and man. My first day there was somewhat
of a disaster, for my predecessor in the clinic had made off with all
the surgical equipment. One of my first tasks was to remove the
stitches from a dog he had recently spayed. Without any forceps or
scissors, I made do with my fingers and a razor blade. The bitch
moved slightly; I nicked myself and a small pool of my blood formed
on its belly. Next thing I knew, the owner, an attractive young lady,
was flat on the floor in a dead faint.

First aid had taught me that under such circumstances I should
loosen all tight clothing, but the thought came to mind that when
she recovered she might think I had been 'interfering', for lack of
a more polite word, with her. While I dithered she did the best
thing she could have done - she rapidly came round. But it was not
a great way to start on one's first day.

Kampala thieves had a habit of putting out poisoned meat or
trailing a bitch on heat near houses they planned to break into in
the hope of distracting any guard dogs. Often the dogs were badly
hacked with *pangas*. Suturing up injured dogs and the treatment of
canine tick fever were my main activities in the clinic. Tick fever
is another of several protozoal diseases transmitted by ticks, and it
causes profound anaemia. Affected dogs show few clinical signs at
first and the owner, unless very observant, is only aware that there
is something wrong in the terminal stages. In those long-ago days
treatment was by injection of a chemical called phenamidine. This
had an unpleasant side effect in that it also caused an acute fall in
blood pressure, which, combined with the anaemia, often resulted
in abrupt heart failure. Having contributed to the demise of a few
dogs in my initial ignorance I soon learned to inject phenamidine

in serial doses under the skin to minimize the drop in blood pressure. In addition to these activities there were the usual vaccination procedures to undertake and the certification of pets which many expatriates intended taking back to their home countries with them.

All this time I was well aware that I was just filling a gap before transferring to Karamoja. I had never even heard of Karamoja, but the commissioner was adamant that if there was any place he could have gone to as a young vet he would have chosen it. Wildlife was plentiful there and, as an aside, he mentioned that the locals, at least the masculine element, all walked about stark naked. This state of affairs was confirmed to me by all the other people who learned I would be transferring to Karamoja in due course. It seemed to be a matter of great importance. There was one other bit of advice the commissioner gave me, and that was that I should not allow myself to be bullied by the administrator of Karamoja. I was not sure how he might bully me or who he even was, though the name suggested he was some sort of administrative officer.[7]

I had also ascertained that there was no electricity in Moroto, there were few shops and that social life centred on the club. The last item came with the warning that I should avoid trying to match the drinking habits of the male members of the club.

With this scant information, I set out in my free time to find a paraffin fridge, charcoal-burning flatirons, paraffin lamps and other non-electric household accoutrements. Thus equipped, in November 1963, I set off in my Peugeot for Karamoja.

---

[7] The senior administrative official in every district was a district commissioner but because of its specific problems, including security problems and its size, the senior official in Karamoja was designated an administrator and had the rank of a permanent secretary.

CHAPTER 4

Early days in Karamoja

There is a spectacular entrance to Karamoja on the main road to Moroto; an entrance so dramatic it is clear to any traveller that they are entering a special place. It is so remarkable that even the locals, the Iteso to the west and the Karamojong to the east, include the place in the folk stories about their origins. To the right, that is to the south, is the block-like mountain called Napak rising to over 8000 feet and to the left another mountain Akisim, shaped like a giant slice of cake. Akisim is small by comparison with its neighbour, at only 7000 feet high. In the valley between them, a valley only about three miles wide, lies the village of Iriri. Although remote, Iriri was familiar to me because my text books referred to a strange disease, Iriri-itis (but more of that later). There, leaning on the pole of a signpost indicating the location of the Iriri Police Post, was a man, naked except for the thin black cotton *shuka* knotted over his shoulder. I had been told often enough to expect this, yet I was embarrassed by his nakedness. This was my problem, because it was clear that he was not embarrassed. If he had been, he would have done something about it.

I had been detailed to drop off a microphone for the radio telephone for the manager of the livestock quarantine at Iriri. Thus I met Steve Stevenson, a large, well-built sandy-haired man of about my own age and his South African-born wife, Fay, who were to become close and valued friends over the following years. Their house was on a little knoll beneath Akisim and from there Steve showed me Moroto mountain rising about 50 miles to the northeast, a hazy blue-green outline over 10,000 feet in height. Stretching northwards from the mountain were the Magos hills, a series of serrations like the teeth of a giant crocodile, They were part of the top of the western wall of the Eastern Rift Valley, and had given their name to the Magosian culture which flourished there in the Palaeolithic era about 9000 BC.

Below, in a valley of the mountain, was Moroto township, which was to become my home for the next two and a half years. It was a town of perhaps a thousand souls with one short tarmac road, a few single-storey shops on each side, leading past a central post office to the police station and administrative offices, the *boma*, and twenty or so houses beyond, nestling on the lowest slopes of the mountain, for senior staff in the various government departments. Moroto also had a prison and a hospital of about fifty beds to serve a district which was one and a half times the size of Wales, a little over 12,000 square miles, with a population of nearly 200,000 people.

There was a very steep learning curve to scale in my first few months and, to be honest, it was about a year before I felt confident about dealing with the many intricacies of the district. Not only did I have to learn the geography of the area but I had to discover much about the people and their husbandry systems before tackling the purely veterinary aspects.

My immediate boss was the district veterinary officer, usually referred to as the DVO. David Morris was a tousle-headed little Welshman who had been in the district for three years. Despite his short stature he was a dominating character. He was also an amusing cynic. Any fiasco was attributed to the Karamoja Buggerance Factor. 'KBF strikes again,' he would chuckle as we experienced another puncture or other mishap. Yet he often expressed his admiration for the Karamojong, for their ability to adapt to the harsh environment and survive. One of his favourite aphorisms was that 50% of animals recover whatever a vet does for them, 25% recover because of what the vet does for them and 25% die despite what the vet does for them. In a way he said it to comfort me when I had been unsuccessful in treating an animal, though I fear not many vets would survive in a veterinary practice with such a high mortality rate. There was one very important lesson he taught me and that was always to make a decision, even if it was the wrong one. On most occasions you come close to making the right decision and when you don't, you can change it. What subordinates hate most is when they have no clear sense of direction, which gives them the opportunity to grumble behind the boss's back.

To show me the geography of the district David Morris took me on safari to the Kidepo Valley National Park in the extreme north of the district, bordering the Sudan. The road was poor, in fact for about fifty miles there was no made road, just a rough track through the bush, so it took two days to drive there. Another of David's maxims was that any fool could be uncomfortable on safari, and as he was no fool he travelled in some style. This was a valuable lesson, for I was on safari about half of each month and sometimes even longer.

One essential was a good safari cook. For a short time I had a Nubian called Zebadayo, but he had too much of a liking for the bottle and after a few months I replaced him with a Kenyan, Waswa, from the Kitale area. That's not to say he was not partial to a drop or two, but he could restrain himself to Saturday evenings after playing centre forward for the Moroto Town XI whenever he was in town. That way we could both indulge synchronously, he in a downtown bar, me in the club, without inconveniencing one another.

The clubhouse was no more than a simple shack with a corrugated iron roof, a bar at one end with an adjoining area for dancing, a small library behind stocked with discarded paperbacks and a veranda in front facing a tennis court. It was simply furnished and lit by gas lamps at night but, most importantly, it was a friendly place. In addition to the tennis court, there was an unroofed squash court in the DC's garden, marked on the map as the DC's garage. This it could never have been, for the back wall of the court would have prevented the parking of any vehicle within it. There also had been a bathing place up the mountain where a dam had been constructed across the stream. Many of the Moroto Club members had complained of itching after swimming and it had taken time to realize that they had contracted bilharzia, an unpleasant disease spread by snails previously infected by contact with human faeces or urine. To prevent further infection the dam had been blown up.

On my first safari to the Pokot country I had been warned by an old man not to foul the river bed even when the water course was dry. I later found that a similar taboo existed among the Karamojong. Watercourses are believed to be inhabited by spirits whose peace is disturbed by human fouling, and the perpetrator is likely to be possessed mentally or become sickly. As a consequence of this taboo the Karamojong and Pokot are free from the disease. The source of the bathing pool infection was found to be a pump attendant from a people who had no such taboo.

Snails however persisted in the dams and valley tanks that had been built in the dry season grazing areas for watering livestock. These then acted as vectors of liver fluke disease of cattle and sheep, a disease very similar to bilharzia in its life cycle. I had come to think of it in Britain as a disease of wetlands and high rainfall, so was surprised in Karamoja that major outbreaks occurred in the dry season, often with considerable mortality.

It took more than a few weeks to get on top of the geography of the district, the political divisions, the roads and the whereabouts of waterholes and other water sources for, apart from the Suam river on the south-eastern border with Kenya, the other rivers ran only in the wet season and then for only a few days at a time when a flash flood would hurtle down the river bed carrying all before it. One river, the Napanyenya, was notoriously treacherous. The crossing was only about thirty feet wide but when there was water in it, the sandy bottom was like quicksand. There was a great temptation to have a go when there were only a few inches of water in it, for the alternative route involved a detour of almost a hundred miles round the headwaters of the river and many hours of bumpy driving. Robbie Robson, the game warden, lost two vehicles in the river and, embarrassed by his folly, he blamed white ants for the second vehicle's loss. Remarkably, nobody in the audit department queried his story.

The great majority of the inhabitants of Karamoja district are of course Karamojong, though there are Pokot living in the southeast adjoining their traditional lands in western Kenya and some small groups - Tepeth, Ik, Napore and Labwor - living in the comparative safety of the mountains and hills in the district. In normal times the cattle owners, Karamojong and Pokot, split their herds and flocks. There were practical as well as security reasons for this. The dry season grazing areas usually became swampy in the wet season, whereupon the herds grazing there withdrew to the higher ground to the east where the villages - the *manyattas*, a Maasai word much used by Europeans - were located.[8] The sheep and goats, collectively called shoats, were the responsibility of the womenfolk and they remained close to the villages throughout the year, as did the cows in milk and their calves where they were herded by the younger boys. After the end of the rainy season the other cattle, steers, heifers, dry cows and the rest slowly migrated towards the dry-season grazing areas, herded by the young men of the group, who were visited at regular intervals by the young unmarried women bringing food and milk for their consumption and other comforts. But the main security reason for the division of a man's herds was that he diminished the risk of losing them all in a cattle raid or from disease.

In times of drought or when a group's herds would have become too large for the available pasture in the locality, there would have been a tendency for the herds to split on a more permanent basis. Even if the split was amicable (and probably in many cases it was not), after two to three generations the ties of kinship would be forgotten and the two groups would compete for grazing and water for their livestock. Among people like the Karamojong, where wealth and status were measured by the number of animals a person owned, the competition was deadly. Young men had a particular

[8] More correctly *ngireria* in Akarimojong

need to acquire cattle, for if they wished to marry they had to kill another person (obviously not from their own group) and pay a dowry of sixty to a hundred cattle to the family of the bride to formalize the union and as a form of compensation, for all the woman's children would henceforth become members of the man's family and clan. A woman's value was enhanced if she could show evidence of fecundity before the marriage, though excessive evidence indicated a degree of promiscuity, which was not considered desirable.

Unless the groom was immensely wealthy, the cattle did not come from his own herd, nor even from his clan's. A man's warrior status would be shown by the lozenge-shaped cicatrices on his shoulders; those on the right shoulder for men killed, those on the left shoulder for women and children. Because of their value as dowry and for prestige, even oxen and bulls were seldom slaughtered for food, although some would be sacrificed to celebrate special events and at the end of each dry season for rain-making ceremonies. However milk and blood from cattle were an important source of protein, as were the milk and meat of sheep and goats which did not have the intrinsic value that cattle had.

Within Karamoja there were five main groups of Karamojong: the Dodoth in the far north, the Jie just south of them; the Bokora and Matheniko in the central part of the district and the Pian in the south.[9] Also in the district was a group called the Labwor, who lived in the Labwor hills in the extreme west; these were not Akarimojong speakers but more akin to the Acholi of northern Uganda. They kept few cattle but were skilled ironsmiths and made spears for the Karamojong warriors, charging two bulls for a pair of

---

[9] Correctly, the term Karamojong refers to the people of Bokora, Matheniko and Pian. Oral histories indicate that the Jie and Dodoth differed from them in their accounts of their dispersal from the vicinity of Lake Turkana in the late 17th and 18th centuries. Nevertheless, common usage refers to all the Akarimojong speakers in Uganda as Karamojong. Other Akarimojong speaking groups are the Turkana in north-western Kenya, the Toposa and Jiye in the southern Sudan and the Nyangatom along the lower reaches of the Omo river in Ethiopia.

spears. Water and grazing were at a premium in the dry season and this was the time of fighting. The weaker groups might make temporary alliances, most often the Jie and Matheniko with the Turkana, but these were never permanent.

There was one benefit from the constant tension between the several Karamojong groups, and that was that between each group there lay a belt of no-man's-land, five to ten miles wide, in which wildlife flourished. But as the dry season lengthened and grazing got scarcer so the adjoining groups had to venture deeper and deeper into no-man's-land with their cattle, and inevitably a time would come when they made contact, with fatal results. If all this sounds somewhat frightening, the Karamojong themselves seemed a happy people and I never ever felt any danger working with them, even spending many nights in undefended canvas tents. Hyena were a much greater hazard and it was essential to close the tent flaps carefully at night so as to prevent them from entering, for they were known to cause dreadful injuries to people sleeping in the open and there were few nights when I did not hear their whooping as they scavenged around the campsite.

Another of my early safaris was with Charles Lamb, the assistant district commissioner for Jie County. Charles had been captured at Dunkirk when fighting with a Guards regiment and had been interned for the rest of the war. This had resulted in a disfiguring skin disease, about which he was very sensitive. This was a pity because, though he was much liked by the expatriate community in Moroto, he shunned European society.

At one stage of the tour around Labwor we inspected a primary school. Everything seemed in order and at the end of the visit he had all the children line up and sing 'God save the Queen.' In the privacy of the Land Rover afterwards I thought to remind Charles that Uganda was now a republic and that the British national anthem might be somewhat inappropriate. 'I know, I know,' he replied 'but it's the only song the children know that I also know.'

I had hardly begun to familiarize myself with the district before I was flung into work. Iriri quarantine had two functions. The first was to identify and prevent the spread of any diseases before trade cattle were despatched to the abattoirs in Kampala and other towns. The second was to isolate any diseased herds of the Bokora and Pian. The quarantine area was large enough, about fifteen miles by four, to be able to separate the two groups. The diseased group was kept at Kopopwa at the eastern end, a place with a low flat hill and a prominent single tamarind tree.

At the time there were about 250 cattle at Kopopwa, the survivors of Bokora herds laid waste by contagious bovine pleuropneumonia, or CBPP for short. The first reliable description of CBPP, lung sickness as it was called in Britain, came from Germany in 1693, though it was almost certainly widespread earlier than that. It was introduced into the United States in 1843 and Australia in 1858 with imports of cattle from Europe. In the absence of written records it is not possible to say that the disease was absent from the African continent, though circumstantial evidence suggests that it did not exist there until infected cattle were imported into Cape Colony from Holland in 1854. It was so virulent that within two years two hundred thousand cattle had succumbed to it. By 1861 the disease had spread to Matabeleland in present day Zimbabwe.

The Scottish explorer Joseph Thomson, the first white man to traverse Masailand, described a terrible outbreak of the disease in

1883 among cattle of the Laikipiak Maasai in present-day Kenya. He wrote of hundreds of cattle dying and the numerous stinking carcases dotting the landscape and the misery of the people. The virulence of the outbreak suggests that the Maasai herds had not been exposed previously to the disease. Thomson made no mention of massive mortality in wildlife, thus eliminating the possibility of the disease being rinderpest. In fact rinderpest did not exist in Africa at the time, though it was only a few years before it too was introduced into the continent.

As its name implies, contagious bovine pleuropneumonia is transmitted by direct contact between animals and causes both pleurisy and pneumonia, which are often fatal. The major problem in controlling it is that many of the survivors remain as carriers of the disease, setting off new outbreaks when traded, used for bride wealth or stolen. Except for this one herd in Kopopwa, the rest of Uganda was at that time free from the disease. Thus the herd at Kopopwa was a dangerous focus for further outbreaks, particularly if some amorous Karamojong decided to acquire them for bride wealth payment.

The disease had almost certainly been introduced by Sudanese cattle which were incubating it when they had been smuggled in for sale in the Kaabong market in the far north of the district. This illicit trade was next to inevitable, for southern Sudan had been in revolt against the Khartoum government since 1956 and this had limited all internal Sudanese trade.

The DVO decided, with the commissioner's agreement, to pay compensation to the cattle owners and slaughter the quarantined animals. The slaughter, fortuitously, also provided the opportunity to compare the efficiency of various diagnostic tests to identify the disease by comparing test results with post mortem findings. The work was led by Nigel Gourlay, a research scientist at the East African Veterinary Research Organization (EAVRO) at Muguga near Nairobi.

It was essential that our intentions were kept secret, for it was very likely that if the Bokora knew their precious animals were to be slaughtered they would disappear overnight. For a couple of days Nigel collected sera and other samples for testing; then when he was satisfied with the results a baraza was called. With a phalanx of policemen armed with sten guns and rifles at our backs, the owners were told of the intention to confiscate the cattle and compensate them. The Bokora women ululated with anger and things looked menacing, but the men were more phlegmatic. Perhaps they thought to take the compensation and recover the cattle later. If that was their intention, they were thwarted, for immediately after the baraza the cattle were moved to a secure boma some miles away and kept under armed guard overnight.

The slaughter started early next morning. After the cattle had been stunned, killed and bled they were skinned, and then it fell to David and me to expose the lungs and chest lining of the dead animals while Nigel identified each animal, recorded any visible lesions and took samples for bacteriological examination. It was bloody work and it went on throughout the morning and most of the afternoon; I don't think I have ever been more filthy or covered in flies. When we were finished, the women of Iriri were quick to carry away the meat, some managing to carry four whole haunches on their heads. What they could not carry off, lions and hyena took during the night.

Nigel subsequently published the results of this survey, though I do not remember either David or I getting any acknowledgement for our help. He showed that the best of all the diagnostic tests then available was the complement fixation test (CFT). Unfortunately it was somewhat limited in its usefulness. It was found to be 100% effective in identifying animals with the acute form of the disease, but these animals presented few problems since they could be identified clinically; they were miserably ill, breathing heavily and coughing intermittently. But it was only 70% effective in identifying chronically infected carriers, and these were precisely the animals one wanted to eliminate from any herd. It has made the control and eradication of this disease very difficult, though recent developments in immunological techniques may soon lead to a more sensitive test.

Christmas came and the New Year of 1964 with parties at the Moroto Club and in individual homes. Steve and Fay invited me to have a traditional Christmas lunch with them and their two children at Iriri. I think it was at this time I learned the truth about Iriri-itis. The animals were usually found dead; the post mortem more often than not showed very congested oesophaguses (or oesophagi if purists prefer), from which scientists at EAVRO had isolated a plethora of viruses, none of which replicated the disease when injected into experimental animals. On the other hand, a few showed massive bleeding into the abdominal cavity. The condition lasted long enough to be included in text books as a mystery viral disease. When Steve was appointed to run the quarantine he insisted that when an animal died its carcase was to be burnt and he prohibited the quarantine staff from eating the meat. Immediately deaths ceased. This was not because of the improved hygiene, as might be assumed, but because the staff no longer had a motive for killing the animals. It turned out the cattle had been killed by drenching them with battery acid, thus causing the inflammation of the oesophagus. In the absence of battery acid some had been killed by the insertion of a sharp stick into the rectum and the aorta perforated.

In the New Year, I thought it time to find out more about the extreme southeast of the district. This was populated by a people we knew as Suk, though they prefer to call themselves Pokot. These people, although pastoralists like the Karamojong and similar in appearance, differed in language and practised male circumcision. Like the Karamojong, they had been pushed out of the southern Ethiopian highlands, probably in the 16th century, by the expansion of the Oromo, a people speaking a language of Cushitic origin, who themselves had come under pressure as a result of Somali expansion.[10] But while the Karamojong had migrated westwards, the Suk had moved south.

The Suk county headquarters was a small settlement called Amudat which lay on the main road to Lodwar, the headquarters of Turkana District, the most north-westerly of the Kenyan districts. Amudat consisted of three corrugated iron *dukas* each with a veranda in front. One sold diesel and fuel, which was much needed in that remote area, and each of the three verandas had its attendant tailor with a treadle-operated sewing machine. The tailors did not have much to do, for the Suk disdained clothing as much as the Karamojong though the few schools in the county did press their scholars into uniforms. There was also a small police

---

[10] The Oromo were and are often described by European writers as Galla which they consider a derogatory term.

post, two hides-and-skins stores and a mission hospital about half a mile away.

On the north side of Amudat ran the Kanyangarang river; it was dry throughout the dry season but a major obstacle when trying to get to Turkana when in flood. Large leafy trees lined the river bank, but otherwise the county was drier than the rest of the district. Low spiky sansieveria, a kind of aloe, were the commonest plants, and pairs of little dik-dik, no bigger than rabbits, would peer shyly from them. They were the most common antelope in that dry bush country, although occasionally a curly-horned striped lesser kudu might dash across the track.

It had been my intention to survey for trypanosomosis in the area, for tsetse flies were said to be present. I was somewhat doubtful about this, for tsetse need shade because of their susceptibility to dehydration and this was open dry country except for the banks of the Kanyarang river and the Suam river, forty miles further south, which there formed the Uganda-Kenya border. But my intention was quickly diverted when news was brought of a major clash between the Pian and Suk over grazing and watering on the Kanyangarang.

I set out with my driver to get more details and soon came upon the body of a Suk boy, about eight or ten years old, bloody and bearing numerous spear wounds. This information I relayed to the administrator in Moroto some seventy miles away on the police telegraph, an efficient radio-based system which used Morse code. He first told me that grazing control was, as specified in the Grazing Ordinances, under the control of veterinary officers, but I replied that as I did not have the control of a police force I really could not prevent more bloody clashes between the rival groups. So an assistant district commissioner was sent to help out.

Douglas Durand had been in Uganda more years than I had been months and carried the prestige of his office with him. He quickly organized a meeting of the elders of both groups, which I also attended, supported by a platoon of well-armed policemen. He opened with the words 'We are met here today to find a *modus vivendi* between the Pian and the Suk…' Neither the Karamojong nor the Suk translators paused to ask what a *modus vivendi* was and I resolved there and then to redouble my efforts to learn Swahili, which I had already started to learn in extra-mural classes at Makerere University while I had been posted to Buganda.

After he had spoken, I rose to answer some questions. I was totally flummoxed when a Suk woman, elegantly dressed in a goatskin skirt sequinned with cowrie shells and topped by an expansive *décolletage* discreetly concealed behind rows and rows of beaded necklaces, asked why the government, now that Uganda was independent, did not print more money so that everybody could have lots of it and not just the white people. I bowed to Douglas, telling him I thought that was an administrative question, not a veterinary one. I cannot remember how he replied.

Then another diversion occurred. The previous month the African population of Zanzibar had risen up against the Omani Arab Sultan and thrown him out. Many resident Arabs suffered a worse fate. The massacre seemed a remote event and did not disturb us much in Uganda. There was more anxiety about the impending independence celebrations in Kenya and the fear that they might be followed by anti-European demonstrations in that country. Fortunately these fears were unfounded. But a month later the Tanganyika Defence Force mutinied in Dar-es-Salaam and the mutiny spread to the 1st Battalion of the Uganda Rifles in Jinja and units of the Kenyan army in Lanet. Whether these events were linked I do not know; it seems very probable.

The 2nd Battalion of the Uganda Rifles was based in Moroto, so there was considerable anxiety that the mutiny might spread there. Douglas Durand was sent a message on the police telegraph ordering him to lock up the armouries of all the police stations around Amudat and he asked me to accompany him. I wondered that two unarmed white men could contain a mutinous police force, but all went well and the station commanders collaborated willingly, which was a great relief. We then returned post haste to Moroto to find the expatriate community, which included the 2nd Battalion's officer corps, in considerable alarm about any possible spread of the mutiny.

I packed my Land Rover surreptitiously with water and food but could not think where to go. There was a civil war going on in southern Sudan and Kenya, with its own mutiny, did not seem an attractive alternative either. The top of Moroto mountain, where there was a climbers' hut, seemed the best place to go. The next day, a Saturday, the nervous expatriate community collected for mid-day drinks in the club; a radio at one end of the bar was tuned to Radio Uganda and another, at the other end, tuned to the BBC, hoping to get news of developments.

Early in the afternoon the Prime Minister, Milton Obote, came on the radio to announce that an agreement had been arrived at with the mutineers and all the British officers would be replaced forthwith. He then announced that Sergeant Major Opolot, who then was the senior non-commissioned officer in the 2nd Battalion, had been promoted to army commander. The ousted battalion commander, Major Groom, who was then with us in the club, immediately sent a driver to collect Opolot from the barracks and bring him to the club, where we plied him with drinks and congratulated him on his new appointment. Opolot seemed overwhelmed by these developments but a nervous peace was restored.

At the time I thought Obote had made too many concessions to the mutineers and in this I was proved right. Within a short time the army had become an undisciplined force of men, completely outside the law. Opolot did not last long. He was replaced by a Colonel Amin, later to become a self-styled Field Marshal and Conqueror of the British Empire, though numerous Ugandans in later years just referred to him as 'the buffoon' or worse. Obote was exiled from Uganda seven years later, never to return again alive, and the country descended into chaos under Amin's rule.

The Kenyan government made no compromises to their mutinous soldiers and peace and stability were quickly restored there. The long-term consequences of the mutiny in Uganda were disastrous, but in the short term I made a valuable gain. Two days after the end of the mutiny an RAF transport plane flew into the Moroto airfield to take away the British officers and NCOs with their families. Many had pets, which David Morris and I were obliged to put down. The adjutant, a man called 'Kuni' Wood, had a young black Labrador, more correctly a sort-of Labrador for he had too narrow a head to be a true one, called Rufus. It seemed a pity to put him down so I acquired him. He remained with me for twelve years - a faithful companion who on one occasion at least saved me from death, though he would more likely have licked any unwanted intruder to death rather than use more vicious means.

On the surface, life continued normally. Club parties were held on Saturday evenings every fortnight and attendance was compulsory just to keep the club finances ticking, for an earlier member had brought it close to insolvency. During a period when he had been a bar member he had enjoyed the best the bar could offer but never paid, and he had managed to hide the hole in the club finances by concealing various invoices from the treasurer. It was only after his departure from Moroto that the supplier, an Indian called Ishverbhai Patel, complained that the club was in arrears in paying his account. It was then the hole was discovered.

Parties were held at regular intervals to boost the club's revenues. There was no shortage of reasons to party. St Valentine, St David, St Patrick, St Andrew and St George were all holy causes for celebration, as were Guy Fawkes and Robbie Burns, Hogmanay and Hallowe'en and, of course, Independence. No excuses for absence were accepted and no member could entertain at home on the designated day. Dress was usually formal on these occasions.

My brother, Philip, came to visit early in the year, for he was then working on the huge Gezira cotton scheme in northern Sudan and could do little during the last weeks of Ramadan and the Idd-ul-Fitr celebrations that followed. He got a little more excitement than he probably expected. On the way to Kampala from the airport we were held up by an illegal army checkpoint on the road, but fortunately we were not robbed.

After a few days in Moroto we set off for the Kidepo National Park, where I had become very friendly with Peter Pegg, the park warden. I could justify these excursions most months by undertaking an official safari to pay the veterinary staff in Dodoth. Staff closer to Moroto would travel into town to collect their wages, some as much as 90 miles on foot or by bicycle, for there was no bus service running within the district though the mail bus ran on alternate days to Soroti, the district headquarters of the adjoining district.

On our second day in Opotipot, the headquarters of the park, Peter announced that Sudanese raiders had tried to storm one of the park's ranger posts at Kanangorok, a place of sulphur springs astride the international border. These were Anya-nya, Southern Sudanese dissidents in conflict with the central government in Khartoum, who were in constant need of ammunition. Though shots were exchanged they had failed to break into the post and had then gone on to a police post in Kapedo, where they had killed two people. Peter intended to set up an ambush, lying up on some rocks above a path often used by people going by foot to and from the Sudan. We drove there after dark, a platoon of rangers and ourselves, leaving our vehicles some distance away so that the noise of their engines would not alert the raiders. The rocks were quite smooth and offered no protection but their height above the path would give us a tremendous advantage in any shooting match and, we hoped, the raiders would not see us in the darkness. We passed a tense night but they failed to appear, so at daylight we returned to Opotipot to catch up on our sleep.

On the way my Land Rover developed a puncture - a common experience and one easily corrected. I jacked up the vehicle as usual but as I picked up the spare wheel, I noticed a pack of African wild dogs, more than thirty in number, circling us within a radius of about twenty yards. We were armed but I did not want to shoot recklessly within the park, nor did I know how the dogs might react if one was shot for there was no way we could shoot thirty dogs in the few seconds it would take them to spring on us. I need not have worried, for they continued to stare at us impassively while I changed the wheel. I think Philip returned to Gezira thinking he lived in a much tamer milieu than I did.

A month or so later I was again spending a couple of nights in Kidepo when Peter heard that a large party of Didinga refugees had entered the park from the Sudanese side. They were not wanted in the park. So while those who were injured remained at the park headquarters at Opotipot where they were treated for gunshot wounds, the rest were moved with their livestock to the park boundary. I found them there the next morning at a place called Karenga. The cattle were very stunted compared to Dodoth animals and I ascribed this to the chronic effects of trypanosomosis, for the Kidepo valley was well stocked with tsetse flies, the vectors of this disease, and the Didinga lived in the Sudanese reaches of the river. The Dodoth were aware of the tsetse hazard near the river, which was a reason they showed little resentment to the alienation of so large a part of their territory for a national park. Tryps, as it is usually called, can be treated, but there was something more alarming; some of the Didinga animals were showing obvious clinical signs of pleuropneumonia, which we had only just eradicated from the country after the slaughter at Iriri.

Using the park's radio telephone I immediately communicated this information to David Morris in Moroto and the commissioner in Kampala. My first priority after that was to allocate some land as a temporary quarantine area for their livestock. But where? The

Dodoth would resent any incursion by the Didinga on to their pastures, besides which any contact was likely to infect their cattle. I therefore arranged with the local chief to locate the refugees around Karenga, a small village on the southern end of the Nyangeya mountains which formed the western boundary of Dodoth.

The inhabitants of this range were called Napore, a people with a linguistic affinity with the Didinga, so the potential for conflict was minimized. The Napore were predominantly agriculturalists, though they kept some livestock. Two Napore characteristics stand out: they thatched their houses most beautifully and their hoes were quite different from the usual. Instead of the blades being at right angles to the handle they were in the same plane and the handles were over twelve feet in length. The weight of the handle gave the blade the momentum to cut into the soil and the vibration of the long handle then broke up the soil.

Over the following weeks more and more refugees crossed into the country. It was obviously a political problem and not just a veterinary one. Big shots flew up to see for themselves, and as I had got to know several of the Police Airwing pilots I had the opportunity to fly surreptitiously, if that is possible, over the lower reaches of the Kidepo river. I saw that whole Didinga villages and their fields had been burned by the Sudanese army.[11]

The commissioner, Hugh Newlands, under pressure from his minister, would from time to time send me instructions on the park's radio telephone that were plainly impossible to carry out. I think Hugh knew that too but was obliged to relay the minister's orders. Fortunately I had learned from David how to handle such situations.

'Say again. Over,' I would bark down the microphone.

---

[11] The use of fixed-wing small planes was common not just for personal transport but for the carriage of vaccines to remoter parts. Another use was for game counting in which I sometimes assisted the game warden. Game counting not only established the location and numbers of each species but was also used to determine the numbers of hunting permits to be issued each year, an important source of revenue for the Game Dept. 50% of the animals were assumed to be males and permits were issued to shoot 10% of the males in any one year. Thus the breeding potential of the herds was not compromised.

Hugh repeated his instruction.

'Sorry, sir, I'm not catching you. Over' I would lie, somewhat plausibly, for the radio telephone was operating at the furthest limit of its range and was often interrupted by electric storms which were frequent at the onset of the annual rains. Other users of the same frequency would try to assist by relaying Hugh's message, and, though I could hear them clearly I continued with the lie.

Eventually, after several weeks contemplating what to do, the administration decided to relocate the refugees to Moruita, about 200 miles to the south, which was part of the no-man's-land between the Pian and Suk and close to Amudat. It was a prudent decision, for it prevented the Didinga from engaging in hit-and-run attacks on the Sudanese army over the border which might have brought Uganda into the conflict. It was also decided to prevent the dissemination of pleuropneumonia by blood-testing all the cattle, killing the reactors and trekking the rest to Iriri, about 160 miles to the south, before selling them to an abattoir in Kampala - the sale money to go to the refugees to assist them in their new life. While these matters were under consideration David and I were trying to improve the health of the refugee cattle by treating them for tryps and vaccinating them against rinderpest, which was enzootic to the region at the time.[12]

Unfortunately the improvement in their conditions and the services provided for the refugees acted as a magnet to those Didinga who had remained in Sudan and within weeks the few hundred refugees became several thousand, with over thirty thousand head of livestock. To assist us in our work, we established a semi-permanent camp a few miles east of Karenga at a place called

[12] The words epidemic and endemic refer to human diseases (Greek δῆμος = people). The words epizootic and enzootic have similar meanings but refer to animal diseases.

Loitanit which consisted of two uniports for drivers and safari cooks to sleep in and in which to keep a paraffin refrigerator for storing vaccines - and keeping our beer cold. Closer to Karenga we had a crush built for vaccinations and blood collections using locally-cut posts and strips of bark to lash the side pieces to the posts. Working conditions were difficult, for the rains were at their heaviest at that time of year. We were all ankle-deep in mud and the smaller animals in the crush slipped and fell; brute manpower was needed to get them on their feet again. It was not an easy time. Fortunately we had one great asset - a man called Nikanor Okema, who was a veterinary assistant (VA) like Fred Mwanje. But whereas there were numerous veterinary assistants in most parts of Uganda, the lack of any secondary schools in Karamoja at that time meant that there was only one VA in Karamoja despite it being the largest district with the most livestock. Nothing was too much for Nikanor and he covered all parts of Dodoth, a county twice the size of most English counties, on a bicycle. Without him I doubt that we would have been successful in dealing with so many refugees. He truly was a remarkable person.

Soon after the decision to test the cattle for pleuropneumonia was made, a mobile laboratory was put together at the Animal Health Research Centre in Entebbe by an FAO expert called Eric Huddart, who had made his reputation at EAVRO by developing the pleuropneumonia complement fixation test for use in the field. Huddart was middle-aged and difficult and expected us to do all the camp chores for him. David, who was no respecter of reputations, informed me that the word 'expert' was derived etymologically from ex, meaning a has-been, and spurt, a drip under pressure. Huddart demanded our full time presence - a demand which was just not possible in such an extensive district with a cattle population exceeding six hundred thousand, not to mention sheep and goats, some camels and numerous donkeys.

The Karamojong staff collected the blood samples and these were then analysed by the laboratory technicians who had come from Entebbe with the mobile laboratory. Each animal was identified by having a letter and numbers stencilled with household paint on its back when its blood was taken so that sample and animal could be correlated in the event that an animal was found to be a positive reactor. There were two major problems with this arrangement. The first was that on rainy days the paint often ran, got smudged or just covered with mud, and the second was that the laboratory results were usually not available until late afternoon, when it was difficult to read the numbers in the gathering gloom. Those animals that were positive and could be found, I shot. One outcome of this policy was that many Didinga preferred the wretchedness of their own country to losing their herds and so returned to the Sudan. Altogether I shot about seven hundred cattle over a period of a fortnight. The refugees took first choice of the meat, while the local people also benefited.

Among all this carnage I noted that many of the animals were affected with hydatidosis.[13] As this is a zoonotic disease[14] I informed the district medical officer, who in time discovered that some of the Didinga refugees were infected also and required surgery to remove the cysts. It was very uncommon to find the disease in the

[13] Hydatidosis is caused by Echinococcus granulosus, a very small, often unnoticed, tapeworm of dogs and other carnivores. Its intermediate stage, the hydatid cyst, can develop in man, domestic animals and numerous wild mammals. The typical cyst may be 2-4 inches in diameter though 20 inch cysts containing 3½ gallons of fluid have been seen in man. Development within the skull causes severe neurological problems and death. Cysts can rupture and form numerous daughter cysts. Dogs become infected by eating raw meat from infected animals. It used to be until recently a serious problem among the human population in Wales where sheepdogs fed on carrion were the principal sources of infection

[14] A disease affecting both man and animals

Karamojong, although there was a high prevalence among the Turkana. Why two peoples with such similar life styles should differ in this way is still not fully understood.

The slaughter of pleuropneumonia-positive cattle at Karenga also attracted lions from many miles around. One night the lions joined me for supper. In the evening we would usually light a camp fire around which we would sit over a beer or a glass of whisky. If I was alone my driver and safari cook would join me. On this night hardly had the fire been lit than the rain came down, so I was forced to withdraw to my tent. After a long interval Waswa, my usually cheerful cook, brought the first course of my dinner to the tent from the uniport where he had been cooking. He put the plate down on the table but then, instead of returning to the uniport to prepare the next course, he sat on my camp bed without saying a word, looking strangely nervous. When I finished the soup I suggested he get the next course, but all he could do was point wordlessly outside.

I took his point and looked outside the tent. There by the light of the fire were six lions, lying contentedly in its warmth. A very long time passed before I got the next course.

This was not my only close encounter with the big cats. On another occasion I was staying at Opotipot helping Peter Pegg with a game count. This was a welcome diversion from veterinary work and one I enjoyed doing for the park authorities and the game department, as it enabled me to understand better the biology of many animals - their reproductive cycles, their territorial priorities and their grazing behaviour. Usually I stayed in Peter's house, a simple mud-and-wattle construction with a fine Napore-thatched grass roof, on a hillside overlooking the Kidepo valley. Though simple, it was stout enough to give reassurance when lions could be heard a few hundred yards away, provoking the many zebra to bark a warning to others in the vicinity.

On this visit Peter had other guests, so I put up my tent in the park's campsite while my driver and cook found accommodation with friends in the rangers' lines. In the middle of the night I was woken by grunting around my tent. I could not be sure whether it was lion or leopard. I was too far from the rangers' lines or Peter's house to shout for help so, armed with a half-empty bottle of whisky and a torch, I challenged the animal to come and get me. Even the sound of my voice and the shining torch did not deter it and it continued to circle the tent until it stumbled on a guy rope; the whole tent shook as a result, but that also shook the intruder enough to encourage it to go away. In the morning while taking down the tent I asked Ali, my driver, who was half Karamojong, half Mkamba, to look for any pug marks. The Wakamba are a Kenyan people famed for their tracking skills and in little time he found the pug marks of a leopard. This was not really surprising. Leopard are very partial to dogs, even entering peoples' homes to get at them, and on most safaris I would take Rufus with me unless I was going to a tsetse infested area. The park was just such an area and I had left Rufus at home, but the doggy fragrance of the tent no doubt attracted the leopard's interest.

In the end about three thousand Didinga cattle were trekked under police supervision and myself to Iriri quarantine for onward movement to a Kampala abattoir. Regrettably, and despite my warnings to Dodoth elders about the dangers, a number of infected cattle were rustled by younger men with matrimonial ambitions and within a few months pleuropneumonia broke out in a dozen or so Dodoth herds. This should have, but probably didn't, teach them a lesson.

It was about this time I had my first contretemps with the administrator, a humourless, prim little man, about whom I had been warned. Knowing that there was to be a club party at Moroto one Saturday, Waswa, Ali and I packed up our camp on the Sudan border early one morning after a very light breakfast and set off, but it wasn't until late afternoon that we got back to Moroto. After a wash and a glance at my mail I retired to the club badly in need of a cold drink and some food. The cold drink went down like an elixir, but inevitably had a predictable effect on my empty stomach, so I resolved to leave the party furtively after I had had some food so as not to make a fool of myself.

On the Monday morning I was summoned to the administrator's office. 'As I am the representative of the Queen, it was an act of disrespect to leave the party before me' was his preposterous assertion. I remembered the warnings I had been given in Kampala not to be bullied by him, so I reminded him that Uganda was now a republic and that he did not represent the Queen.

'Well, as representative of the president' he corrected himself. To which I replied that I had not been aware that the President had been invited to the club party. I imagined that he would, behind my back, make a complaint to the commissioner about my perceived impertinence, so I fervently hoped the commissioner would back me up.

Soon afterwards I had a second clash with the administrator. It followed a safari I made to Upe in the southeast of the district to discover the cause of a sudden outbreak of a fatal disease among Suk cattle. I was always prepared for these emergencies and my safari boxes were ready for them.[15] What I was not prepared for was that the deaths had occurred half way up Kadam Mountain, and at seven and a half thousand feet with the rain coming down incessantly it was uncomfortably cold. I slept just a few hours the first night and when Waswa brought morning tea to my tent he complained that neither he nor Ali, who had been in a second tent, had been able to sleep at all. So the second night we all bedded down in my tent while the rain continued falling. A pressure lamp and Primus stove contributed to warming us up and we were able to sleep comfortably that second night.

By late the next morning I had got sufficient histories and samples to enable me to make a diagnosis - it was East Coast fever that was the cause of mortality - and we could then return to Moroto. Somehow the administrator heard about this incident and I was summoned again and told never, ever, again to share a tent with my staff. What I did not share with the administrator was his attitude to race and class, so I ignored his admonition but kept my own counsel.

It would be wrong to think that all our work was confined to the handling of emergencies. In fact the routine work, the organization of annual vaccination campaigns and the management of livestock markets, made up the bread and butter of veterinary activities, a fact of which Huddart seemed unaware. The major disease affecting cattle in many parts of Africa at that time was rinderpest, or cattle plague as it used to be called in Britain. Rinderpest was originally an old world disease and was

---

[15] An earlier veterinary officer I knew well had been disciplined for being unable to explain the deaths of ten animals in one village — this in a district one and a half times the size of Wales with poor communications.

often associated with wars, since the only movable assets the peasantry had when dispersed by war were their animals. It was an acute viral disease characterized by very high mortality in susceptible cattle. Before the advent of vaccines, restricting the movement of animals was the only means of control available. Harsh methods were used to enforce movement restrictions and in Romania in the 15th century the penalty for breaking the law was death (though clerks in holy orders were exempted from this punishment and were merely defrocked). In a later era, Catherine the Great of Russia and Frederick the Great of Prussia in 1770 connived to annex large swathes of Poland as *cordons sanitaires* when rinderpest hit that country. The last outbreak in Britain occurred in 1865 when it was introduced with cattle from Russia. Queen Victoria ordered that prayers be said in all churches throughout the kingdom for 'relief from the murrain' although it is likely that the quarantine and slaughter measures that were instituted at the time were more effective in controlling the disease.

Different accounts are given to explain the introduction of the disease into Africa in 1889. The most likely is that the Italians imported infected cattle from Aden, of southern Arabian or Indian origin, to feed their garrisons in their newly conquered colony of Eritrea. In no time at all the disease spread throughout the upper reaches of the Nile and into Uganda. The effects were devastating among both cattle and wildlife. In some areas in the Zambezi valley and southern Africa even the tsetse fly were eliminated, for there were no warm-blooded animals left for them to feed on. The cattle-keeping pastoralists of East Africa including the Karamojong, Samburu and Maasai were severely affected, though the camel keepers such as the Rendille of present-day northern Kenya and the Somalis were not.

By 1896 the disease had reached South Africa; its advance checked only temporarily by the Zambezi river. The government of the Cape of Good Hope made two attempts in 1897 to hold back the advance. A double line of fences was erected around the town of Mafikeng, where the disease was first found, and when that failed to restrict the advance a second fence, over a thousand miles long, was built along the Orange river from the south-western corner of the Bechuanaland Protectorate (now Botswana) to the Indian Ocean and reinforced with mounted guards. The story goes that despite these precautions a drover with a span of oxen travelling along the fence saw a dead eland on the other side and stopped to skin it. Others say he saw a sack of biltong. Whatever it was, within a few days his farm was affected and from there the disease spread throughout South Africa.

In 1897 the German bacteriologist Robert Koch was appointed by the Cape government to advise on control of the disease. Koch was a man of great distinction, who had in 1884 formulated the eponymous postulates linking causation between microbes and disease.[16] He had been the first to show that diseases such as tuberculosis, cholera and anthrax had a bacterial origin at a time when the conventional wisdom was that disease was caused by poisonous miasmas or the consequence of sin.[17] Evidence of the

---

[16] Robert Koch, together with Louis Pasteur, were the first to develop the germ theory of disease in the 1860's and 1870's. Koch's Postulates were:

i - the microorganism must be found in abundance in all animals suffering from the disease but should not be found in healthy animals;

ii - the microorganism must be isolated and grown in pure culture;

iii - the cultured microorganism should cause disease when introduced into a healthy animal

iv - the microorganism must be re-isolated from the inoculated, diseased experimental host and identified as being identical to the original specific causative agent.

These original postulates have since undergone amendment since some animals are carriers of disease microbes but show no clinical signs

[17] Tuberculosis was the cause of almost a quarter of all human deaths in northern Europe at that time.

former superstition still persists in the names of a common tropical malady, malaria, and the city of my birth, Buenos Aires, and one can only wonder if moral philosophers of old considered animals capable of sin. Within a short time Koch produced a useful vaccine using bile from cattle that had died of the disease, but not before over two million cattle had died in South Africa.

It had long been known that people and animals which had recovered from certain diseases were subsequently resistant to further infection. It was the English physician Edward Jenner who first demonstrated that it was possible to immunize people actively against smallpox by scarifying their skin with infected material taken from cowpox lesions. Louis Pasteur improved the technique of immunization by using killed vaccines in which the causal bacterium or virus was destroyed by chemicals such as formalin. Being dead, the organisms could not reproduce the disease, though unfortunately in many cases the organism was so altered by the chemical that it produced no antibody response, or one of very limited value in protecting the subject. The problem in making vaccines has been, and still is, to neutralize the virulence of the causal organism so that it neither causes clinical disease nor disseminates the disease but still retains its effectiveness to promote immunity. The commonest means to achieve this result is to attenuate the causative organism by passaging it through many generations in an unnatural host, such as chicken or duck eggs, or in a culture medium, but it is a very hit-and-miss procedure. Koch's vaccine, though a godsend at the time, met few of the criteria of a safe and effective vaccine. So during the first half of the 20th century many attempts were made throughout Asia and Africa to find better vaccines against rinderpest.[18]

---

[18] More recently a few vaccines have been produced using molecular fractions of the causative organisms

At the time I went to Karamoja the vaccine in use was the Kabete Avianized Goat vaccine. KAG had been developed in the Kabete laboratories of the Kenyan department of veterinary services with a virus that had originally been isolated from a goat and had then been 'passaged' through a succession of chicken eggs. It was effective in protecting vaccinated cattle, yet sufficiently virulent to produce clinical signs of rinderpest. Although milder than the fully virulent field strain it was malignant enough to kill animals in a poor state of health caused by malnutrition or chronic disease. Consequently, vaccination campaigns were carried out at the end of the rainy season when the cattle were in good condition and, if there was evidence of tryps in the area, the cattle were treated for that about a fortnight before vaccination commenced.

There was another advantage for vaccinating at the end of the wet season; all the animals were concentrated around the Karamojong villages and not dispersed in the remote dry-season grazing areas.

The chiefs of all the villages were obliged to build and maintain cattle crushes, which they did using local materials and labour. This was no problem, for there was considerable cooperation and trust between cattle owners and the veterinary department. Although the vaccine gave a lifelong immunity to adult cattle, this was not so if administered to young calves, so the policy was to vaccinate all calves and yearlings each year. The yearling animals were then branded on the hump using a hot iron with a K brand (in other parts of the country and in Kenya an R brand was used, so assisting in identifying stolen cattle).

The vaccine, being a live one, had to be kept on ice in large vacuum flasks until used, and getting ice to the remoter sites was always a logistical problem. The vaccine came in glass vials of a hundred doses and was reconstituted with saline solution immediately before use, the solution being made up at each vaccination site as it was needed. A vaccination team consisted of six to eight men; two to drive the cattle into the crushes, usually assisted with great noise by the cattle owners, two to administer the vaccine, two to maintain the fire and brand the cattle, and a recorder. Under ideal conditions a team could vaccinate up to two thousand animals a day, but conditions seldom were ideal and were further exacerbated by the Karamoja Buggerance Factor, so more typically a team vaccinated about six thousand animals in a week. The aim was to vaccinate about three hundred thousand animals annually and with four teams working simultaneously about a hundred thousand could be covered in a month.

The vaccination teams operated closely to minimize the use of transport to move teams from site to site and provide them with vaccines, ice and other requirements. Consequently staff from all over the district were grouped together, which meant putting men of different Karamojong groups, who would under normal circumstances be hostile to each other, to work at the same site. But they all got along well, so well that the greatest risk posed to the vaccinators was the possibility of getting sore heads from the hospitality offered to them by appreciative livestock owners. In fact the only grievance I received was from a man in Karenga who complained that one of the alien vaccinators had been too free with his daughter and she had become pregnant during the previous vaccination round and was now in danger of becoming pregnant again.

I would try to spend as much time as possible with the vaccination teams but with four teams operating simultaneously I could not be everywhere at once. The work was hot, dusty and repetitive, but it was rarely boring and my presence built up a sense of camaraderie with the vaccinators which was useful when settling other disputes. Getting ice to teams within sixty or seventy miles of Moroto was not a problem, as a Land Rover could get to the site and back in a day. Dodoth presented a bigger problem as it took about seven hours hard driving to reach Kaabong. Fortunately I struck up a friendly relationship with the Verona Fathers who ran a Catholic mission on the outskirts of the little town and would store the vaccine in their refrigerator. It was one of the rules of their house that they could not drink unless they had guests, so I was usually very welcome, especially if I brought a demijohn of Chianti with me. This suited me well as I seldom arrived in Kaabong much before dusk, so while my cook and driver were putting up tents and making camp in the gathering darkness and preparing their food I would repair to the mission to store the vaccine and stay for supper.

On one occasion, and it must have been a day when there were no problems in Moroto to sort out before departure, I arrived in Kaabong in the middle of the afternoon. Since it was still light, a kind Italian father insisted on showing me around the mission station. There seemed to be rather a lot of *café-au-lait* children around and I remarked on it as Kaabong was so remote it seemed unlikely that they had been born locally.

'The reason, Mr Minor' he explained in his thick Italian accent, 'is we take a vow of celibacy but not one of chastity.'

The second routine activity of the veterinary department was

73

to conduct monthly cattle markets at each county headquarters. There were seven such market sites in the district and the markets would last for two days at the bigger centres and one day at others. All the elements of the trade were managed by livestock marketing officers. Initially there was a single buyer, one of the marketing officers, but there were objections, since the local politicians thought the buyer could manipulate the price to the detriment of the cattle owners. To counter these objections, auction yards were built at each site and butchers from the larger towns in central Uganda attended.

The largest numbers of cattle were offered for sale early in the year, when not only school fees and other taxes had to be paid but with the advancing dry season there was a shortage of food and cash was needed to purchase maize meal. Within a month or so of the onset of the rains in May, when the cattle were beginning to thrive, the supply of animals dried up. In years when food was short, up to sixty thousand animals were marketed, a tenth of the whole population. This was much encouraged by the administration, for in those days it was believed that overgrazing caused desertification. Modern theory, however, is that it is over-cropping that causes permanent and irreversible soil degradation, whereas overgrazing causes only temporary, reversible damage.

I enjoyed market days, which gave me the opportunity to meet and pay local staff who came in from the outlying areas for the purpose. The auctions were fun and I would try to guess what would be offered for each lot. At the end of each market the animals would be trekked under escort to Iriri quarantine where they were sprayed against ticks immediately on entry and twice a week thereafter. This was to prevent them from contracting East Coast fever, to which they were very susceptible as most parts of the district were free from the disease, it being too dry for the survival of the brown ear tick. Only around the mountains such as in Akisim and Napak, which attracted higher rainfall, did the vector ticks flourish.

Cattle entering quarantine were also vaccinated against rinderpest and anthrax and had to remain at least a fortnight in quarantine to see if any other disease was present, of which foot-and-mouth was most likely. Later, when pleuropneumonia spread to some areas, all cattle transiting the quarantine were also tested for the disease and the reactors slaughtered. Once a week, and sometimes more often, one of the veterinary officers would be obliged to go to Iriri to examine the outgoing animals before they were trekked the fifty miles or so to the railway line at Soroti, from where they were entrained to the abattoirs of the major towns.

It was also fun was to watch the Karamojong men who would gather at the markets to watch the proceedings. Generally they were a handsome crowd, fine-bodied and long-limbed, and barely covered with a black cotton shuka; their shoulders were often covered with cicatrices arranged like medals in geometrical patterns to show the number of people they had killed. Even the older men, wrinkled as they might be, retained a certain gracefulness. The younger, unmarried men had headpieces, cylindrical in shape and covered with red ochre, while the married ones had skullcap-shaped headpieces over their hair decorated with white, blue and red clay. Ostrich feathers or brass rings might further embellish them. Some men wore ivory or bead bracelets and older men often had an aluminium or ivory lip plug inserted in a hole below their lower lip. All the men carried a neck rest, shaped like a T or the Greek letter π, to prevent damage to their elaborate headpieces when sleeping. There was an amusing vanity about them and they would collect around the wing mirrors of my Land Rover, as fascinated by their own images in a mirror, which many had never seen before, as by their ornamentation. They also had no false modesty about displaying their masculinity, for they had little reason to be modest. This was brought home to me in another way by my young office messenger. At the end of each day he carefully folded up his uniform and hid it behind a filing cabinet; when I asked him one day why he didn't return home with his uniform he replied that the girls might think he was deficient in some way if he were to wear it.

CHAPTER 5

District Veterinary Officer

In due course, David went on leave and I took over as DVO of Karamoja district. There were some reservations because, although I was qualified, I was the youngest and least experienced of all the senior staff. Fortunately David had supported me, remarking to the commissioner, Hugh Newlands, that the only reason for hesitation was that I was 'shy of files', which was true. I did not think it a very damaging criticism. Nor, it seemed, did Newlands.

The most important of my new duties was the financial administration of the veterinary department in Karamoja. At the beginning of each financial year funds were voted to cover a range of items from the employment of casual staff to transport costs. This gave me considerable autonomy from head office, since I could go ahead and employ casual labourers or buy goods without having to apply for consent. Standing orders made it clear, however, that any over-expenditure would be deducted from my salary, a policy which ensured financial responsibility. On the other hand, if there was a large surplus left in the budget for any item, one could be sure that there would be a reduction in funds for that item in the following financial year, which meant that one tried to spend almost up to the limit. An engineering colleague, who later became a senior official in the World Bank in Washington, advised me that should

I overspend I should do so by a large amount; too much to be deducted from my salary. Perhaps spendthrift habits were considered a virtue in Washington.

It was not long before I had to face up to these financial responsibilities; there was a 10% cut overall in the new vote allocated to me. The most obvious saving was to reduce the numbers of casuals, which I did by using the 'last in, first out' formula. This had the local Member of Parliament, Joshua Loruk, storming in to my office demanding I re-employ them. Gently I tried to explain to him that the money allocated to me had been voted by parliament and as he was a member of the ruling party, the United Peoples Congress, he had supported the government's budget proposals. Not only that, he had voted for a government bill to raise the minimum wage, so that the money apportioned to me was even more limited. I suggested that I might be obliged to explain this to the recently discharged men but, of course, he did not wish to be seen to have connived in their dismissal, so he removed himself from my office and the matter was quietly dropped.

Another role I inherited from David was that of visiting magistrate to the Kotido jail. It was a high-security prison for long-term prisoners, but the greatest disincentive for them to escape was the fearsome reputation of the Karamojong living around the prison. This was an era before the advocacy of human rights was as pressing as it has now become, but I always considered my first priority was to protect the prisoners from any abuse and that my second was to defend the prison officers from criticism when, in fact, they had acted quite lawfully.

I would drop in unannounced whenever I was in the area.

When I did, I always found the prison immaculately clean; a great deal cleaner than the district hospital. It also had a flourishing vegetable garden fed with water from the prison's kitchen and wash places which seemed to me quite remarkable, as Kotido was, and is, quite the most dusty of the dust bowls in Karamoja.

One of my duties was to interview all prisoners in solitary confinement. After each visit I would have to write a report to the commissioner of prisons. However I had not long been in the post when Uganda's Prime Minister, whether prompted by paranoia or not I don't know, suspected that some of his cabinet colleagues were disloyal and had them locked up in Kotido jail. I thought that there might be questions asked about their condition, so I decided it would be prudent to make an unannounced visit, but I was politely but firmly prevented from seeing them. From previous visits I had developed a high regard for the prison officers, so I suspected that they were acting under orders to refuse me access to the high-profile prisoners. This suggested that they might be being subjected to some maltreatment which I could not prevent. Rather than appear to collude in this possible abuse, I resigned as visiting magistrate to the jail.

Another role, but not an inherited one, was my appointment as a licensed circumciser by the district medical officer. One of our veterinary staff had converted to Islam and had been circumcised with a broken beer bottle, which resulted in considerable injury to his manhood. A beer bottle seemed to me a singularly inappropriate object with which to initiate the man into the Islamic faith. At least as a vet I was equipped with more suitable tools than that.

Aside from these unusual roles, the normal work of the veterinary department still had to go on. It was soon apparent that not only the Dodoth but the Bokora and Pian had illegally acquired some of the Didinga cattle which had been intended for slaughter, and reports of new outbreaks of pleuropneumonia started to come in on the police telegraph network. Clearly something had to be done, but it was not clear what. The commissioner, Hugh Newlands, as well as Tom Coyle, the chief research officer, and Eric Huddart all flew up for a policy-making meeting. It was beyond the resources of the department to test the blood of three hundred or so thousand cattle in the three infected counties and politically inexpedient to slaughter the large number of reactors that were likely to be found, so a vaccination policy was agreed on. I say agreed on, but I voiced profound reservations about the use of vaccines to control the disease, since previous vaccines had failed to protect the animals and some had even disseminated the disease to uninfected herds. In the end, however, my objections were overruled by Newlands.

At the time a new vaccine was being developed at Muguga using a strain of *Mycoplasma mycoides*, the causal organism of pleuropneumonia, which had been isolated in Tanganyika and then serially passaged through many generations to reduce its pathogenicity. This vaccine came to be known as T_1 broth culture vaccine, the T being for Tanganyika. There were numerous drawbacks to its use, one of them being that it had never been tried on a large scale before. It was also not known if vaccinated animals might not prove positive to the CFT, thereby rendering the test useless in identifying infected animals. There were doubts also about the vaccine's pathogenicity, about its immunogenicity and about the length of time it would protect cattle, yet I had to persuade the Karamojong to accept it.

Like previous pleuropneumonia vaccines it was injected in the end of the tail, so that if there was a severe reaction the tail could be amputated. This was another problem, for the tail tip is often contaminated by faeces, so it was impossible in the field to decide whether a tail reaction was due to faecal contamination of the injection site or to the vaccine itself. An even greater problem was logistical; the experimental vaccine had a shelf life of two months and had to be kept on ice at all times. The short shelf life meant that I had to predict the district's vaccine requirements and order sufficient quantities of vaccine from Muguga well ahead of the time it was to be used and when I did not know whether roads would be passable and all the other Buggerance Factors that inevitably affected vaccination schedules.

It was about the time when the annual rinderpest vaccination campaign was about to commence, so I set about organizing a combined vaccination campaign using both rinderpest and CBPP vaccines. This brought up two more problems. The first was that a new rinderpest vaccine, an attenuated tissue culture vaccine, TCV for short, was also being introduced at this time. The Karamojong, and the Dodoth in particular, did not like it. The old KAG vaccine converted to a red suspension when reconstituted in the saline solution and produced mild symptoms of disease; the new vaccine was colourless and non-virulent. As a result the Karamojong were profoundly distrustful of the new vaccine; to them it looked no better than water. The second problem was that there was a possibility that the use of two vaccines simultaneously might interfere with the development of a high degree of immunity to one or both diseases. In an attempt to overcome the Dodoth's distrust of the new colourless vaccine I tried to persuade Walter Plowright, who had developed the vaccine, to add a dye to the vaccine, though I was not surprised when he countered the suggestion saying that any dye was likely to be detrimental to the viability of the vaccine.

The logistical problems were also increased. Whereas the dry TC vaccines could be kept on ice in vacuum flasks, the fluid T_1 vaccine was bulky and had to be stored in specially- constructed ice boxes when used in the field. Added to this difficulty was that the numbers of animals to be vaccinated were greatly increased, since the vaccination campaign would have to cover cattle of all ages, not just the calves and yearlings.

It took a little while to persuade cattle owners to accept the new rinderpest TC vaccine, but eventually there was considerable cooperation from the Dodoth and Bokora and vaccinations went smoothly in their counties. Bokoran cooperation was also shown in another way: some of their infected herds were isolated at the Kopopwa section of Iriri quarantine, but one of the herd owners decided to break out. Within a few days he sent me an emissary with the proposition that he would return his herd to the quarantine if I agreed not to prosecute him. It turned out his neighbours had threatened to kill all his cattle if he did not. I was happy to agree and glad that the cattle owners themselves were willing to enforce quarantine regulations.

This incident showed the degree of trust that existed between cattle owners and veterinary officials. In this I benefited from the veterinary officers of the previous fifteen years, who had introduced effective vaccines and treatments and had thus earned the confidence of the Karamojong for, quite certainly, the Karamojong had had, and still have, their own remedies, and it was unlikely they would change their ways just because a white man in Moroto said they had to.

Only in the southern county of Pian was there a lack of cooperation, and ironically it was led by the Member of Parliament for that area, a man called Daniel Lobunei. According to the MP, the pleuropneumonia vaccine would make cattle sterile, so he advised his people not to get their cows or heifers vaccinated.

One of my new duties as DVO was to write a monthly report to my immediate senior officer, the provincial veterinary officer. I could blackmail the field staff, most of whom were literate to a degree, to hand in their reports on pay day around the end of each month and I then submitted my own report by the tenth day of the following month. A similar obligation was required for the annual report at the end of December. In many ways it was a tedious procedure; the numbers of cattle sold or slaughtered by butchers were easily calculated, but the numbers of chicken eggs sold and their prices at markets all over the large district required an active imagination. The monthly and annual reports, however, were an extremely useful management tool; not only did they allow me to keep tabs on the field staff and, I suppose, allow the PVO to keep tabs on me, they allowed me to see trends in disease patterns over time.

The most important of these trends was to note that within two months of vaccinating 90% of the cattle, firstly in Dodoth and subsequently in Bokora, no new herds became infected with pleuropneumonia. Given my initial scepticism about the T_1 vaccine, this was exceedingly satisfying. But sadly in Pian, where MP Lobunei was frustrating the department's efforts, new herds were becoming infected every week. Months went by, then half a year, and still fresh herds became infected whereas in the two more northerly counties the disease was contained. Then Lobunei did me a favour, though not of his own volition. His own herd was found to have the disease.

It so happened that the principal member of veterinary staff in charge of Pian county was Lobunei's brother. As it was far more likely that he was in the MP's camp than in mine it seemed prudent not to delegate any actions to him and to take charge of events myself. Accordingly I arranged for Lobunei's herd to be moved to Namalu, another of our quarantine stations in the south of the district, and I fixed a date with Lobunei, the county chief (a government-appointed official known locally as the *Ekapolon*) and other chiefs to meet them there. Quite a crowd assembled at the appointed time, possibly in the hope that there might be some free meat going at the end of proceedings, and while I addressed them about the evils of the disease I instructed my staff to separate the sick animals from the healthy ones. When the baraza was finished we all walked over to look at Lobunei's herd. Hoping that they had all taken in my words with care, I asked the crowd if they noticed anything special about the sick animals, in the expectation that they would repeat the clinical signs of the disease which I had gone through in painstaking detail.

'They're all cows and heifers,' answered the Ekapolon.

It was not the answer I had expected, but I was grateful to him for making the point that the unvaccinated animals were the ones to succumb to the disease. It certainly embarrassed the MP and from then on the control of pleuropneumonia went on apace in Pian.

There was another important lesson derived from this event. The fact that the disease was controlled in those counties where there was a high level of vaccinations was only circumstantial evidence that the vaccine protected cattle against the disease. But Lobunei's herd provided a comparison between vaccinated animals and unvaccinated control animals, and the evidence was overwhelming that even in a herd with a high proportion of actively infected cattle, the vaccinated animals were protected by the new T1 vaccine.[19]

This was a significant observation, since previous vaccines had so often been ineffective and, on occasion, had produced serious lesions at the vaccination site and even disseminated the disease so, when time permitted, I published a paper on the use of the vaccine under field conditions. One of the questions I felt sure would be asked about the vaccine was what deleterious effect it had on the tails of cattle. To try to determine this I examined the tails of a mob of about four hundred trade cattle at the Kaabong cattle market in Dodoth, where vaccine usage had been high, and compared the rate of tail loss among them with those of trade cattle in Kotido, where no vaccine had been used. Surprisingly, there was a greater rate of tail loss among the Jie cattle in Kotido market than among the vaccinated cattle of Dodoth - an observation which prompted a colleague to remark that I had shown that T_1 vaccine protected cattle's tails. It was only after publication of the paper that I realized the cause of the difference. The Jie people used oxen to a much larger extent than did the Dodoth for ploughing and from time to time the oxen's tails were injured when caught between the links of the chain drawing the plough, resulting in crushing of the tail tip or even severance.

No sooner had the first vaccination campaign been completed

---

[19] Because of the logistical problems associated with the keeping and transport of the broth culture vaccine, a freeze-dried derivative was later used. The potency of a vaccine is measured in ID50 units. One ID50 is a dose sufficient to immunize 50% of animals given the vaccine. A single dose of the broth culture vaccine contained 100 ID50 units. In initial experiments freeze-drying had a deleterious effect on the fragile, live Mycoplasma mycoides organisms and killed 99% of them — in other words the original freeze-dried vaccine had only 1 ID50 left in it, sufficient to immunize only half the animals given it. Although freeze-drying techniques have improved since then I have yet to see compelling evidence that later attempts to freeze-dry CBPP T1 vaccine have been more successful.

than Huddart advised a second round of vaccinations, for at that time no one knew how long any immunity persisted in vaccinated animals.[20] This, of course, increased the workload on an already over-pressed group of men.

In my annual report at the end of 1965 I was able to state that over a million vaccinations had been carried out and that, for the first time on record, there had been no reports of rinderpest in the previous twelve months. Hugh Newlands, who was about to retire as commissioner, made a last trip to Moroto and, after reproaching me for my inability to hear him on the radio-telephone, congratulated me on this outcome.

During this time I was finding myself overwhelmed by the demands made on me. Most weeks I was out of the office checking trade cattle, supervising vaccination campaigns, diagnosing disease outbreaks and other activities. I would return to Moroto on Saturday evenings and would have my clerk in on Sunday mornings to prepare pay vouchers and other documents for my signature before returning to the field on Monday. So I asked Newlands for some help. This came to me in the form of an overseas graduate volunteer. I was not best pleased, because Jim was not a veterinarian so could not make diagnoses, and he was not a government officer so could not authorize payments. He had studied a biological subject at university, so I suggested he undertake some of the laboratory work, but he said he did not know how, even when I provided him with a manual of laboratory techniques. He was worse than useless, for under the terms of the contract with his voluntary organization he was entitled to have the use of a vehicle and one of the limited number of houses allocated to the veterinary department. 'Salaried tourists' was what

[20] It was later shown by two veterinarians at Muguga who afterwards became colleagues, Walter Masiga and Roger Windsor, that under experimental conditions of severe challenge the vaccine gave excellent protection for a year and substantial protection for two.

one senior Ugandan officer called them.

I thought the volunteer might at least be of some use in undertaking pay safaris, but in that I was disappointed too. For his first safari I took Jim to Iriri, where there was a permanent camp of uniports to accommodate the veterinary officer who was obliged to make a visit at least once a week to supervise the release of trade cattle. The talk that night was of snakes; it seemed he had a dread of them. I tried to reassure him that they were seldom dangerous unless cornered. As if on cue, when we went out later to water Africa before turning in, a snake slithered away in the darkness, but though it was not aggressive he was not reassured. Next day I thought to have an early morning shower, but when I went to turn the taps I saw to my horror a snake coiled around them. I leapt out of the shower without bothering to collect my towel. Seeing my nakedness, both Ali and Waswa went into fits of laughter, enough to wake the volunteer. He emerged from his uniport bleary-eyed and asked why I was unclothed. Even though I hadn't been bitten, my explanation just reinforced his idea of the ubiquity of snakes and the risks they posed.

The following week I took Jim on safari to Lokales, where we were building a cattle dip. The area was close under Kadam Mountain, which attracted more rainfall than on the plains and was therefore another place where the brown ear tick thrived and spread ECF. This time I allocated him his own vehicle and a driver who spoke English. Albert was a nice lad who had been in a Catholic seminary, but after putting one of the nuns in the family way he had been considered unsuitable material for ordination so took up being a driver.

I insisted that Jim and Albert erect a tent from the store to ensure that all the poles and pegs were with it. While doing so a colleague passed by and warned me to keep Rufus close to me as he had seen a leopard nearby the previous week. On hearing this, the intrepid volunteer suggested he sleep in my tent, to which I said a firm 'No', thinking he must get used to safari conditions. During the night I was woken a few times by the bleating of goats in a manyatta a few hundred yards away, but this to him was another terror, for he admitted next morning to having had a dreadful night because of all the scary noises.

Nevertheless I persisted in trying to find some use for his limited capabilities and sent him out on a pay safari with Albert, who knew the country well. I suggested he leave on a Monday morning, spend a couple of nights in Kaabong paying the Dodoth staff, a couple of nights in Kotido doing the same and then a night in Labwor and ascertain the positions of the major waterholes in those areas while there and return on Saturday. But he was back late Monday night, having covered more than 400 miles in one day and paid exactly one man. As he was not an employee I had no way of disciplining him, which put me in an invidious position because it looked as if I favoured him over the African staff.

Some weeks later while on safari, Ali mentioned to me that he thought the new *mzungu* was useless. I tried to cover up, but to no avail. Ali, and no doubt many others of my staff, had recognized him for what he was. But true to form, the 'salaried tourist' managed to visit at least half a dozen game parks in his two-year stint - and nearly drove me up the wall. Jim was, obviously, quite the wrong person to be recruited to work in the bush.

His dread of the bush precluded him from enjoying what, to

me, is one of the most abiding memories of those years - the sheer pleasure of nights in camp marked by the high-pitched buzz of cicadas in the foreground with the occasional bark of an alarmed zebra, the whoop of a hyena or the grunts of lion hunting somewhere beyond the light of the camp fire. Above, the great sweep of the stars moved majestically from east to west, returning back to the same place the following night. Like aliens among these natural phenomena, one or two man-made satellites glided serenely and silently from horizon to horizon most nights; satellites which within a few years of the flight of the first sputnik in 1957 the Karamojong had learned to distinguish from other celestial objects and named. In the stillness of the bush the magnificence of the cosmos above quite overwhelmed me, in much the same way as a Mozart concerto can. It was easy to understand how early men in their attempts to explain the awesome reality of the universe invented whole pantheons of gods to give meaning to it.

Inevitably I was interested in what diseases affected the Karamojong in particular as, for example, hydatidosis was a particular problem for the Didinga and Turkana peoples. Late one night, when everybody else had long gone home, just three people were left in the club bar - the district agricultural officer, John Wilson, the district medical officer, Graham Hulley, and myself. It seemed a suitable time to discuss what others might think was a sordid subject. At first Graham mentioned pneumonia as a particular hazard of children in the wet season. This was understandable, as few were adequately clothed against the wet and cold when herding sheep and goats around their villages. Graham also mentioned that there was a much higher prevalence of liver cancer among the Karamojong than in neighbouring groups. This interested me as I had just been reading about a new disease of turkeys - Turkey X disease - which had caused massive mortality in the turkey industry in Britain a few years previously. This had been caused by a fungal toxin caused aflatoxin.[21] At this stage John interjected with the observation that the Karamojong preferred eating mouldy sorghum because it was sweeter. This, of course, did not prove that the Karamojong's preferred diet was implicated, but within a year the medical faculty at Makerere University had arranged a symposium on medical mycotoxicoses. I like to think that that late-night discussion started something.

There was a constant stream of visitors, not all of them welcome. Particularly irksome were European tourists who travelled inadequately equipped, without spare tyres or drinking water and with incorrect maps, and who expected government officers to assist them when they got into trouble. One of them, a Swedish journalist, whose name I have long forgotten, caused considerable annoyance. I found her ensconced in my camp in Kaabong one morning after I returned from vaccinating a mob of cattle. Naturally I was affable but after an hour or two I suggested she move on as I had a lot of work to do. It seemed it was her intention to go to Gulu. When I told her that it would be impossible in her small saloon car, she maintained that her Shell map showed that it was an all-weather road. Eventually I persuaded her of the impossibility of her plan, saying that I wouldn't even attempt the road in a 4-wheel drive vehicle without a back-up.

'So what do you suggest?' she asked.

I proposed she go to the Kidepo National Park about 50 miles

---

[21] Aflatoxicosis is now found to affect many species including fish. In a brilliant investigation Ruth Allcroft, working at Weybridge in England, discovered that turkeys whose diet contained groundnuts from Brazil were not affected while those fed groundnuts from West Africa were. The difference was that West African groundnuts were often mouldy as a result of contamination with a fungus called *Aspergillus flavus*. Extraction of a toxin from the mouldy groundnuts which was then fed to rats caused liver tumours in the rats..

further on or return the 120 miles to the Moroto rest house where she had spent the previous night. After dark she returned to my camp saying the park's fees were too high. I had no choice but to arrange to accommodate her in my camp, for it would have been far too dangerous to drive to Moroto at that time of night. It was pleasant to have her company and I was somewhat indiscreet, but it did not take me long to realize that she had been touring Uganda on the cheap, relying on white residents to put her up most nights. Later I saw her book on Uganda, in which she described me as a cross between James Bond and Tarzan; she also repeated some of the indiscreet remarks I had made about Ugandan politicians. Fortunately the book was written in Swedish, so the indiscreet remarks got no further, as I would surely have been dismissed if a Ugandan official had read them - and the description of my physical charms would have sent my friends falling about with derisive laughter.

My Swedish girlfriend Else certainly thought it funny. She had come out to visit me in Uganda about a year after my arrival. I had hoped very much in the intervening time that her visit would lead to an engagement, but David Morris put a spoke in the affair by intimating to me that the ladies of the station would not take it well if we cohabited for any length of time without a formal engagement. Clearly the new sexual *mores* current in Europe at the time had not reached the Europeans in Moroto - though it was equally clear that the locals had never embraced the old Victorian morality. I was angered by this criticism, for I had good reason to believe the pot was calling the kettle black. Although I tried to conceal the altercation with my boss from Else, she was quickly aware that the station's ladies were talking about her and thought she should move on.

I was in two minds. I had known her for three years and my more than fond feelings for her had not changed, but I was also thoroughly enjoying my job and did not wish to be domesticated just yet. For her part, she had no desire to live in Africa.

Another welcome visitor was a professor of entomology from Cornell University in New York, John George Matthysse, on a sabbatical leave. Matthysse's speciality was the study of ticks. I assisted him on several occasions to make tick collections throughout the district, mainly from cattle but also from sheep, goats and dogs. Before his visits I had had only a superficial interest in ticks, but he quickly inspired me. Later I took over his laboratory in Entebbe, though my interests were mainly about the role of ticks as vectors of disease, whereas Matthysse's interest was in the classification of ticks- in other words the taxonomy of ticks.

On one of my rare visits to Kampala I had met up again with my old assistant Fred Mwanje. Fred at this time was reading for a veterinary degree at a Pakistani university but was home on leave. I had always liked him and I suggested he might like to come and spend a few days with me in Moroto. We drove back together and on the first evening I took him up to the club. By this time my *bête noire*, the humourless administrator, had been replaced by a Ugandan, Paul Tamukedde. Paul was a short man but he could serve aces over the net like a Wimbledon champion, after which he would retire into the club house for a Guinness. Good manners prescribed that I introduce Fred to him, which I did. After a few pleasantries we both retired to the bar but I soon noticed Paul was beckoning to me to come back.

'Do you know who he is?' he asked me softly, obviously referring to Fred.

'Yes, he is Fred Mwanje' I replied.

'Evidently you don't know who he is' said Paul. He then explained to me that Fred was the Katikiro's son. It was indicative of Fred's modesty that he had never boasted about his paternity, though I now could understand why all the Baganda farmers had been so effusive when we visited them.

Many years later I met Fred's mother at his dairy farm just a few miles outside Kampala. She was a widow by then and I guessed close to eighty, but nevertheless, she insisted on curtsying right down to the ground when greeting me. I was touched as well as being impressed by her great dignity. In those early years after independence there were some very fine Ugandans in the administration, police force, university and elsewhere. Apart from the terrible harm done to the economy by Idi Amin, the greatest other damage he did to Uganda, and from which it still suffers, was the killing or exile of many of these fine people.

The year 1965 was a dry one, that is to say it was a drier year than most and the long rains came later than usual. In those long weeks before the onset of the rains the Karamojong had exhausted their food reserves from the previous year's harvest and had been obliged to eat their seed grain. Cattle, commonly in a weakened condition at the end of every dry season, were pushed over the dividing line between life and death and bleached, desiccated carcases lay open-gutted over the plains and on the few roads in the district. Only the vultures did well; too well, for many were so satiated they could not rise off the ground when approached by a vehicle so their bodies, too, lay about with the other carcases on the sides of the roads.

The district medical officer proposed at a district team meeting, where heads of all departments would meet monthly, that famine relief measures be introduced. Under pressure from me, he admitted that the only deaths from famine he was aware of were of elderly people. To me it seemed that the cattle owners put a greater value on their cattle than on the elderly members of their group.[22] I had noted that there was plenty of maize meal in the dukas around the district but that the numbers of cattle offered for sale at the newly-constructed auction yards had not increased at all. Giving away free food would put no pressure on cattle owners to sell their cattle. When pasture belongs to the whole community, what is called a common good, no one man is going to limit his herd size for the benefit of his neighbour, which means that herd sizes increase uncontrollably if not checked by drought at intervals. It is a sad irony that the more successful disease control programmes are, the worse the overgrazing problem becomes. Destocking measures had been tried by the colonial authorities among pastoralists in northern Kenya and, not surprisingly, they were very unpopular. In independent Uganda, political considerations would have made it impossible to introduce similar measures. Unlimited herd expansion has two deleterious effects: first it puts even greater demands on the grazing resource and as a consequence, secondly, it exacerbates the tensions between neighbouring groups as they compete for that resource.

African cattle have been selected for their hardiness by exposure to drought through many generations, and the females

---

[22] Many Karamojong, perhaps the majority, are now Christian, but in past times they had no belief in an afterlife nor had they any funeral rituals so that corpses were often consigned to hyenas for disposal. One can conjecture that in such a society, without belief in an afterlife, the highest priority would be the survival of the present society, particularly the warriors, child-bearing women and children, and their cattle.

counteract starvation by stopping lactation and ceasing to ovulate. So the two groups most vulnerable in times of drought are suckling calves and the older animals, which succumb a year or two earlier than they might in years of plenty. But come the first flush of grass with the rains and all the quiescent heifers and cows begin to ovulate within a few weeks. The bulls don't waste their opportunities and within a year the premature deaths of the previous year have been compensated for by a new generation.

Slowly, however, as hunger took hold, the numbers of cattle offered for sale mounted. The buyers were all butchers from down-country, for the export of breeding cattle from Karamoja was prohibited to prevent possible carriers of pleuropneumonia from extending the disease to areas free from it. To give the buyers some confidence in the security of their cattle after purchase when they were trekked to the quarantine station at Iriri, they were held there under the safeguard of the department's own force of askaris. The men selected were all Turkana, who themselves spoke Akarimojong but were in no way friendly with the Karamojong, which, we hoped, would avert any conspiracy between Karamojong and askaris to steal the trade cattle. In this, happily, we were right.

To comply with the law and to allow them to be armed, the askaris were inducted as special constables; however the police authorities limited the department to only sixteen men, so they were spread very thinly at seven markets, along the 350 miles of stock routes to Iriri and at four different bomas on the quarantine station. Consequently these brave men usually operated on their own. As was only to be expected, one night a raiding party tried to get away with a mob of trade cattle from one of the bomas at Iriri.

They were foiled by the solitary askari, who shot and killed one. I was informed of this on the radio-telephone early next morning and went to report the death to the Moroto police station.

'Did your askari challenge the raiders before shooting?' was the first question.

Being seriously outnumbered and armed only with a single shot Greener shotgun, I did not suppose he shouted out 'Who goes there?', thereby giving away his position.

'In that case it could be murder' said the policeman.

I quickly realized that if the man was jailed for shooting a raider the other askaris would very likely be reluctant to fire their weapons when attacked, so I drove rapidly down to the scene of the shooting, found the man, paid him his arrears of pay, leave pay and other allowances and ordered him to commence his leave immediately. Of course I could not admit to anyone that my real intention was to frustrate the police and prevent them from arresting him. Unsurprisingly, the other askaris believed that their colleague was being rewarded for killing the raider, so over the next few months more raiders were shot, which brought an end to attacks on our trade cattle. Fortunately hyenas, of which there were many, disposed of the evidence very effectively, so the police were never aware of these incidents.

Apart from fairly frequent visits to the Kidepo National Park, where the warden, Peter Pegg, was a close friend, another place where I could enjoy some diversion from the constant veterinary problems was Lake Rudolph in north-western Kenya, now known as Lake Turkana, the world's largest permanent desert lake and well-known for its fishing. On one of my jaunts there I went with

Donald Parminter, my provincial veterinary officer, and Graham Clegg, one of the livestock officers involved in cattle marketing in Karamoja. On arrival at Ferguson's Gulf on the western shore of the lake we put up our tents, then went to see the local fisheries officer, a large, very blond man, Bob McConnell, to arrange to hire a boat. At the same time we invited him to join us for a drink and some supper, but he declined, saying he had his own guest.

The lake is fed by just three rivers, the main one being the Omo which pours down from the Ethiopian highlands with lesser ones coming down off Mount Elgon and the Kenya highlands. In common with other Rift Valley lakes there is no outlet and the water is so alkaline it feels soapy, something I knew well because on my first visit there, when the air temperature had been close to 45°C (113°F), I had swum in the lake despite notices warning against crocodiles.

The lake at the time was well stocked with Nile perch, though a later drought in Ethiopia so reduced inflow that the water became too alkaline and most of the fish perished. Interestingly, the presence of Nile perch seems evidence that in the past the lake level had been much higher and had been joined to the Nile river system. We spent the second day successfully trolling the lake. More sport was to be got from the smaller fish, for the larger fish - and some Nile perch go up to 200 pounds and more - have disproportionately less gill area relative to size and therefore rapidly become exhausted for lack of oxygen if not moving forward through the water to ventilate their gills. Donald had brought with him two large insulated boxes full of ice, so we were able to fillet the fish and keep them to take home.

We were joined the second evening by Bob McConnell, who,

it turned out, had become weary of his guest. Bob was a reserved man, but it was the whisky that broke the ice. Or to be more precise, it was the ice that we could provide for his whisky that brought him on side. Like me, he had been presumed upon too many times by inadequately-equipped tourists to make himself amenable. The most egregious of the wrongs he had suffered had been the appropriation of his only can-opener by one of the fishing parties, so he was suspicious of them all. Having established that we were completely self contained he stayed for supper and invited us to join him the next evening.

There we met the guest of whom he had grown weary. He was another veterinarian, Professor Bernhard Grzimek, director of the Frankfurt Zoological Society, who had made a name for himself on television for his wildlife films and as author of the book *Serengeti shall not die*. During the evening I spoke to him about the game in Karamoja, which at the time was plentiful. Just the previous week on a drive over the southern plains of the district near Namalu, an area of black cotton soil interspersed with wait-a-bit thorn trees, I had seen over 3000 animals in a morning.[23]

'It should be made into a national park' was his comment.

I pointed out that the Pian used the area for dry season grazing and were themselves not hunters; indeed it was a common sight to see gazelle grazing in among cattle with a herdsman looking on nearby.

'The people can be moved. The area should be made into a national park' he persisted.

Since there was always competition for pasture, any compulsory movement of people to another area would certainly have resulted in violence by the people whose grazing was taken over, but it was

---

[23] Including zebra, Rothschild's giraffe, jackal, Jackson's hartebeest, eland, lesser kudu, waterbuck, roan antelope, oryx and Grant's gazelle

an argument Grzimek would not accept. I could easily understand why McConnell had grown weary of his presence. Sadly, a lot of people, many of whom have ready access to the media, and including Dutch and British royalty as I found out later when in Botswana, put the welfare of wildlife above that of pastoralists, instead of trying to work out a compromise and finding ways to reinforce the traditional coexistence of pastoralists and wildlife.

Another man I used to see from time to time in his red Land Rover on the Kaabong road was Colin Turnbull, an anthropologist who was studying the Ik people who lived among the mountains of north-eastern Dodoth. I had never really got to know him, but one night in Kaabong I noted he was camping down by the river below my camp so I invited him to join me and my other guests. The stories he told of the people he was studying were horrifying and were later repeated in his book *The Mountain People*. The Ik, in common with the Napore of the Nyangeya hills and Tepeth of the southern mountains, probably had inhabited the plains of Karamoja before the arrival of the Karamojong. Forced to retreat into the mountains, they were hunter-gatherers and honey collectors.

The Ik territory covered the mountains of Morungole and Zulia in north-eastern Karamoja as well as a part of Turkana and mountains in southern Sudan, but they had been much reduced at the coming of independence, for the new governments of Sudan and Kenya maintained they were Ugandans and restricted their entry. A second disaster befell them when the Kidepo valley was gazetted as a national park, for it was their principal hunting area and they were now excluded. Starvation threatened them and in their despair they turned on each other. All the bonds of affection and kinship ceased to exist. Three-year-old children were sent out to forage food for themselves, but if they found any it was likely to be stolen by their older, stronger siblings. When I asked Colin how the smaller children survived he replied that they did so by standing under wild fig trees and snapping up what monkeys dropped, for monkeys are dirty eaters. There were other stories which were equally distressing.

As Colin got up to go, one of my guests asked what he would suggest to remedy the situation. He responded bleakly that since society had completely broken down he would not recommend that it was worth saving; it were better that it ceased to exist and that some opportunists, women in particular, might seek to integrate themselves with the Karamojong. There are plenty of instances in history of societies breaking up and reintegrating with others.

Turnbull was later much criticized by other social anthropologists for his terrible depiction of the Ik, some even suggesting that he named them Ik for its onomatopoeic implication of disgust. But in that his critics are wrong, for the Ik do, in fact, call themselves Ik, whereas their neighbours, the Dodoth, call them Teuso. Happily, he was wrong in anticipating the group's disintegration, for I had news of them fifteen years later when working in southern Sudan and as I write, more than forty years later, I have been informed by a Dodoth friend of their continued existence in the mountains of Morungole and Zulia.

CHAPTER 6

Lango and Entebbe

The time came when I had to think about renewing my contract. It was clear that there was no long-term future for me in Uganda as more and more qualified Ugandan veterinarians returned to the country from their up-grading courses at Kabete. On the other hand, I had little enthusiasm for returning to Britain; life would seem very dull by comparison. But I had to keep in mind that although I had acquired some experience of dealing with people, paperwork and finances, I had not significantly improved my veterinary skills since graduating. So I hinted to the new Ugandan Veterinary Commissioner, Herbert Nsubuga, that I would like to be posted to the Animal Health Research Centre in Entebbe - though I had no very clear idea what I might do there.

But it was not to be. On my return from leave I found I had been posted as district veterinary officer to Lango, a district in the centre of the country. On its eastern side it was bounded by Karamoja and on the western by the Nile and Lake Kyoga, which can best be described as a broad flood plain along the course of the river. It was a gently undulating grassy landscape with papyrus-choked swamps in the folds where the locals caught catfish and bilharzia. It was wooded in places, but there was not a mountain in sight and very little wildlife. The district headquarters was Lira, very much in the centre of the district so that all parts could be reached by car in a few hours thereby making tented safaris unnecessary. In other words the district was unexciting compared to Karamoja.

Waswa followed me to Lira with his burgeoning family. When I had first employed him he had had four children, but it was very clear soon after my arrival in Lira that a fifth was on the way. So I wasn't surprised when one morning Waswa told me his wife had started contractions. I took her to the local hospital as soon as I could. They sent her away, saying that it would be several days before she was ready, but it wasn't so and late the following night Waswa woke me and told me his wife had started delivering. The hospital had been so off-hand the previous morning that I suspected there would be even less care for a woman in labour at two in the morning.

It was clear as soon as I saw her that I would have to assist in the delivery there and then. Waswa didn't feel able to assist, though whether this was because of some taboo or just fear I don't know. However I insisted he stay with me because I could not speak his wife's language. There was only one problem; the lady was quite excessively modest and kept pushing her dress down below her knees each time I turned to wash my hands. I pressed Waswa to tell her she need not be so modest, for certainly childbirth is not the time to be overwhelmed with erotic inclinations.

Fortunately the delivery went off without a hitch, but it was rather like delivering a baby with the lights off and using the sense of touch to feel where everything was. Later in my career I was compelled to assist in three more deliveries. I was perhaps lucky, for my limited experience of human obstetrics is that it is a great deal easier than large animal obstetrics. The human foetus, for a start, is smaller and lighter and therefore easier to handle; nor does it have a long neck allowing the head to lie twisted under the chest or on either side of it nor four long limbs with numerous joints which so often seem to be flexed in every position but the right one.

The Langi themselves are a sedentary people who practise agriculture as well as keeping cattle and shoats. There being no great security problems, most lived close to the fields where they worked. Being sedentary, education had flourished in the district, to such an extent that the first prime minister of Uganda, Milton Obote, was a Langi, later becoming president while remaining Member of Parliament for Lira town. The advantage to me of the higher level of education was that there were a number of veterinary assistants, a corps of non-graduate but trained aides, to whom I could delegate the running of each county, a benefit I had been denied in Karamoja, where Nikanor Okema was the only veterinary assistant in the whole district.

The political connections in Lango, however, were no advantage. Indeed, my predecessor in the post, a Ugandan veterinary officer called Francis Kitakule, had fallen foul of one of Obote's kinsmen, who was minister of Agriculture, and had been summarily transferred elsewhere as a consequence. I thought it prudent, therefore, to visit the minister's farm, some forty miles from Lira, as soon as I had settled in my post.

What I found was a disgrace for a man supposedly in charge of such an important ministry, although I had to be cautious even hinting as much. It wasn't even clear what the purpose of his farm was. Was it supposed to be a dairy farm or a beef ranch? If the first, the market for milk was a long way off; if the second, the acreage was too small to be commercially viable. Fencing consisted of a few strands of barbed wire tacked on to trees, too high and too loose to restrain any cattle from either entering or leaving the farm - although giraffe, if there had been any in the vicinity, might have found it a little hazardous. What was even worse was that at the time of my arrival at the farm in the middle of the morning I found all the cattle still in their night bomas, not out grazing. In my report to the minister I stated that cattle thrived better on grazing, to which he replied that he found it difficult to manage his farm labour since they were all his relatives. It seemed to me that Kitakule had been disciplined for something completely out of his control and I could only hope that I, too, would not fall foul of the minister.

On the positive side, the two great plagues of rinderpest and pleuropneumonia were absent from the district, though rinderpest vaccination campaigns were still carried out annually in the counties bordering Karamoja to prevent any potential spread. But other diseases abounded, principally foot-and-mouth disease, tryps and East Coast fever.

Foot-and-mouth, FMD for short, was my major headache, for it regularly interrupted cattle markets. FMD is rarely lethal, but it can cause abortions, which results in considerable loss in production. This is a matter of great concern to commercial farmers but less so to peasant livestock owners who live with numerous other more lethal scourges, as well as enduring the ravages of intermittent droughts. Animals that contract the disease in the wet season are set back briefly; the lesions on their feet and in their mouths are painful so restricting their grazing, but within a week or so the lesions heal and the animals are back on their feet. It is a more serious matter in the dry season because the animals are in a poor condition and their grazing is restricted for considerably longer because the grass is drier and more fibrous and therefore more painful to chew.

There are six principal types of foot-and-mouth disease virus and several sub-types, so no single vaccine will protect against all the types in circulation. Added to that disadvantage, the vaccine is expensive and gives only a short-lasting immunity and vaccinated animals, although not showing any clinical signs, may still harbour virus thereby being a potential source of infection to other animals. Thus in many parts of Africa vaccination was, and still is, normally confined to high-value animals. The main means of controlling the disease therefore were movement restrictions and aphthization, a process whereby a piece of cloth is passed through the mouth of a diseased animal and then relayed through all the rest of the herd in order to infect them all at the same time. This may sound the antithesis of good veterinary practice but it ensured that the outbreak was over in a very short time, thus limiting the period when movement restrictions had to be in force.

There were no formal cattle markets in the district as there were in Karamoja, and I got the impression that cattle owners were getting a bad deal in their private arrangements with traders, so soon after my arrival in the district I resolved to try and open up some markets. There are two advantages in formal markets in fixed places on fixed dates. The first is that the producer, in this case the cattle owner, is able to look for the best price for his animal, while the second is that veterinary staff can monitor the health of the animals at the market and, should they identify any communicable disease, and foot-and-mouth was topmost of the likely hazards, can close the market and limit the spread of disease. But opening up the markets needed the cooperation of the county council, where I soon found some vested interests did not want change.

There were about a quarter of a million cattle in the district, so the potential for export seemed to me to be about 25,000 animals annually. Two export quarantine stations were in use. One was at Aloi in the eastern part of the district astride the northern spur of the Mombasa-Kampala railway line. This had been built with the purpose of linking up with the Sudanese railway system but while that never materialized, it did facilitate transport to the main towns such as Kampala and Jinja. The other quarantine was at Atura in the west. From here the cattle were ferried across the Nile and trekked the 150 miles or so south to Kampala.[24]

There was another livestock-associated trade of which I was little aware before I reached Lira and that was the trade in hides and skins. At the time it was by no means negligible, for in Kenya and Uganda hides and skins formed the fourth largest source of foreign exchange after coffee, tea and tourism. African hides of good quality got premium prices for they were not holed by warble flies in the middle of the back as were many hides of the northern hemisphere, and so were much esteemed for upholstery, especially car seats.[25] Little capital, other than working capital, is required to trade in hides and skins and as they are very durable they can be stored for long periods and transported easily in the backs of lorries. Rats and

---

[24] One odd piece of trivia comes to mind when I think of loading cattle on to wagons at Aloi and that was that all the steel sleepers (wooden ones would have been susceptible to termites) were marked 'Krupp 1917' and I wondered if they were the remnants of WW 1 reparations

[25] Warble flies live in the temperate zones of the northern hemisphere and are active in summer months when they lay their eggs on the bodies and legs of cattle where they hatch in about four days. The larvae burrow through the skin and then migrate through the body undergoing various development stages before erupting through the skin of the back a year later. The flies are also known as gad flies because their constant attacks cause cattle to gad about the field while desperately trying to shake them off.

ants are the main cause of damage and by simple brief legislation encompassed in the Hides and Skins Ordinance the production of good quality hides and skins could be ensured. One of my duties was to inspect hides and skins stores before issuing trading licences under the ordinance. I learned a lot more about the trade from the traders than ever they learned from me. One incident I remember clearly: Nikita Kruschev, the Communist Party Secretary, announced in 1966 that by the end of the next Five Year Development Plan all citizens of the Soviet Union would have leather shoes. As a result of this the export price of leather doubled.

By no means could I claim that my work in Lango was very arduous, certainly not by Karamoja standards. And by Karamoja standards there were much closer distractions - the closest being the second hole of the club's golf course, which was right in front of my house not more than thirty yards away (the fourth fairway was also the town's landing ground for small aircraft). Further away, at the western periphery of the district, was the Murchison Falls National Park, where there was good fishing for Nile perch in the river if one was not too concerned about meeting the buffalo which came down to the river for water. The falls are an impressive feature of the Nile, as they tumble down the eastern escarpment of the Western Rift Valley to make their way to Lake Albert in the floor of the valley. At the falls the river plunges into a roaring vortex barely twenty feet wide before making its final drop to a pool 150 feet below where crocodiles abound, sated with the stunned fish that crash down from above.

The existence of the national park had come about as a result of a terrible epidemic of sleeping sickness which overwhelmed

Uganda in the early years of the protectorate administration. It is believed that almost a quarter of the population died but with no census figures and a total absence of a disease reporting system it can only be an informed guess.

The story of sleeping sickness is an interesting one. It was an army surgeon, David Bruce, who had been the first to recognize, in 1895, that the cattle disease, *nagana*, affecting native cattle in Zululand was caused by a trypanosome, a blood parasite.[26] There was some confusion initially in classifying the parasite that caused nagana because the samples he sent to Britain did not reproduce the disease in experimental cattle and only later was it realized that his first sample was a mixed one of two species of trypanosome which were duly named as *Trypanosoma congolense*, which is pathogenic to cattle, and *Trypanosoma brucei* which is only mildly so, though pathogenic for man, horses, dogs and other animals.

It was not long before it was recognized that trypanosomes also caused sleeping sickness in humans.[27] In 1903 Bruce headed a commission of enquiry which was established by the Royal Society in London to investigate the massive human mortality in Uganda. What he found was very disturbing, for he found both forms of disease were present and, although the Ugandans had acquired some degree of resistance to the East African form which was endemic, they were very susceptible to the West African form. Thus he reasoned the West African form had been introduced recently.

[26] Bruce had already made a name for himself in 1887 when posted to Malta where he identified a bacterium from the spleen of a person who had died of Malta Fever as the cause. British army and navy personnel were most seriously affected whereas native-born Maltese were usually resistant. It was later shown that people were infected from consuming milk or cheeses from infected goats. He named the causative organism *Micrococcus melitensis* although later workers established a new genus of bacteria into which it was included which they named Brucella in his honour — the cause of brucellosis.

[27] There are two forms of sleeping sickness – East African sleeping sickness is rapidly fatal and caused by *Trypanosoma brucei rhodesiense* and the West African sleeping sickness which is a more chronic disease, although fatal eventually if not treated, and caused by *Trypanosoma brucei gambiense*. Both forms of the disease are predominantly transmitted from man to man by the bites of tsetse flies although some antelope and wart-hogs probably act as reservoirs of T. b. rhodesiense.

The blame fell upon Henry Morton Stanley. Stanley had first gained prominence after finding David Livingstone at Ujiji in 1871, an event which has been immortalized by his famous greeting 'Dr Livingstone, I presume', a phrase he never used, for who else could he have met in that remote location? But as Stanley was a newspaperman he knew it made good copy. Stanley had subsequently led an expedition to trace the course of the Lualaba river, which flows out of Lake Mweuru in present-day Zambia and which Livingstone had wrongly thought might be a tributary of the Nile. In fact it is a headwater of the mighty Congo river and Stanley was the first white man to follow it to its outlet in the Atlantic Ocean.

Stanley had been only a few months back in Britain when in 1878, as a consequence of his knowledge of the river, he was recruited by King Leopold of the Belgians to develop the king's personal colony in the Congo. Stanley held the post for five gruelling years, setting up trading stations on the lower reaches of the river before falling out with the autocratic king over the maltreatment of the indigenous Congolese by Belgian officials.

Much further north a messianic figure, the Mahdi, was leading a rebellion against the Anglo-Egyptian condominium in Sudan. In January 1885 General Gordon was killed by the Mahdi's followers in Khartoum, leaving the governor of Equatoria Province, Emin Pasha, isolated in the south of the country. In Britain there was considerable anxiety for Emin Pasha's welfare and that of his men. The Nile route was closed by the Mahdi but by this time there was fairly constant traffic between Zanzibar and the African interior, so this was considered the most rational means of reaching him.

Emin's first letters of distress arrived in Britain in late 1886 and prompted a rapid response, for public opinion there had been much angered by the British government's procrastination in sending an expedition to relieve Gordon. In his letters Emin described how he had retreated to an area close to Lake Albert to avoid the Mahdi's followers. William Mackinnon, a Scot with commercial interests in East Africa, was chosen to head a committee to establish the Emin Pasha Relief Expedition.

Because of Stanley's reputation Mackinnon approached him to lead the expedition but, despite his falling out with King Leopold, Stanley was still under contract to him and the king would only release him from his contract if the expedition approached Lake Albert by going up the Congo river. This had certain advantages, because steamers could go a considerable distance up the river and Emin had asked for large quantities of arms and ammunition to maintain his forces around Lake Albert. The king, not surprisingly, had an ulterior motive, which was to use the expedition's resources to extend his fiefdom right up to Lake Albert. It was a terrible expedition in terms of hardship and the cost in lives, and when eventually Stanley met with Emin on the lake, Emin seemed strangely reluctant to be rescued.

Actually it was not so strange; Emin Pasha was in fact Dr Eduard Schnitzer, a short-sighted German doctor who, failing to get a licence to practise in Germany after qualifying, set up in practice in Albania - then a Turkish province - and subsequently joined the staff of Ismail Hakki Pasha, governor of northern Albania. Before long he started an affair with Madame Hakki and on the governor's death he lived with her openly. In 1875 penury threatened and he moved back to Germany, taking her with him as well as her four children and six slave girls. So large an entourage merely compounded his financial problems, so he abandoned his mistress, fled the country taking her money and jewellery and eventually reached Khartoum, where he took the name of Emin and set up his plate. It was here that Gordon first met him. In due course Gordon recruited him as governor of Equatoria province.

What Emin certainly did not want was to have his name publicized in the world's newspapers as having been 'found' by Stanley as Livingstone had been some eighteen years previously. But a mutiny by his own troops and the possibility of capture by the Mahdi's followers ultimately persuaded him that he had no other option but to accompany Stanley to Zanzibar. On reaching the coast, a celebratory party was organized for him by German and other officials at Bagamoyo, a port on the mainland opposite Zanzibar Island, but the celebrations came to an abrupt end when Emin fell off a veranda into the street below and was badly injured. At the time it was put about that he had met with an accident due to his short-sightedness and, possibly, a surfeit of alcohol, but it seems possible, since his former mistress had already issued an international warrant for his arrest, that it was a suicide attempt. Whichever it was, Emin was dead within the year, beheaded by Arab slave traders in the Congo.

So, all in all, the Emin Pasha Relief Expedition was a disaster. Hundreds of men had died; the object of the expedition was unappreciative of the efforts made on his behalf - and, circumstantial evidence suggests, West African sleeping sickness was introduced by Stanley's men to Lake Albert and its environs.

Following Bruce's report in 1903 and in a bid to minimize deaths, the British protectorate government in Uganda forcibly ejected the inhabitants from the surrounding area, which included the north and south banks of the Nile. This became in time a game reserve and subsequently was designated the Murchison Falls National Park. Remarkably the park has gone through a complete ecological cycle in the century that has followed. The Acholi to the north of the river and the Banyoro to the south were great hunters, probably because the tsetse fly made it impossible for them to rely on cattle keeping. The removal of the human population and the subsequent prohibition of hunting in the park then allowed the wild animal population to explode. Elephants, with their voracious appetites, destroyed much of the woodland, removing the shade cover that tsetse need to avoid desiccation, and the hippo grazing the margins of the river stripped it of much of its vegetation, leading to considerable sheet erosion for two to three miles on either side of it, so the tsetse were almost eliminated. Then Idi Amin destroyed the elephants and hippo for their ivory to prop up his foreign exchange holdings, the bush and trees recovered, and the tsetse fly returned with a vengeance; so much so that the last time I was in the park, a decade or so ago, I was attacked by them as if they were a swarm of angry bees.

There was another river I fished, though with much less success, and that was the Aswa which rises in the hills of Labwor in western Karamoja and flows through Acholi and into the Nile about ten miles north of the Uganda-Sudan border. My friend Steve Stevenson had left running the quarantine station at Iriri and was employed in setting up a cattle ranch on the eastern side of the

Aswa river, an area which had recently been cleared of tsetse fly.[28] It was a drive of only about a hundred miles north from Lira, so I was able to visit fairly frequently. It wasn't the fishing that attracted my real interest but the ranching, which had interested me since a boy in Argentina.

Two things stand clear in my mind. The first is that the East African shorthorn zebu has considerable potential as a beef animal. In a traditional system much of a cow's milk is taken for domestic consumption and the calf gets only the leftovers, thereby stunting its growth. In setting up the ranch Steve was buying heifers locally as foundation stock but what was significant was the fact that their calves at a year old were already taller than their dams at the shoulder, although still trying to reach their udders to suckle. The second thing that stands clear is the speed which a good lea can be established with native grasses by judicious grazing, especially if leguminous plants such as *Styloxanthes* are introduced.

I had not been in Lira very long when two American volunteers about to leave the country brought me their pet patas monkey to put down. It was an enchanting little animal and I asked if I could keep it, to which they consented. Patas monkeys are also known as red hussars for their ginger-coloured coat and white bellies. They live in groups of about a dozen on the ground and frequently raid peoples' shambas for food. He quickly bonded to me and on the first night would not be separated, so I allowed him to sleep on my pillow. But monkeys cannot be house trained and I woke in the night with the strong smell of urine next to my head. Obviously there had to be another way of keeping him. For a few days I kept him on a long-running chain in the garden but soon realized that

[28] The ranch later became the HQ of the infamous Lord's Resistance Army.

113

it would not do, for monkeys are intelligent and gregarious animals and keeping him so restricted was plainly cruel. So I let him go free and wondered what he might do. Instead of making off, he bonded with Rufus and it was a common sight to see them sleeping together, the little monkey curled up between the dog's front legs. I would often take them for a walk on the golf course, where hawks would stoop down on him, so he learned to run under Rufus's belly to avoid their attacks.

Rufus had discovered how to find his way to my office and to the club, so dog and monkey together would find me at one or the other if left alone at home. It was easy to confine Rufus, but the monkey was soon able to open doors, so nowhere was safe from his depredations or his excretory habits. In the club he was very partial to both beer and gin, which members were only too happy to give him despite my protests. Considering his size and his liking for alcohol, I suspected that he woke many mornings with painful hangovers.

Milk in Lira was sold on an informal basis, with milk producers pedalling around the houses of regular customers on their bicycles with milk in a churn fixed to their carriers and ladling out whatever amount was required which prudent consumers would then boil. What was not sold was unloaded on the Lira Dairy Cooperative, a small block-built structure with a galvanized iron roof in the town centre. There was however a downside to this arrangement, as the cooperative charged a cess, which found little favour with the producers. This was no surprise, for when I had been working in the Kabaka's government in Buganda I had found that dairy farmers much preferred marketing their own milk, even though it took up three or four hours of their time each day, in preference to selling it to a dairy.

In a fit of unthinking charity the US Agency for International Development (USAID) donated a milk cooling machine to the Lira Dairy Cooperative and in due course a beautiful stainless steel cooler was delivered to the cooperative's premises. The back wall of the dairy was knocked down so it could be installed and it was duly set up and the wall rebuilt. But it didn't work because, being American, it operated at 110 volts and the local supply sometimes approximated 240 volts, so the back wall was knocked down again and the cooler sent away for alteration before being returned and the wall bricked up yet again.

Meanwhile the town council, under pressure from central authorities, passed a bye-law prohibiting the informal sale of milk in the township. This did not go down well with the producers, who got a lower price for their milk. It also did not go down well with the district medical officer who realized that the bulking up of the milk supplies in the cooler and in the absence of a pasteurizing unit meant than any contaminant (tuberculosis and salmonellosis were his main concerns) would be distributed to all milk consumers in the town and not just to a section of consumers. But the final irony was that the cooler was turned off every night to allow the milk to sour before the morning, because the Langi preferred their milk that way - a preference many African people show, which may well be related to the high rate of lactose intolerance in some African populations.

As in Karamoja telegrams were an essential means of communication but, unlike Karamoja where the police network was used internally, it was the post office's network that was used.

There were telephones but they were tedious things to use. To get the attention of the operator one had to turn a little handle on the machine; he would then try and get the attention of the next operator down the line and so on. Getting a call through could easily take a couple of hours and, likely as not, the person you wanted to contact was out at the time.

There was a certain etiquette about sending official telegrams. All outbreaks of notifiable diseases, that is those epizootic diseases prescribed by law that had to be notified, were relayed to district veterinary officers in adjacent districts and to the commissioner by telegram. Another rule of the telegram was that when any instruction was received the requisite action had to be taken the same day. A post office messenger on a red bicycle was a common sight; one evening he found me on the golf course but with considerable forethought he had brought with him a pad of telegram forms, so there and then I wrote a reply 'Have received your instruction Stop Will investigate disease outbreak tomorrow first light Stop' and got on with my game.

Another essential of a civil servant's office was the Uganda Gazette, a publication of mind-numbing dullness, which was issued weekly and in which were recorded the various appointments of civil servants, commissioning of officers in the armed forces, any new legislation or orders made by ministers and, lastly, all patents and copyrights claimed for products, brand names and logos. In one of these I noted that the Minister of Animal Industry (who was not to be confused with the Minister of Agriculture) had gazetted an order declaring Lango to be a tick-free district. It seemed an extraordinary directive but in due course I received a letter informing me of the order and instructing me to put it into effect.

It was a very tall order for I estimated that with a quarter of a million cattle and as many sheep and goats at least fifty dip tanks would be required to dip the animals even at weekly intervals. It would have been more appropriate to dip them twice weekly to achieve a reasonable level of control, for most ticks remain only three to four days feeding on their hosts. Water for the dips was available in many of the swamps but bore holes would have to be sunk at other locations.

After several weeks' consideration I submitted a plan with maps and estimates of development and annual recurrent costs. I need not have bothered with the effort, for all I got by return was a letter from my former mentor, Sam Walshe, informing me, in case I was unaware of it, that when a minister made an order it had to be obeyed, and offering me the equivalent of about £100 to put the order into effect. I felt let down by Sam but my friend, Steve, who was a deal more versed in the ways of officialdom than I was, came up with the suggestion that I get a local printer to produce a poster with a tasteful picture of a dead tick with the words 'This area is now declared tick-free by order of the Minister' and to spend any surplus funds on hammers and nails so that my staff could then post them up throughout the district.

Throughout all this time I was continuing with my efforts to improve the cattle marketing facilities in the district. It was gratifying that several county councillors were beginning to come round to my thinking, but I was constantly frustrated with new outbreaks of foot-and-mouth disease, which entailed the gazetting of quarantine restrictions and stopping all trading. What I could not understand was why Lango district had almost more outbreaks of disease than all the other districts in the country put together. Then one day I caught a trader moving cattle from one county to another on the main road, in direct contravention of a quarantine order. The animals were obviously trade cattle, for there were few females and no calves in the herd as there would be in a normal breeding herd.

I took the trader to court. The police, who were not conversant with the Diseases of Animals Ordinance, asked me to lead for the prosecution. The proceedings were conducted in Swahili and the magistrate asked if I needed a translator. This suited me as, though I was able to follow most of the proceedings, the translation gave me time to think up another question in the hope of entrapping the defendant. In his defence he argued that he was only moving the cattle from parish to parish. This was, in fact, a lawful movement but the magistrate, who was probably as conversant with the Diseases of Animals Ordinance as the police, took this as an admission of guilt, in which I did not contradict him, and the defendant was jailed.

I hoped that this might be the first step in stopping illegal movements and thereby limiting the spread of foot-and-mouth disease. A month or so later I caught another trader moving animals across county borders. He was emboldened to say that he had been instructed by the Minister of Agriculture to ignore the movement restrictions and buy cattle. I was not sure whether to believe him or not as other traders, white as well as black, had tried to bluff me with tales of ministerial connections. I certainly could see why traders benefited from buying during a quarantine period since it would have been a buyer's market with little or no competition from other buyers. But the trader was not bluffing, and a week later I received a telephone call from the commissioner instructing me to stop the prosecution of the miscreant.

I pretended that I could not recognize his voice and made it clear that I would need a signed instruction if I was required to bypass legal procedures and implicate myself in a criminal activity. Within a few days I got a signed order from the commissioner transferring me from the district forthwith. I left without even a formal handing over, since no veterinary officer had as yet been appointed to take over from me.

My next posting was to the Animal Health Research Centre in Entebbe, which was where I had wanted to be in the first place, though I had not been sure in what role. That was decided for me by the chief research officer, who put me in charge of the parasitology section which Professor Matthysse had recently vacated. He had trained half a dozen or more laboratory technicians in the techniques of tick collection and identification. I knew about tick collection since I had helped him on several occasions when he had visited Karamoja, but my knowledge of tick taxonomy was woefully deficient. I made up for this in the late afternoons after the staff had gone off duty and I could teach myself without them becoming aware of my deficiency. I soon realized that mere comparisons with diagrams in relevant textbooks was not good enough as it was difficult to remember all the distinctive features of individual ticks, so I resolved to draw each species from collected specimens. I am a dreadful draughtsman and I think I wore out more rubbers than pencils, but within a short space of time I became fairly confident in recognizing all the common ticks.

Most people have a revulsion to ticks, but they are interesting creatures to study and I was soon hooked.[29] Most of Matthysse's taxonomic work had been completed by the time I reached Entebbe, but there was continuing work on testing a variety of acaricides, chemicals for the control of ticks, against a standard which at that time was toxaphene, a chlorinated hydrocarbon, which was then in general use throughout East Africa. For this study the research centre had a mixed herd of about forty cattle consisting of both the shorthorn zebu of eastern Uganda and the long-horned Ankole cattle of western Uganda which were kept on a hilltop at the southern end of the Entebbe peninsula where now is the main runway of the international airport. It was back-breaking work as there would be about twenty animals in each trial divided into four groups of five. Every second day, come rain or shine and there was plenty of the former in Entebbe, each animal in the trial had to be thrown to the ground and its whole body searched for ticks, which were classified and counted. The process took about a quarter of an hour for each animal.

As a veterinarian, I was particularly interested in the role that ticks played in the transmission of diseases. So, while the acaricide trials continued, I diversified in two directions. The first was to study the potential role of buffalo as reservoirs of East Coast fever and the second was to investigate the causes for the breakdown of tick control measures on ECF affected farms.

[29] There are two major types of ticks – soft ticks which mainly parasitize birds and people and hard ticks which parasitize other animals. A prototype hard tick hatches from a clutch of several thousand eggs which are laid on the ground and after an incubation period of about a month or more depending on climatic conditions it hatches and progresses through three stages – larva, nymph and adult – the adult differentiating into male or female forms. All three stages need to feed on a host to complete their development. In some species the larvae, nymphs and adults only remain on the host for 3-4 days to feed before falling off to complete their development – these are known as three-host ticks. Two-host ticks remain feeding on the same animal in the larval and nymphal stages before falling off, moulting to the adult stage and then attacking a second host. One-host ticks remain on the same animal from the larval stage until adult. Fertilization of the female occurs while she is still on the host after which she engorges on the host's blood before falling to the ground where she lays another clutch of several thousand eggs before dying exhausted.

Two-host and three-host ticks can transmit infections from one host to another after moulting and attaching to another host – this is called trans-stadial infection. One-host ticks can only transmit disease through the eggs – transovarial infection.

My interest in the role of buffalo followed from my experience in Karamoja, where sporadic outbreaks of ECF occurred when cattle moved up the mountains for grazing during the dry season and where they were likely to come into contact with buffalo or, at least areas which had previously been grazed by buffalo and on which infected ticks remained.

As was well known the brown ear tick, *Rhipicephalus appendiculatus*, was the only natural vector of the protozoal parasite *Theileria parva*, which is the cause of ECF and the brown ear tick could not survive the arid conditions and thrived only up on the wetter and cooler mountains. *Theileria* were first discovered by Robert Koch in 1898, but he confused them with another blood parasite and failed to recognize them as the cause of ECF. So it was Arnold Theiler, a parasitologist of Swiss origin in South Africa, who with other workers elucidated the role of the blood parasite in causing ECF which was named after him a few years later.

A semi-tame buffalo calf was available in the Entebbe zoo, more an animal orphanage actually, and from this animal, after a Herculean effort on the part of all six laboratory assistants, we collected a blood sample in which I found numerous Theilerial parasites. But that alone was not sufficient evidence that it was *Theileria parva*, for there are other parasites of the same genus, though they are much less pathogenic.

The next step was to infect an experimental steer with the parasite to see if it caused typical ECF. Workers in Southern Rhodesia (now Zimbabwe) and Kenya had already gone down this route and a heated debate, which is not yet fully resolved, developed over the identity of the causative Theilerial organism.

The Rhodesian workers believed the buffalo parasite was a species in its own right which they named *Theileria lawrencei*, and claimed it caused a disease similar to ECF which they called corridor disease. The Kenyan workers, on the other hand, believed that the buffalo parasite was the same as the bovine one, *Theileria parva*, and that the difference in size between those isolated from buffalo and those from cattle was due to the fact that buffalo red blood cells are smaller than those of cattle, so the parasites inhabiting them never reached their full size.

Part of the development of theilerial parasites occurs in the gut of the host tick, so it is not possible to transmit ECF by injecting experimental cattle with blood from infected ones since that would by-pass the essential development within the tick. Having had one vigorous wrestling bout with a young buffalo I was in no mood for a second confrontation to collect infected ticks from it. However there is a way of getting around that problem, and that is to inject infected blood from buffalo into splenectomized rabbits and feed the tick larvae on the ears of the rabbits.[30] When the fully engorged ticks drop off, they are collected, allowed to moult to the nymphal stage and then placed on a susceptible bovine host in an attempt to reproduce ECF.

An interesting observation developed from this activity. Particular species of ticks generally feed on specific hosts and in specific locations. Thus *Rhipicephalus appendiculatus* usually feeds on cattle and all stages attach in and around the ears. Other species feed on birds in their early stages and only on cattle in their adult stage, while some prefer to feed on tortoises and snakes and some on elephant and rhinoceros. Rabbits can tolerate being used as

[30] Rabbits from which the spleens have been removed surgically

hosts for *Rhipicephalus appendiculatus* ticks once, but to try and feed such ticks a second time on a rabbit is rarely successful; the rabbit's ears swell up and the ticks fail to attach. This suggests a specific immunological reaction by a host animal to a second exposure to an 'unnatural' parasite, while retaining a tolerance of those species which normally parasitize it. It would seem to me that much benefit could be obtained if an immunological reaction could be stimulated in animals against those ticks which are its natural parasites as an alternative to using acaricides to control them. It's just a thought.

My second interest while at the research centre in Entebbe was to investigate the causes for the breakdown of tick control measures on certain farms. This required the equipment to assay the concentration of acaricide in a dip or spray and also facilities to breed ticks so that they could be used to determine the minimum concentration of acaricide necessary to kill them.

The first farm I investigated was a cotton-growing research station just north of Kampala which used cattle to graze fields before they were re-sown with cotton. Although being sprayed regularly twice weekly, these animals were dying of ECF. This was a classic case where low-strength acaricide solutions had led to the development of resistance. The assay of acaricide strength showed the concentration to be less than half the manufacturer's recommended concentration and the ticks collected from the station and bred up in my laboratory proved to have become so resistant that the acaricide concentration required to get a 100% kill would be sufficient to kill the cattle. When I showed the results to the farm manager he admitted that as a cost-cutting measure he had used the acaricide at half the recommended dilution. Further investigations showed that the resistant ticks had spread to all the farms on its perimeter, including the university's research station. I therefore advised the commissioner to make an order promoting the use of an alternative acaricide in all the affected premises, but my advice was ignored and the cattle continued dying of ECF.

A similar problem developed in one of the veterinary department's own experimental herds near Mbarara in south-western Uganda. Here considerable money had been spent on building 12-foot-high barbed wire fences to protect the cattle against lion at night; sadly not the same amount of money was used to protect them against ticks and only one hand-operated stirrup pump was available. Hand pumps are suitable for spraying small numbers of cattle but here there were 200. It usually takes five minutes to spray an animal adequately, so it took little mathematical ingenuity to realize that it would take almost 17 hours to spray the whole herd. It is true that while the local veterinary officer and I looked on, the job was done very satisfactorily but I really could not believe that the sprayers would be so assiduous in our absence. There are not that many hours in a normal working day.

A sad episode happened at that time, an indication of the way the department was heading. One of my laboratory assistants, to whom I had taken quite a liking, kept pressing me to visit his uncle's farm north of Kampala, where most of his herd had died. I was reluctant to do so for it would have been intruding on the work of the local veterinary officer but I eventually agreed to make an informal visit on a Sunday. The old man had been a watchman for many years at Gayaza Girls' School, quite the most prestigious girls' school in the country, and had recently taken retirement. Instead of a pension he had accepted six Friesian cows from the school governors with which to start a small milking herd.

At the time of my visit only one undernourished calf remained; the rest were dead. None of the preconditions which were required for keeping 'exotic' cattle that had to be met when I had been a very new veterinary officer in Buganda were present and yet the old man had been given a licence, which he showed me, to keep such cattle. As a result he was destitute.

I was sufficiently angry to go and see the commissioner to complain that the preconditions for keeping 'exotic' cattle were being disregarded, only to be told that the preconditions had been dropped as they had been instituted by the colonialists to prevent Africans from keeping high-producing cattle. To which I retorted that it was disease that prevented Africans, as well as others, from keeping 'exotic' cattle.

At about the same time, the latter part of 1967, a much more fearsome incident occurred. Simultaneously in Germany and Yugoslavia a number of laboratory workers producing polio vaccines died from an unknown disease which spread rapidly to their families and attendant medical staff with similarly fatal consequences. The common factor in both places was that the kidneys of vervet monkeys of Ugandan origin were used for vaccine production in both laboratories, so suspicion rested on Uganda, though the Ugandan veterinary authorities were quick to deny it.

The virologist at the research centre, Catrinus Terpstra, and I were ordered to investigate. Catrinus subsequently became a well-regarded academic veterinary virologist in his home country of the

Netherlands. The epidemiology of the disease strongly suggested a viral origin and I was a parasitologist, not a virologist, so I asked why I had been co-opted to the team and was told that I had been selected because I was unmarried. I take no credit for my input, which was limited to suggesting that we investigate any unusual mortality in monkey catchers; in fact there was none. Catrinus took the brunt of the work collecting blood from captured vervet monkeys and injecting it into experimental animals such as mice, guinea pigs and hamsters. Again this was without result, though it was nerve-racking work nevertheless.

Fortunately within a very short time the German scientists had isolated a virus as the cause of the disease which is now known as Marburg haemorrhagic fever or green monkey disease. The virus is naturally found in muscle tissue, so only monkey eaters and research workers are exposed to it. Hence collecting blood was not in itself a dangerous procedure, though Catrinus did not know that at the time and deserves commendation for his courage.

My little patas monkey was now dead. I had taken him for a walk one evening with Rufus across the fields in front of my house on the research station's property when I came on one of my colleagues also walking his dog. The monkey took fright and skipped up the nearest electricity pole. In Uganda power lines are not insulated, resulting on dark, windy nights in splendid displays of fireworks, but on this occasion it was the monkey that was electrocuted as he put his hands on two live wires to reach the top of the pole. He was dead instantly. I mourned him briefly but was relieved that I would not have to give him to the Entebbe zoo where the facilities for monkeys were very inadequate, as seemed increasingly necessary because of the many houses and people close to my own home. On post mortem he was found to be hosting several intestinal parasites harmful to man. I was lucky not to have been affected. Another veterinary colleague in Uganda, Hugh Clifford, developed a polio-like disease after being bitten by someone else's pet monkey and spent the rest of his life in a wheelchair. As a consequence of these three incidents I feel very strongly that people, especially families with children, should not keep monkeys as pets.

Once again my contract was approaching its end. I was very much enjoying my work on ticks as well as enjoying the social life of Entebbe where eight nights a week were necessary to enjoy it to the full. My posting to Entebbe had come towards the end of the contract period and I needed a lot more time to complete the work on the role of buffalo in the epidemiology of ECF. Accordingly I applied for another contract, but all I got in return were vacillating responses.

Meanwhile I had been approached by two former colleagues enquiring about my future intentions. The first, Matt Cunningham, had done valuable research at the East African Trypanosomiasis Research Organization (EATRO) in Tororo on the Kenya-Uganda border and was attempting to put together a team to develop a vaccine against ECF at Muguga. This promised to be stimulating work since no vaccine at that time had been developed against any protozoal disease, not even malaria. Unfortunately Matt could not give me a date for the commencement of the project, nor an absolute promise that I would be employed.

The second colleague was the former commissioner, Hugh Newlands, who had rebuked me previously for failing to hear him on the radio-telephone and who had since taken up a post with FAO in Rome. He was looking for possible recruits to instruct Ethiopian field staff in anticipation of a major vaccination campaign to eradicate rinderpest from Africa, a programme called JP15. He also could not give an absolute promise that I would be engaged but the project seemed to have a better chance of coming off in the near future than Matt's.

So in 1968 I came to the end of the contract and kept my options open, not knowing whether I would be returning to Uganda or taking up a job in Ethiopia. I retained my house on the research station property, put Rufus to board with Steve and his family up on the Acholi ranch and then took ship to England. My contract stipulated that I was entitled to an outward and return passage by sea on the first and last contract respectively. General Nasser had conveniently closed the Suez Canal the previous year, so I was able to return around the Cape. My work in Entebbe had brought me into contact with several commercial firms producing acaricides and other compounds, and these companies arranged for me to visit a number of research stations in South Africa. The country was still divided by apartheid, a policy which I found totally hateful. The separation of the races was so complete that even saying 'good morning' to an African was received with a sullen stare and frowned on by whites as being excessively familiar.

One visit stands out in my mind. It was to the veterinary research station at Onderstepoort near Pretoria where Gertrude Theiler, the daughter of the pioneering protozoologist, Sir Arnold Theiler, invited me to lunch at her home. Onderstepoort was one of the three great veterinary research stations on the African continent together with the Kabete/Muguga complex on the western outskirts of Nairobi and Fort Lamy in French Equatorial Africa (now Ndjamena in present day Chad). Dr Theiler's research interests were in tick taxonomy and she was anxious to instruct me in the identification of immature ticks. I had only just become familiar with the identification of adult ticks, so identifying the species of immature ticks seemed a step too far.

In our conversation I mentioned that the equipment at Entebbe was fairly antiquated, to which she rejoined that all young people made the same complaint. She then went to a kitchen cupboard and brought out an old monocular brass microscope with a mirror for illumination and told me her father had used it for all his ground-breaking work. I felt suitably chastened.

A little later, while passing through Cape Town on my way to Southampton on the Union Castle ship Oranje (though it might have been more appropriately called a Union Cattle ship), I received a telegram with an offer of a post with FAO in Somalia. I questioned this, as I had originally been asked about my interest in Ethiopia and I had set my mind on going there. Nevertheless, in Cape Town I tried to buy any books available on Somalia to read while at sea. All I could find was Richard Burton's *First Footsteps in East Africa*, which had been first published in 1856, and Bill Travis's account of an attempt to establish a turtle canning industry along the Somali coast, *The Voice of the Turtle*, which had been published in 1967. In due course, the offer was amended to Ethiopia and I very promptly accepted it. At least Ethiopia was better served in terms of literary work by English-speaking authors.

CHAPTER 7

Ethiopia

Ethiopia – just the name of the place conjures up romance and mystery. It was not then, in the late 1960s, on the tourist route, so few people knew much about the country other than it was ruled by an intriguing little man, the Emperor Hailé Selassié, His Imperial Majesty, Elect of God, Conquering Lion of the Tribe of Judah and King of the Kings of Ethiopia (others who were less than impressed just referred to him as Highly Salacious).[31] We were seldom allowed to forget the accessory titles, for they were quoted repeatedly in the lead story on the front page of the *Ethiopian Herald* every day, taking precedence even over the news of Buzz Aldrin and Neil Armstrong's landing on the moon in 1969.

My terms of reference from the Food and Agriculture Organization in Rome stated that I was to instruct field staff in vaccination techniques in advance of the JP15 campaign that had been established by the Organization of African Unity in conjunction with the United Nations and various donors to eradicate rinderpest from the African continent using the new TCV vaccine developed by Walter Plowright in Muguga. Included in the terms of reference was a dress code, with the advice that project managers (I was not one), should come with full morning dress and their ladies with elbow-length white gloves for presentation at the Ethiopian court.

---

[31] Many years later I was informed by a person with contacts to the imperial court towards the end of the emperor's life that the emperor loathed the British. One can only wonder at his reasons since the British had restored him to the throne. Presumably he felt they had slighted him in some way.

After having being briefed in Rome I arrived in Ethiopia in September 1968. In the Ethiopian calendar this was the month of Meskerem in the year 1961, for the Ethiopians still follow the Julian calendar, which is seven years behind the Gregorian one. It was at the time of the Meskal festival, a time when the fields are ablaze with yellow meskal daisies, which commemorates the discovery of remnants of the True Cross by the Empress Helen, mother of the Emperor Constantine, on a pilgrimage to Jerusalem in 327-8 AD, a story which is almost certainly a myth. Much later the Dutch philosopher Erasmus surmised that Jesus had been crucified on a forest of trees, since there were so many relics of the true cross in existence.

I was soon joined by an Irish vet, Charles Lyttle, who had had considerable experience of disease control over many years in Kenya, and a Danish one, Ejgil Overby, who had been in Nigeria but had left during the Biafran conflagration. Charles was a family man with an overriding interest in horses and an extensive knowledge of Jockey Club and National Hunt rules and stud books, while Ejgil was a more phlegmatic character.

We set up our headquarters in an attic room of the Animal Health Assistants' School in Debre Zeit, a small town thirty miles south of Addis Ababa on the railway line between Djibouti and Addis. Our project was defined as a 'blister' attached to the school and this proved a very substantial weakness. The principal of the school, who was also the project manager, had little interest in or knowledge of large-scale vaccination programmes or of the new vaccines available. Yet Ethiopia, with over 25 million cattle, had the largest cattle population in Africa and one of the largest in the world, so the vaccination campaign had to be on a very large scale indeed, requiring a field staff of many hundreds to be trained. My experience in Karamoja suggested we needed about one man for every ten thousand cattle, so I reckoned about two and a half thousand animal health assistants and vaccinators would require training. Ideally this could best be achieved by training a core of trainers who, in turn, would train staff in all of the provinces of the empire.

For the first few weeks, before finding a small and undistinguished corrugated iron-roofed house nearby to rent, I stayed in the Debre Zeit Hotel. The hotel overlooked a volcanic crater lake, Lake Hora, like an hourglass in shape, which hinted at the likelihood that there were two craters side by side whose lakes had merged. The soils around were of volcanic origin and densely cultivated and when the wind blew a fine dust covered everything. DZ, as we called it, was a popular resort and the Emperor, Crown Prince, Prime Minister and other notables all had homes around the lake shore, so they were often seen at weekends.

A certain etiquette surrounded the emperor. If you were a foreigner and you met him while driving a car, you were obliged to stop, get out and bow while the emperor passed (foreign women were excused the formality and could remain in the car), Ethiopians, on the other hand, were obliged to get out and kneel with their foreheads touching the ground until he had passed.

DZ also was the home of the Imperial Ethiopian Air Force. Many of its officers had trained abroad, mainly in the United States, and they were a cosmopolitan lot and good company. Soon after my arrival I met a young air force officer, Messai Dejené, at a party and asked him if he would teach me Amharic. It was an uphill task, for there was no 'teach yourself' book available and the

Ethiopian alphabet bears no resemblance to the Roman one, though some of the consonants are similar to Greek letters, attesting to the origins of the Ethiopian Coptic church and its connection to the Orthodox Church in Egypt. Messai struggled and it was no fault of his that I made little headway. After half an hour or so of each lesson we found it was more fun to sample some of the nightspots of DZ, which were numerous though not always of a salubrious nature.

Unlike any other African country, Ethiopia was at that time a Christian monarchy, so with my interest in history, I tried to relate it to similar states in Europe. A constitutional monarchy it was not; in fact it was much more like England had been under Henry VII in the early 16th century with sovereign, church and barons, what might be called warlords now, competing for power. The emperor was a devout man but poorly educated and the church allied itself to him to further its own interests. Unfortunately the priests were even less educated than the emperor; their learning was confined to memorizing the scriptures in Ge'ez, the forerunner of Amharic, which they started learning as deacons at the age of seven and had completed by the age of sixteen when they were ordained as priests.

Edward Gibbon famously wrote of Ethiopia in *The Decline and Fall of the Roman Empire* 'Encompassed on all sides by the enemies of their religion, the Ethiopians slept near a thousand years, forgetful of the world by whom they were forgotten.' Compared to other African countries there was little sign that the country had woken yet. There was an excellent airline operating both internationally and within the country and a few hundred miles of tarmac road but the medical service was wholly inadequate and the telephone system was so archaic that it might well have been supplied by Alexander Graham Bell. The transport system was primitive and the bulk of agricultural products were still transported to and from markets on the backs of animals - donkeys, mules, miserable-looking horses and long trains of supercilious camels.[32]

Whereas in the western world the church had been instrumental in promoting education from earliest times, the priesthood in Ethiopia might almost be said to have been hostile to it because of the probablity that any modern education might undermine their authority. As a result the students in the Animal Health Assistants' School were often barred from entering churches because of their study of such unholy subjects as biology and medicine. In the newly-developing African countries, the Catholic and Protestant churches took a leading part in providing education, but their activities were severely restricted in Ethiopia, where the indigenous church feared that they might proselytize the local people. Early Catholic missionaries, for example, had to enter the country in the guise of traders.

To some extent the emperor had lost face when he had gone into exile after the Italian invasion in 1935, and he was criticized in some quarters for not staying to fight the enemy, leading the people to turn to their feudal lords for leadership. On his restoration in 1941 by the British and the Ethiopian Patriots who had remained in the country during the occupation, he had tried to wrest back this leadership from the barons and progressively he drew power into his own hands, delegating authority to the few he trusted. Thus his former driver, Abebe Retta, was Minister of Agriculture when I was there. Though he had burnished his

---

[32] The muscles raising the eyebrows are called the superciliaris muscles; hence the probable origin of the word supercilious

credentials by fathering children on the emperor's eldest daughter he was not considered of sufficient social standing to marry her. Eunuchs were often favoured, for they clearly had no dynastic ambitions of their own. This failure to delegate authority and the emperor's delight in making frequent visits overseas to the United Nations and elsewhere meant that little progress was made within the country.

Despite the grave weaknesses in government machinery, the people I met, many of them peasant farmers, were intelligent and industrious and might have done well with good leadership. But the peasantry had a great burden upon its shoulders. Much of the arable land on the highlands, which was used for the growing of barley and *teff*, a tiny-seeded, short-stalked grain used for the making of *njera* pancakes, the staple food of the highland people, was in the hands of the royal family, the church and the barons. Slavery had been officially abolished and with it serfdom, so that such land was worked by tenant farmers. Tenancy agreements were harsh and lasted only a year, so the tenant had no interest in improving the land or in soil conservation. Landlords insisted that the land be ploughed right to the boundaries every year so none was left fallow, and when harvesting time came in October and November they or their agents would appear to ensure that as much as a third of the crop was theirs as rental. Under these circumstances and with no assurance of continuity of occupation, the tenant farmers kept livestock for their own use and as security against being dispossessed, though not, of course, on their landlords' property except after harvesting, when the animals were permitted to graze the stovers, which for a short time restored some fertility to the soils with their dung. At other times livestock grazed the roadsides, the forest reserves and the steep screes on mountainsides and river banks, thus contributing to even more soil erosion. The long-term consequences have been disastrous and a very large proportion of the Ethiopian population is now on permanent famine relief.

The Ethiopians are, in general, a finely-featured, handsome people. The women, in particular, are often striking. Countrymen, though often unshod, wore white jodhpurs with white shirts and fine cotton shawls - *shammas* - over their shoulders, while women wore white skirts with finely-embroidered multi-coloured hems, pale blouses and shammas which more often were draped over their heads, though Oromo women more usually covered their heads with a black cloth. Among the educated classes most spoke good English so it was easy to relate to them. They certainly were an asset if I invited them to a party, for if a Beatles number was put on they would have everyone cavorting on the floor or doing a conga through the garden - and the women were no shrinking violets - whereas the French guests would congregate at the bottom of the garden, conversing in their language but adding nothing to the bonhomie. I still retain some very happy memories of some very lovely people. The Italians may have occupied the country but they never colonised it and the benefits were obvious, for Ethiopians, men and women, retained their pride in themselves and were self-reliant and confident. The downside was that their economy was nowhere near as developed as that of the former African colonies. Furthermore there was no sense of racial segregation as there was, and still is to some extent, in the former colonies. This is not to say there was no racism, for the Ethiopians were patronizing towards darker-skinned people on the fringes of the empire and referred to them as *barya* - slaves.

In a situation in which there seemed to be no great interest in the objective of rinderpest eradication, Charles, Ejgil and I made some forays into the remoter areas of southern Ethiopia, more to fill in time than for any more serious purpose. The first was to the province of Bale on the south-eastern side of the Rift Valley with the intention of continuing to the Ogaden area of the country, which was inhabited by Somalis. FAO had provided us with quite inadequate vehicles and tents. In the southernmost parts of Bale we would be closer to Mogadishu than Addis Ababa and there were no petrol stations in between, so we were obliged to take all our fuel with us. Unfortunately the short-wheel-based Land Rovers we were supplied with were too small to carry spare tyres, tents, fuel and other paraphernalia for a round journey of nearly a thousand miles. This problem was solved by acquiring a very old lorry. Unfortunately, we had hardly completed the first day when it caught fire with all the fuel aboard. We could go no further. We had reached Goba, the principal town of the province, high up in the Bale mountains, almost 8000 feet, and cold. Most mornings we would wake to see a light covering of snow on the grassy hills above us. As we had expected to be travelling in the hot, arid lowlands of the Ogaden, we had come with inadequate clothing for the cold, so we sought shelter in the only hotel in the town, which doubled as a whorehouse. During the day we took some long walks about the town, while we spent the evenings drinking the local *araki* and playing poker according to Royal Limerick Yacht Club rules at Charles's insistence.

We were accompanied by two pleasant young Ethiopian animal health assistants (AHAs) who showed an interest in learning the game, so we obliged and they joined us each evening. Being aware that they were not as well off as we were we showed them some indulgence, but they were quick to learn and soon cleaned us out. We were stuck in Goba for the better part of a fortnight before a replacement lorry reached us from Addis with more fuel and during that time we ran out of money, so we played with matchsticks for stakes and promised to honour them on returning to Debre Zeit.

While in Goba we heard rumours of a military lorry being blown up by a land mine set by Somali bandits, or *shifta*, as the government called the Somalis who were fighting a guerrilla war for their independence from the Ethiopians who had annexed the Ogaden during the reign of the Emperor Menelik II. Numerous fatalities were reported. On going to see the provincial governor he confirmed that the rumour was true but he was confident that we would be safe. It was not a confidence I shared.

However we proceeded to El Karre some three hundred miles southeast of Goba, well inside Somali-inhabited territory. The track first ran over the rolling hills of the Arusi highlands, skirting for a short distance the rim of the spectacular gorge of the headwaters of the Wabi Shebelle river, tiered in great steps of a thousand feet and more, before dropping to the arid thorn scrub of the Ogaden. El Karre stood on a hillside from which a spring supplied clean water to a conduit which ran through the little town. Despite its isolation it was a remarkably well-kept place; a few years later I met with Dougie Collins, a former British army officer, who had been a district officer there and responsible for the town's orderly condition. Although a part of Ethiopia, the British had administered much of the Ogaden from Mogadishu after ousting the Italians in 1941 before handing it over to Ethiopian administration in 1955. This was a process Dougie had opposed, for he had a great affection for the Somali people, as his book *A tear for Somalia* bears witness. We returned safely to Debre Zeit but it was clear to us that it was not a suitable training area because of the *shifta* insurgency in the area.

While we were stuck in Goba a World Bank-sponsored team of experts stayed at the hotel for a night. They were part of a mission proposing to establish a dairy industry around Addis, which badly lacked an adequate supply of fresh milk. Of course, as veterinarians we were interested in their proposals, so the team promised to give us a copy of their first draft when we returned to DZ.

In a sense veterinarians are natural pessimists. We look at a situation, be it a dairy farm, a poultry production unit or whatever, and anticipate what might go wrong. If we see that the water supply might be contaminated or the buildings are inadequate, we seek to put them right before some misfortune hits. My own opinion is that if there is a flaw in the management system, a farmer has no more than a year to put it right before being subject to some calamity and in East Africa, where East Coast fever is a problem, experience in Buganda showed that even ten days might be too long if there is a fault in the dipping schedule.

The World Bank proposals filled Charles and me with alarm. Among them was a proposal to import 5000 Friesian heifers from Kenya to establish a hundred dairy farms around Addis over a period of five years. Aside from the fact that there probably were insufficient heifers in Kenya for sale and those that would be offered for sale would likely have been of poor quality, the numbers of farms proposed meant that a new farm would have to be established every eighteen days over a period of five years, and we had seen no evidence that there were sufficient skilled people in the country to do this. For example, I had seen no indication that anybody in the country knew how to erect a decent wire fence. Needless to say, it was obvious that the landlords would not do the menial work, so the employment of farm managers was proposed. The recommended wages were considerably lower than those of animal health assistants, so competent people would clearly not be attracted to take up posts of such responsibility.

Another anomaly in the proposals was that their selling price for the milk in Addis would be higher than the current price, which itself was on the high side because of the overall shortage, though likely to fall when more milk came on the market. When we pointed this out to the team they replied that they thought people would be prepared to pay a higher price for Friesian milk. I had never heard such nonsense. Few purchasers care whether their milk comes from a Friesian cow or any other breed (in fact the milk of the low-yielding native cows is more nutritious and sweeter that of high-yielding Friesians).

There were numerous other snags in the proposals but the greatest of all was that at that period there was no properly constituted diagnostic laboratory in the country, so nobody could forecast the disease hazards to which imported cattle would be exposed. This meant there could be no well-considered programmes for vaccinations, tick control or other precautionary measures. Charles and I spent a considerable time writing a paper drawing attention to the deficiencies in the dairy project and sent it to the mission. After a few weeks we had had no response from them, so we enquired if they had received our paper. They admitted that they had but considered the criticisms so pessimistic that they had decided to ignore them. I heard much later that the dairy programme had been a failure and I suspect several Ethiopian farmers were drawn into debt as a result.

Ostensibly there was a Department of Veterinary Services in Addis with an Ethiopian director and another as deputy, but the real policy maker was an elderly French veterinarian, Dr Blanc, who had the ear of the emperor. Dr Blanc, a spare, greying man, had been brought up in Algeria and had all the wit of a *colon*. There was also a French vaccine production laboratory in DZ next to the Animal Health Assistants' School and an American veterinary task force led by an ex-army veterinarian, Frank Madden.

Ten months passed after my arrival before the Minister of Agriculture, the emperor's former driver, decided to start an anti-rinderpest vaccination campaign in Sidamo province in the south of the country. But in a country where the emperor held power by a policy of divide and rule, the fact that a decision was made by the Minister of Agriculture did not mean that it would inevitably become fact.

Frank and I drove down to Awasa, an attractive little town lying on a Rift Valley lake of the same name which was the administrative capital of the province, to see the governor and to get his consent to a campaign in his province. He was agreeable but he could promise no funds, since that was the responsibility of the provincial treasurer who was not subordinate to him but to the Minister of Finance who was himself subordinate only to the emperor. I began to see why policy decisions took so long to come into effect in Ethiopia.

There were other structural weaknesses I began to be aware of. The provincial veterinary officer was a Frenchman but he lived in Addis, where there were better schools for his children, and visited the province infrequently. Another even more serious weakness was that the majority of field staff had not been paid for five months and some not for nine months. It was rumoured that a minister kept the designated funds in a personal bank account, drawing interest on the sum until just before the end of the financial year, when he would finally release them. It was also said that the field veterinary staff were not averse to charging livestock owners for their services, but I could hardly blame them when they were deprived of their salaries.

I got to know Awasa well over the next year; it was at the end of one of the few tarmac roads in the country and was a popular weekend holiday destination for the expatriate community in Addis. The *Bellevue du Lac* hotel, run by a Swiss, was the best of the hotels in Awasa and when it was fully occupied I would stay at a more ramshackle one run by a German. He was interesting company. One day he told me he had been with the Afrika Korps in Libya, so I told him that the British held Rommel in high regard. He did not take it lightly. 'He was a shit!' he exploded. 'I know, I was his batman.'

The trouble with Awasa was that it was at the extreme northern edge of the province of which it was the capital and over a hundred miles from Negelle, which was to be the main centre of our activities. Sidamo is a large province stretching along the border with Kenya from Somalia in the east to Lake Stephanie (Chew Bahar in the local language) in the west, a distance of 350 miles, and roughly 250 miles from north to south. There were only two roads in this vast area, one leading from Awasa via Yavello and Mega to Moyale on the Kenya border, the other via Negelle to Dolo on the Ethiopian-Kenyan-Somali border. Neither of them were maintained, though the section from Negelle to Dolo, built by the Italians during their six year occupation, was of such superior construction even after almost thirty years of neglect that it seemed like a veritable highway. It was marked at regular intervals by marble milestones crested with a *fasces* and indicating the distances to Rome, Addis Ababa and Mogadishu. Other roads were mere tracks, and where they passed though some landlord's territory a barrier was set up and a toll demanded. Where there were no roads or tracks, vaccination equipment, water and the rest was packed on cradles and loaded on to the backs of camels and mules. The main livestock owners were the Borana, a sub-group of the Oromo people, in the central part of the district and the Somalis in the east.

I was certainly pleased to have something constructive to do at last. The Ministry of Agriculture provided a few clapped-out Land Rovers and with these and a group of about twenty animal health assistants and a few more lowly vaccinators the rinderpest campaign started off. With few exceptions the AHAs were excellent and, although inadequately equipped and working under difficult conditions, they never complained. They were also remarkably resourceful and proud so that they seldom worried me with their difficulties but set out to overcome them themselves. An example of this occurred when one of the dilapidated Land Rovers gave up the ghost in a remote spot. Rather than send to me for help, the animal health assistant got together a team of oxen which towed it some fifteen miles to the Italian-made road, where he got a lorry driver to tow it into Negelle for repairs.

FAO was of no help. The Effing Awful Organization, Charles dubbed it. As soon as a decision was taken to commence the vaccination campaign I ordered six paraffin refrigerators from suppliers in Addis for use in the field to conserve the vaccines. The order was, however, immediately countermanded by the procurement section in Rome, which maintained that I did not have the authority to make it. Half a year later six electric refrigerators were delivered from Rome - they were cheaper, said the procurement section. They were, of course, quite useless in the remoter areas of Sidamo where there was no electricity supply.

Accommodation in the remoter areas was a problem. FAO had provided us with tents suitable for housing a platoon, weighing a hundredweight and more. On one safari Ejgil and I had put one up and it had taken us the best part of an hour and a half to do so which we found very disagreeable in the gathering darkness after a heavy day's work in the field. As these huge tents filled most of the space in our short-wheel-based Land Rovers I resolved not to use them. Where I could, I stayed in local hotels and brothels. The beds often looked like bundles of bedbugs and other wildlife and so I got into the practice of spraying the bed with an insecticide, then laying a large polythene sheet over it to deter marauders and kipping in a sleeping bag on top of the pile. In one place the bed looked so disgusting that I asked for it to be removed completely and slept on my own camp bed. I was pleasantly surprised next morning to find my account had been halved, for the original bed had been set up in a passageway and rented out to other occupants.

It amused me that in many of the brothels the pillow cases were embroidered with little hints such as 'His' and 'Hers' or 'Mr' and 'Mrs' so as to intimate to occupiers that they should not be sleeping alone. There were other hints. If late in the evening a girl had not found a client she would come knocking on the door, asking for a cigarette or a light. They were fun, they were attractive and they were better company than my own. But the greatest advantage of a brothel room was that one could lock the door from the inside, which was important as I often travelled with considerable sums of money to pay vaccinators, purchase fuel and for other needs. I was well aware that two of my veterinary colleagues, including Frank, who persisted in sleeping in tents, had been woken up by armed shifta in the middle of the night and robbed of all they had.

The Somalis are Muslims, so there were no bars in the Somali part of Sidamo and apparently no hotels or brothels either, so on occasion I slept in school rooms. The Somali are nomads and somewhat disdainful of education, so I was seldom disturbed by schoolchildren.

Rufus, whom I had retrieved from Uganda, usually accompanied me and saved me from one potentially nasty experience. It happened this way: I was returning one late evening after spending a day servicing various vaccination teams when the Land Rover struck a tree stump hidden in the grass, bending the track rods underneath. The track rods are part of the steering assembly of the vehicle, so I now found myself with two front wheels facing inwards and clearly could not proceed. It was too dark to take them off and straighten them, so I realised I was stuck there for the night. Fortunately I was accompanied by two Ethiopians so we made camp but lit no fire lest we attract the attention of shifta.

In the middle of the night Rufus, whom I had tied to the end of my camp bed, started barking. He had two kinds of bark - one a hesitant bark against a vague noise in the night and the other a determined bark against a real threat. This was the second kind. I had a torch by me, so I switched it on and looked out in the direction I supposed he was barking. There, not thirty feet from where the three of us were sleeping, was a lion. In a trice I was in the cab of the Land Rover and so were the two assistants, leaving poor Rufus tied to the end of my camp bed barking furiously. I turned on the vehicle's lights and hit the horn savagely, deciding the shifta were a lesser threat, and slowly the lion retreated back into the darkness. Not knowing where he might be, I supposed we would have to spend the rest of the night in the cab but, despite my warnings, the assistants very soon climbed out, rolled themselves up in their bedding and went back to sleep. I admired their courage and after about an hour without any more alarms I emerged gingerly and joined them for what was left of the night. At sunrise we lit a fire and cooked some breakfast and then used the embers to heat the track rods and beat them back into a semblance of straightness. Then we made our way back to our base camp.

The shifta posed a real threat to the vaccination teams, for the majority of the animal health assistants were Amhara from the highlands and these were precisely the people the Somalis were fighting against to gain their autonomy. There was only one Somali vaccinator and he was just in his early twenties, but he had one great advantage - his uncle was a very powerful political figure from one of the major clans and the local Somalis were well aware of the lad's lineage. Meanwhile I had met an elderly Somali who had fought with the King's African Rifles during the war and still remembered some Swahili, so I recruited him. So with the lad and the veteran I was able to assemble two vaccination teams to operate effectively in the Somali-inhabited areas.

In fact the Somalis had few cattle and were much more interested in the health and welfare of their camels. The biggest disease problem of camels was trypanasomosis but in this very remote area of Ethiopia there were no appropriate drugs. Not many drugs have been developed for the treatment of the disease in camels and not all the bovine remedies are suitable but I managed to find one in Addis - suramin. The major concentration of camels was around Dolo, a dry hot desert land with no trees except for some doum palms along the river banks. Dolo was in the extreme east of Sidamo at the confluence of the Dawa Parma and Ganale rivers which meet there to form the Juba river, which all but runs into the sea between Mogadishu and Kismayu. I spent several hot days in Dolo injecting camels and insisted on being paid in the East African currency which was then in use, as there were some reasonably well-stocked shops on the Kenyan side of the border whereas nothing was available on the Ethiopian side. Occasionally I did some fishing in the rivers in the evenings when it was a little cooler, but all I caught were catfish and not even Rufus deigned to eat them.

In Dolo I slept in a schoolroom, but with its corrugated iron roof it gave little respite from the heat during the day. At Melka

147

Wara, overlooking the Dawa Parma river, I slept in a Somali encampment with their camels and goats in close proximity, protected by a thick thorn barricade. I assumed the best place to sleep was curled up round the central fire but was quickly put right by the old veteran who advised me to sleep next to the thorns, explaining that if lions leapt over the barricade they would take an animal near the centre before leaping out again with their prey. Not that the sides of a boma were always safe, for in Debre Zeit I had treated a sheep which had been attacked by a hyena through a gap in the thorns. Unable to drag it through the small aperture, the hyena had ripped off its foreleg, including the shoulder blade and all the muscles attaching it to the chest wall. It was an appalling injury and I felt the sheep had little chance of survival, so I suggested to the owner he slaughter it and eat it before it succumbed. He was insistent that I treat it, so I sewed up the skin tear and filled the animal with antibiotics, though with little confidence that it would survive. A fortnight later, however, I saw the same three-legged sheep grazing on the side of the road, which really surprised me for sheep are notoriously fragile animals. As a Scottish shepherd once said to me 'There's one thing that sheep do easily and that's die.'

Across the Dawa Parma river on the Kenyan side was a small town, Ramu, with remarkably well-stocked shops. The river was not particularly deep and could easily be waded, but it had an evil reputation for crocodiles and the Somali would beat the water with sticks when they crossed. I did the same, but took the added precaution of putting the long-suffering Rufus in the water ahead of me. Several brands of gin and whisky were available at give-away prices, all marked as NAAFI stores, which was the reason I had demanded to be paid in East African currency for treating the Somalis' camels.[33] What the source of the liquor was I don't know, though I suspected that it had been shipped from Aden and then carried overland on camel back. I was surprised also because I had thought the Somali, as Muslims, were an abstemious people. Perhaps the low prices merely reflected the transport costs for products not in great demand and whose original wholesale prices had been zero.

Away from the rivers, water in that hot arid land was the greatest necessity and in my small Land Rover I carried as much as I could to supply the vaccinators. I took to growing a beard to save on water, but it was a false economy because the sweat evaporated, leaving salt behind. This caused considerable itching, so I found myself using more water to wash my beard than if I had shaved regularly. At nights only a sheet was necessary as covering and on some nights not even that, but it served a useful purpose tucked around my neck in that it prevented me from smelling myself after many days unable to bathe.

Negelle was a much more comfortable billet and it became the centre for vaccination campaigns among the Borana people. The governor of Negelle, a major-general, was the brother of one of the animal health assistants and he became a useful ally, providing me on occasion with a modern but unfurnished house to stay in. His hospitality was prodigious and his gin and tonics perverse. While I might put two or three fingers of gin into a glass and then top up with tonic, he would put in two or three fingers of tonic and then top up with gin. Two of those and you were knocked out for the

[33] Navy, Army and Air Force Institutes which provided British armed forces with recreational facilities as well as duty-free cigarettes and liquor.

day. Perhaps his source of gin was the same as mine down in Ramu but I didn't ask.

Inevitably in such remote areas injured and sick people would be brought to me for treatment, and I kept a few antibiotics and dressings for the purpose. Fortunately my undergraduate education had been integrated with medical students, which made me familiar with some of the conditions I saw. Quite the nastiest was the case of a Somali boy who had somehow injured his knee. A local healer had followed the traditional method of dealing with joint ailments and used a hot iron to cauterize the knee. He had destroyed much of the surrounding tissue, including so much of the joint capsule that I could see the innermost ligaments of the knee joint. Clearly the boy needed modern surgery if there was to be any hope of reconstructing the joint capsule, though I thought it probably too late as the whole was badly infected. I gave him a mighty dose of antibiotics and told him to return in the morning with his father, saying I would take them into Negelle where there was a mission hospital run by an Australian doctor. Sadly I saw him no more. As I had found previously, a syringe and needle was considered a magical combination curing every sort of ill, and nothing more was considered necessary.

On another occasion, while we were vaccinating cattle, a young man turned up who was quite obviously afflicted with smallpox. He too failed to appear when I was ready to leave for Negelle, which probably was just as well as I could not be sure that all the vaccinators had been immunized and the Australian doctor would certainly not be pleased to have a smallpox case in his little hospital where there were no isolation facilities.

One day I was returning from vaccinating some large herds of Borana cattle with an animal health assistant when he drew my attention to two women sitting on the side of the road a dozen miles or so from Negelle. I chose to ignore them at first, thinking they were merely hoping for a free lift, but the assistant pressed me to stop. One of the women was very obviously pregnant, so I suggested she sit in the cab, but she was clear in her mind that she preferred to lie on some bundles in the back with her woman friend and Rufus for company.

I had not driven five minutes when I heard a piercing scream from the back of the Land Rover. I stopped abruptly and went to the tail gate to see the floor of the vehicle covered with blood and other fluids in which Rufus was taking considerable interest. It was only a half hour drive on to Negelle, but a quick look up the lady's skirt showed that there wasn't a minute to spare, for a little down-covered head was already in the breech. My hands were filthy and I had given all my water to the vaccinating team, so there was no way to wash them unless I used the water in the radiator and that, I thought, was likely to be scalding. The second essential was to get an engrossed Rufus out of the way.

I supposed that with the head already delivered the rest would come easily, but for some reason it would not and it took me a little time to realize that the umbilical cord was looped around the infant's neck and pulling just tightened the loop. This is not usually a veterinary obstetrical problem, though I was aware that it did happen with humans. My mixed undergraduate training came in handy, for I remembered that the problem is easily resolved by just slipping the loop over the baby's head. This is what I did and immediately I had the baby out. But it wasn't breathing spontaneously and was quite blue, or as blue as a dark-skinned infant can look. A quick smack on its bottom set it howling and in no time at all it looked relatively pink.

At this point I was in a dilemma, for my hands were so dirty that I didn't want to handle the cord any more than necessary for fear of infecting the baby with tetanus, so I just handed the baby, still attached to its mother, for her to nurse while I drove on to Negelle to get her to the mission hospital there.[34]

I had not driven many miles before there was an eerie silence from the back of the vehicle, so I stopped again to make sure all was well. It wasn't; the baby had stopped breathing and returned to its blue colour again. I spanked it again and it howled and mercifully kept on howling the rest of the way back to Negelle. Meanwhile, as I drove, I realized that in my anxiety I hadn't looked to see what sex the baby was, so when I reached the hospital I asked the mother. She hadn't noticed its sex either.

Two days later I dropped into the hospital to ask the Australian doctor how mother and baby were doing, to be told that he had released them in excellent condition the previous day. He chided me for my obstetrical methods, which seemed to me an unreasonable criticism in view of the successful outcome. He also told me that the mother had thought the baby dead, but it always

---

[34] Whereas in human obstetrics it is common practice to clamp the umbilical cord before severing it, in veterinary practice it is left to nature. The 18th century physician, Erasmus Darwin, grandfather of the pioneer of evolutionary theory, himself suggested that clamping the cord was likely to be detrimental and modern obstetricians are increasingly coming to the same opinion. It was only in Thoroughbred studs that foaling mares were treated with almost as much care as expectant mothers and the cords ligated as in human practice. This led to a condition of newborn Thoroughbred foals called barker foal syndrome in which foals coughed continuously and died within a few days of birth and on post mortem were found with lung tissues only partially inflated. Two Newmarket veterinary surgeons had pondered on why it only happened in Thoroughbreds and not in other horses and realised there was a link between tying the cord and the coughing syndrome. Usually a mare foals lying down and, exhausted by the straining, will take a few minutes before standing up again or, alternatively, it is the foal that lurches to its feet and it is this action which breaks the cord but in those minutes the uterus contracts quite considerably thereby squeezing the placenta and pushing one or two pints of foetal blood into the newborn foal, sufficient to expand its lungs normally.

started screaming when it saw a white face. Poor baby: starting life with an acquired racist attitude.

Many of the Somali and Borana herdsmen carried arms, probably the remnants of the Italian occupation some thirty years previously. As a consequence wildlife was scarce and what there was was extremely shy. The long-necked gerenuk and tiny dik-dik were the commonest animals. One day I saw a remarkable sight near Filtu in the Somali sector - looking across a blackened lava field I noticed dozens of strangely shaped rounded brown rocks. Then one moved and I realized they were all giant leopard tortoises.

The wildlife had little chance, even in designated game parks. On one occasion I was driving with a local governor through a national park lying to the west of the Awasa-Yavello road on the shores of Lake Abaya and Lake Chamo when a wart hog dashed across the track. In an instant the governor had drawn his revolver and blasted away at its fast disappearing rump. For him it was just target practice, for Ethiopians follow the Mosaic Law and don't eat pork, nor do they eat the meat of water fowl, which at least gives the duck and geese on the rift valley lakes and elsewhere a chance of survival.[35]

Dotted around in the dry Borana country are a number of wells which according to legend were dug by a race of giants. While vaccinating cattle at one of them, El Lei on the track between Negelle and the Kenya border, I saw numerous herds of cattle and camels coming to drink. A ramp cut through the rock about a hundred yards long led down some forty feet to an open space in the ground where the troughs were and in the centre of which was the actual well which was another forty feet or more deep. Water was lifted in giraffe-skin bags by men standing one above the other

---

[35] See Leviticus, cap 11

on small platforms within the shaft of the well. Only when one herd had finished watering and returned to the surface was the next herd driven down the ramp to the troughs. What was remarkable was their patience in awaiting their turn, for they had probably had no water for two or three days.

There were other small towns within the Borana area where I based myself while supporting the vaccination teams operating in the area. Moyale is a border town with Kenya and, as at Ramu, the shops on the Kenyan side were much better stocked with goods. This was very welcome since I could always obtain spare parts and tyres for Land Rovers without having to call Addis for them. Another welcome feature was the Kenya Army company camped there as their officers were always most hospitable.

The Emperor Menelik II originally had ambitions to extend his empire southwards in accordance with the legend that the lands of the first Menelik extended to the Indian Ocean, what is now Somalia, and right down to Mount Kilimanjaro.[36] Aware of this, officials in the new British East Africa Protectorate pressed the Foreign Office to urge the emperor to come to an agreement about the southern limits of his country, but there was considerable complacency in King Charles Street over the matter and it wasn't until 1902 that negotiations started and a Boundary Commission set up. With the agreement of both sides, much of the border was established along the bottom of the Megado escarpment and a frontier inspector was appointed to ensure that the Emperor's forces did not encroach over the agreed line. Oddly, a Greek, Philip Photios Zaphiro, a resident of Addis, was chosen by the Colonial Office for the job. It was an inspired choice, for he was an extremely resourceful

---

[36] Menelik I, legend asserted, was the outcome of a diplomatic encounter between the Queen of Sheba and King Solomon in Jerusalem (See I Kings 10, v.13) and the first of the Solomonic line of Ethiopian monarchs

man in a lonely post. With the agreement of the local Borana people he established one of his outposts from which to oversee the 400-mile boundary line on Churre Moyale hill, where it was considerably cooler - though five miles north of the agreed border.

The problem with the alignment was that it divided the traditional grazing areas of the Borana people in two, so early on a British consulate was established in Mega about 70 miles north-west of Moyale with a resident British consul to ensure that the Kenyan Borana were accorded common grazing and watering rights on both sides of the border, as had existed before the border demarcation. I always felt there was something sinister about Mega. It was high and cold and often wrapped in mist. Perhaps it was the cold that gave it the sinister feel. Beside the road a couple of miles north of Mega was an Italian fort which to me seemed like the remnant of some film set, so unusual was it in that setting. And always in front of the fort, strutting their stuff, were a platoon of kori bustards.

Perhaps it was a story told by one of the consuls posted there, 'Tich' Miles, before the Italian occupation that gave Mega its baleful distinction. The consul had been invited to lunch by the provincial governor, Dejazmatch Balcha, a eunuch of Oromo origin who had been one of the Emperor Menelik's generals.[37] On arrival at the governor's compound on his mule the consul was led through an outer courtyard, where numerous soldiers presented arms and then through a second courtyard where more soldiers presented arms and finally into a third courtyard and the entrance to the private quarters.

On sitting down to lunch a line of slaves, about twenty in all,

---

[37] Dejazmatch was a title of nobility meaning a marshal of provincial headquarters and roughly equivalent to a count.

brought in dish after dish and laid them on the table before turning to face the wall. In conversation, the governor mentioned that Hailé Selassié was half man, half snake but the snake was more conspicuous. The consul was taken aback. Though he might have had a similar opinion he certainly wasn't going to express it, so he urged the old Dejazmatch to be more cautious in case the slaves repeated his disloyal conversation.

'They can't. I've had all their tongues cut out to prevent such a happening' was his reply.

Though I was glad to be doing something constructive, I was profoundly dissatisfied with the conduct of the vaccination campaign. At no time did the FAO project manager confide to Charles, Ejgil or myself what the national rinderpest control policy was, so I had to ask the USAID veterinarian, Frank Madden, what had been decided in Addis Ababa. My terms of reference were to train vaccination staff in anticipation of the JP15 rinderpest control programme, not to organize local vaccination campaigns so that the provincial veterinary officer could continue to reside in Addis for the benefit of his children's education.

At a personal level it was also dissatisfying, for I was doing the job of a driver delivering vaccines, water and other necessities which could as easily be done by a livestock officer, not a veterinarian. I was also dissatisfied because the area was so vast and the vaccination campaign so transitory that despite learning a few words of Borana I was never able to feel much rapport with the people or the place, as I had in Karamoja five years earlier. Equally clearly the provincial veterinary officer had no rapport either, so the opportunity to build up a sense of trust between livestock owners and veterinary officials did not exist, nor was any continuity established in veterinary activities, such as the regular reporting of disease outbreaks, which is essential if eradication of disease is the objective.

However, by far my most serious criticism of the campaign was the quality of the vaccine itself. I had no problem with the quality of the rinderpest tissue culture vaccine but Walter Plowright, who had developed the vaccine at Muguga, had shown clearly that there was a very considerable deterioration of the vaccine, sufficient to nullify any immunizing capability, if reconstituted in ordinary water rather than in saline solution. I had spent nights by the Dawa Parma river boiling water from the river and filtering it and then adding household salt in measured amounts so that there would be a proper saline solution for reconstitution of the vaccine for use in the morning, but it seemed to me that the vaccine laboratory in DZ was in a much better position than I was in the field to produce a sterile saline solution. When I mentioned this to Dr Blanc his only response was 'Pouf! Who is this man, Plowright? I've never heard of him' a comment which only showed his own ignorance.

Far worse was the quality of the pleuropneumonia vaccine. As a cost-cutting measure old rubber bungs were used to seal the bottles of vaccine but these leaked and, depending on changes in temperature and barometric pressure up and down the precipitous roads, they either forced out or sucked in material as the liquid vaccine expanded or contracted. The broth culture in which the vaccine was produced was not exclusive for the growth of pleuropneumonia bacteria and so numerous contaminants found an ideal environment in which to grow. The fact that no provision was made to keep the vaccine iced merely accelerated their growth. So on many occasions I found I had bottles of vaccine ranging through all the colours of the rainbow except blue. They were clearly contaminated so I discarded them, but I had no way of knowing if bottles that had not changed colour were also contaminated. In fact there was some evidence that contaminated vaccine was used, for I once got a report that over ninety cattle had died in one village a few days after the vaccinators had been there. A full bottle contained 100 doses of vaccine, so the numbers added up. I wasn't brave enough to go and investigate for I would surely have been lynched if I had and, almost certainly, there would have been nothing to examine anyway for people and hyenas would have removed all the pathological material.

Both Charles and I were concerned about the vaccine quality and thought that if someone made a complaint to the disciplinary committee of the Royal College of Veterinary Surgeons we could both be accused of unprofessional conduct for knowingly using substandard vaccines. The problem was that our professional opinions were totally ignored by the project manager.

A few weeks later Dr Blanc flew down to Negelle with more of the same dubious vaccine but no saline solution. I told him I would not distribute it to the vaccination teams. He then ordered me to distribute it, so I informed him that he had no authority to give me any orders. If he was insistent on the vaccine being used, he could do it himself and I would return to Addis on the plane in which he had flown down. It was an unpleasant altercation but I hoped it would lead to something. It led nowhere, though I found out six months later that Dr Blanc had written to FAO headquarters in Rome complaining of my refusal to support the vaccination programme. Neither the officials in Rome nor the project manager in DZ took up the matter. I felt I had been a voice in the wilderness.

One of my obligations was to write a quarterly report to Rome, so in my next quarterly report I brought up the issue of the poor quality of the vaccines as well as the fact that we were conducting vaccination campaigns on behalf of the government but not training staff, as we were required to do in our terms of appointment, other than the forty or so men in the teams in Sidamo. This report would most certainly have been seen by the project manager before it was forwarded to Rome, but still he did nothing.

Two areas of animal welfare and production took my attention in Ethiopia. The first struck me within minutes of landing at Bole airport for the first time. I was met at the airport by John Scott, who had been with the Royal Army Veterinary Corps in Burma during the war and had later risen to deputy director of veterinary Services in Tanzania. Whereas in most of the towns and cities of the world taxicabs are a ubiquitous sight, the commonest form of local public transport in Ethiopian towns was the gharri – a light two-wheeled horse-drawn vehicle for two or three passengers. Sadly, I noticed on the drive in from the airport that most of the horses were lame. I mentioned this to John, who suggested I tell him when I saw a horse that was sound. Perhaps, more than anything, that indicates the size of the problem. It was a result of ignorance of simple farriery. In Ethiopia, where the gharri horses were driven on hard tarmac roads, the usual form of protection of the sole of the hoof was a bit of old rubber tyre tacked to the walls of the hoof. With no wear on the heels they just grew longer and longer, tipping the hoof forward.[38]

The other deficiency was in the field of animal production,

---

[38] Normally a horse's hoof looks like a wedge when viewed from the side with the long part at the front of the hoof, the toe, and sloping down to the heels on either side. In between the heels is the frog consisting of an elastic horny material and it is this part which takes the brunt as the foot hits the ground thus cushioning the impact; but with the heels too long the frog never touches the ground so the impact is taken by the bones of the lower limb and the cartilaginous joint surfaces between the bones leading to the development of a painful arthritis of the joints. But this is not all; by tipping the foot forward the lower part of the limb, the pastern, takes a more vertical position unlike in a properly conformed foot where the pastern is at 45° to 60° from the horizontal ground surface. This angling has a further cushioning effect for the three terminal bones of the limb act somewhat like a leaf spring in a lorry. A simple knowledge of farriery would have ensured that the heels were cut away so that the pastern was angled correctly and the frog touched the ground thus saving many horses from much pain. This was, and is, most certainly a case where prevention is better than cure for once the arthritic changes have set in it is impossible to reverse them.

where there was no appreciation of the proper way to prepare hides. The only criterion for buyers was the weight of the hide and not its quality so, of course, to increase the value a lot of fat and other tissues, including hooves on occasion, were left adhering to the hide. As a consequence they were only fit for the making of glue. This was a considerable economic loss, for while in Uganda and Kenya the export of hides and skins formed the fourth largest source of foreign exchange, Ethiopia, despite having by far the largest number of cattle of any country in Africa, missed out in the trade.

Of course, there were diversions. With Messai as a guide I spent one New Year visiting Gondar, an ancient seat of the empire and famous for its castles. It is just north of Lake Tana, the virtual source of the Blue Nile, though others might argue that the springs that feed the lake are the real source. There were some wonderful things to see including the Blue Nile gorge, deeper even than the Grand Canyon and quite as spectacular, and the Tississat Falls, where the river plunges out of the lake on its way to join the White Nile and continue on to the Mediterranean. On our way back southwards the road up the side of the gorge was blocked by large procession of priests with their colourful parasols, and people celebrating Timkat - the Feast of the Epiphany.

Messai also took me to visit his parents, who lived in a large sprawling home on the western wall of the Rift Valley near Debre Sina overlooking the Danakil desert on the road to the Red Sea port of Assab. The Shewan plateau, over which we drove, is a high, fertile plain and treeless except for clusters of eucalyptus trees around the scattered homesteads. The road climbed steadily to 9,000 feet and more, at what was then called the Mussolini Pass, before dropping many thousands of feet to the floor of the valley in which the Red Sea lies. Captain Dejené, Messai's father, had been in the Imperial Guard and had fought the Italians before taking refuge in Kenya, where he had been confined in an isolated camp with other Ethiopian exiles at Manyani close to the Tsavo National Park. Later he joined the forces under Lieutenant-General Cunningham which pushed the Italians out of southern Ethiopia before linking up with the British under General Platt from the Sudan and restoring the emperor to his throne. The old man was proud to show me his campaign medals with King George VI's features on them and insisted I take his photograph with them.

Hard times had come later in 1960, when the Imperial Guard had rebelled against the emperor. There was heavy fighting around Addis, but eventually the rebels were defeated. All officers of the rank of major and above were executed but Captain Dejené's life was spared, though he was sent into exile to Jijigga, a town southeast of Harar in the Ogaden area of Ethiopia.

By the time I met him his exile had ended. One evening the three of us went out shooting francolin, a bird like a partridge but somewhat smaller. I hit two but didn't bag them. The first flapped weakly on and then tumbled down the escarpment and fell a couple of hundred feet beneath us and could not be retrieved, while the second dropped and was instantly snapped up by a leopard which made off with it into the undergrowth. Captain Dejené took off after it with a shotgun, which I thought a rather foolish thing to do, but he didn't find the leopard, which was just as well as I doubt that there would have been much left of the francolin if he had.

But the most memorable visit I made was to the Church of St

Gabriel, a few miles west of Dirre Dawa, a town on the railway line between Addis and Djibouti, a port on the Red Sea. Every year a great festival to celebrate the saint's day was held there which the emperor attended. It attracted, in particular, barren women who hoped the saint would remedy their failure to conceive. Messai and I drove down to Dirre Dawa some days before the event and managed to find rooms in a hotel near the railway station but, as the town filled up with supplicants, the hotel manager had to turn us away for customers who had made earlier bookings, thus obliging us to drive to Harar to find accommodation.

Harar is a walled city sitting on highlands on the south-eastern side the Rift Valley. For years it had been a Muslim stronghold and for a while was held by the Khedive of Egypt, until conquered by the Emperor Menelik. The approach to the city from Dirre Dawa was unremarkable, with the usual advertising hoardings for fuel and local hotels on the outskirts but passing beyond it on the road to Jijigga and looking back one could see the ancient walled city virtually unchanged from the pen and ink drawing in Richard Burton's book *First Footsteps in East Africa*..

Then the Harar hotels also filled up with pilgrims, so we returned to Dirre Dawa on the eve of the festival. Thinking we had a long night ahead of us and no place to sleep, we met up with some of Messai's colleagues in a local bar and played cards to while away the time until morning. I cannot say I was enthusiastic about a night without sleep, so I was pleased when Messai negotiated with one of the ladies of the twilight to rent her room. I managed a few hours' sleep before the lady returned with a client who presumably was a more lucrative proposition than the rental, so I returned to the bar to find the card players in a very merry mood.

In the early hours of the morning it was decided it was time to move in the direction of the church before the crowds built up. Then one of Messai's friends remembered that it was usual to take a gift so, finding a flock of sheep in one of the streets, we chased them and caught a fine ram as an offering. We bundled it into the back of the Land Rover. At the entrance of the church grounds were three long trestle tables marked in Amharic 'Gold', 'Cash' and 'Others'. We handed over the stolen ram at the appropriate table as our gift to the monastery.

It was a cold and grey morning; it had been raining all night and the ground was muddy and slippery. The blind, the halt and the maimed were there, shivering in their rags. Close under the church were numerous little stalls, separated by hessian sacking, selling coffee and cakes and relics of the saint. Admission to the church was restricted and, as we were all single at that time, we would very likely been refused entry because of our sinfulness which was taken for granted if one was a bachelor (stealing a ram might be considered a sin but it wasn't the sin the priesthood had in mind). After two hours or so the emperor arrived and after that the crowd pressed so hard we thought it better to retire. I imagine the great mediaeval pilgrimages to Jerusalem, Rome, Santiago de Compostela, Canterbury and elsewhere were similar.

The British Embassy in Addis Ababa was a welcoming place, unlike most British legations in other capitals where I have worked. When not in the south of the country I was a fairly frequent guest. Sir Thomas Bromley, the ambassador, was a genial host and not always the most discreet, especially after the last official guest had left. He admitted to me on one occasion that he made sure I was on the guest list frequently as he found me a more useful source of information about events in southern Ethiopia than his own staff, whose information came from the cocktail circuit of the capital. On another occasion he told me he was expecting Harold Wilson, the then Prime Minister, to visit the following week, to which he added the words 'worse luck'. In this he might have been speaking for his own chief, the Foreign Secretary, George Brown, who was well known to be no admirer of Wilson. In fact at that time a note was in circulation, purportedly signed by George Brown, asking for donations for a statue of Harold Wilson to be erected in Parliament Square in London. According to the note the organizing committee had thought long and hard about where to place it but had eventually decided to erect it between the statue of George Washington, who never told a lie, and Lloyd George, who never told the truth, because Harold Wilson could never tell the difference.

On the diplomatic front both Sir Thomas and the American ambassador were trying to persuade the emperor to name his successor, for the imperial crown had never passed peacefully from father to son and in the interregnum, while various candidates fought over the succession, the country had always fallen into years of chaos. The Crown Prince, Asfa Wossen, was a sick man, having suffered a stroke earlier in his life, and was not trusted by his father after he had taken the rebels' side, probably under duress, in the December Revolution of 1960. Although Sir Thomas never told me who the American ambassador's favourite candidate was, his own favourite was Lij Iksander Desta, the Commander of the Imperial Navy and the grandson of the emperor, being the son of his eldest daughter, Tessagne Worq, and Ras Desta Damtew.[39] Ras Desta had been

---

[39] Lij – literally 'boy' was a courtesy title for the sons of noble families. Ras was roughly equivalent to a Marshal-Duke

executed after falling into the hands of the Italians during their invasion and subsequently, while they were in exile in Britain, his widow formed a liaison with the emperor's driver. I had met Commander Iksander very informally some time previously. We were in our bathing costumes at the time having a swim in the pool of the Ghion Palace Hotel in Addis. I found him an easy man to talk to, made easier because he had been educated in England - Stowe and the Britannia Royal Naval College at Dartmouth to be precise. It was only after he had picked up his towel and disappeared through a small gate into the grounds of the Ghion Palace itself that an air force officer told me of his identity. It is a debatable point whether the 1974 revolution could have been averted if the emperor had named a successor. Sadly Iksander himself was the first member of the royal family to be killed by the Marxist revolutionaries.

I even had a very brief conversation with the emperor himself. He had a small palace overlooking the Debre Zeit crater lake, Lake Hora, where he spent many weekends and a farm close by and it was not unusual for him to walk down to the farm, well escorted by aides de camp and his pet Chihuahua which went everywhere with him. One Sunday evening, my watchman had left the garden gate slightly ajar, allowing Rufus to escape. Sensing another dog in his patch, he wanted it off and by the time I got into the road the Chihuahua was firmly in his jaw. I managed to free the little dog and get Rufus in hand. My schoolboy French and knowledge of Mérimée's story of Carmen had not prepared me for conversations with royalty, least of all under such circumstances, but I managed to blurt out 'Votre majesté, je vous prie de m'excuser.' 'Ce n'est rien' was his brief but benign reply. And that was it. I still think Rufus would have been shot by one of the aides if I hadn't intervened so quickly.

Three months went by and it was time to write another quarterly report; three months in which no action whatsoever had been taken to bring vaccine usage up to standard, so I repeated my criticisms and added that unless action was taken I would not feel able to continue to work in Ethiopia. Another three months went by and still no action was taken, at which point I made clear to the project manager that I would not extend my contract any further. And so I prepared to leave.

One of the obligations under my contract was to write a final report, without which I would be denied my final emoluments. A few weeks before my departure Hailé Jesus, one of the students at the school, dropped by my house to ask a favour. I had strong opinions about the imperial court, though I prudently avoided making them known to the students, but one day Hailé Jesus had told me he thought the emperor's claim to the Solomonic line was a myth, so I felt more at ease in talking to him about the regime. Expecting that what he wanted was a loan, I was surprised when he said the favour he wanted was that I write the truth in my final report. I did not intend to give up a lucrative position, and at that time United Nations' salaries were much greater than those of other agencies, without making it very clear why, and Hailé Jesus's request just reinforced my intention.

After enumerating the numbers of cattle vaccinated and the areas covered, I made clear in my final report, as if I had not already done so in my previous quarterly reports, about my serious doubts about the vaccines' efficiency and the project's very limited success in training field staff. I concluded that based on my experiences in Sidamo province I had full confidence in the ability of the field staff to execute a vaccination campaign, but I did not have similar confidence in the ability of the men at headquarters to manage a national vaccination campaign.

Rome came down on me like a ton of bricks. Ten days before my departure I received a telex ordering me to destroy all copies of my report, including my own. Assiduously I went around collecting the copies I had distributed and destroyed them, though I took care to keep my own copy because I could be denied my final emoluments if I did not submit a final report and there was nothing in the contract to say that the final report had to be written in a way acceptable to the men in Rome or the Ethiopian authorities.

Before returning to Rome on my departure I took a few weeks' leave in East Africa, mainly to find a temporary home for Rufus while I looked for another job and also to take a brief holiday at Malindi on the Kenya coast, a resort I had come to like over the previous five years. To my great good fortune, though not to the owners', the hotel caught fire and several rooms were totally destroyed. So as to assist the hotel manager I offered to give up my own room, which was undamaged, and took the opportunity to fly up to Lamu, an old Arab-Swahili island town of which I had heard some good reports, a hundred miles to the north. I stayed at the Peponi Hotel, a modest-sized place with impeccable service run by a Danish couple a mile or so beyond the town facing an open beach. I was totally entranced by Lamu, the people, the islands and waterways around it, and vowed to return as soon as I could. In fact I didn't just return once; five years later I bought a derelict 18th century Swahili stone house in the town in which I now live.

In Rome I first went to see the head of the animal health section, a man called Bill Ross Cockrill, whom I had first met and invited to give a lecture to the veterinary society in Cambridge, and was somewhat surprised when he asked if I wanted another job with FAO, for I was sure I had burned my boats with the organization. With no other job yet in sight I said yes, whereupon he suggested I go and see another veterinarian in the section. Reg Griffiths was not a man I knew, although I was aware of his reputation, so it was with some trepidation I found my way to his office and knocked on the door.

Immediately I was summoned in. He looked at me querulously, so I told him my name was Minor.

'Ah, yes; Roland Minor from Ethiopia.'

I was a little surprised that he should know who I was, for he would have had no forewarning that I would call on him, so I asked him how he knew.

'I've been reading your final report,' he explained.

'Well, you shouldn't have' I responded, 'all copies of my report should have been destroyed.'

'I know' he said, 'but it's only those kinds of reports which are worth reading.'

It is a sad reflection on the workings of the international organizations that their staff have to be constrained from reporting honestly lest the host countries should be offended by the comments. Meanwhile the precious livestock of the Borana and Somali people continued to get injected with vaccines of very doubtful quality so as to save giving embarrassment to incompetent officials. One asks how services to people can be improved if criticism is inhibited for, certainly, the Ethiopian press was far too censored to draw attention to any government deficiencies.

CHAPTER 8

Private practice in Mombasa

Back in England I pursued the few jobs advertised overseas for veterinary surgeons, as I had limited confidence that a suitable post would be found for me within FAO. The post that attracted me most was advertised by the Crown Agents in the Veterinary Record, the most important of the veterinary journals in Britain, to be head of a laboratory in Mzuzu on Lake Malawi to study tick-borne diseases. I had not lost the interest in ticks I had developed in Entebbe and, in fact, I had continued to make tick collections in Ethiopia. Accordingly I applied for the post and was interviewed by Sir Glyn Jones - the last Governor of Nyasaland and first Governor-General of Malawi when that country gained its independence. The interview went well, and before it ended Jones confided in me that he would recommend me for the post.

There was, however, one little fly in the ointment. In 1966 when I had driven down to Fort Johnson at the southern end of the lake to visit my younger brother Basil, who was working there at the time I had spent a night in Mzuzu. I remembered very clearly that there was no electricity in the small town. The activities of a laboratory would be very constrained without power, so I wrote to find out whether a power supply had been extended to the town. It had not, nor was there even a laboratory there. It was rather ominous.

But life goes on and while trying to sort the matter out I learned to fly, at Kidlington, just north of Oxford. Having got my private pilot's licence early in 1971, time lay heavy. Winter is not the most pleasant season to be in Britain, so it seemed an opportune time to return to Lamu and spend some time sailing about the islands. This I did by chartering a small local fishing boat about 25 feet long with a lateen sail - what is called a *mashua* in Swahili - and with a *nahoda* (captain) and two crewmen we spent some weeks sailing among the half dozen islands of the Lamu archipelago. None of the islands are very big, the largest being about eight miles long. Mangrove forests surround them, interspersed with pristine sandy beaches and coral reefs which provided good goggling and an abundance of crayfish.[40] When we weren't sailing or fishing, I spent many fascinating hours clambering about the stone ruins of the palaces and mosques that mark the ancient towns on the islands.

All good things must come to an end eventually, and so I made my way back to Nairobi where good friends had told me I could always find a bed. While there I had a chance to meet with Robert Mares, the director of veterinary services in Malawi. He confirmed that there was no laboratory in Mzuzu nor any intention to build one and that I would be posted there as a district veterinary officer. He justified this by saying that this was necessary as a contingency measure, but it seemed to me to be thoroughly dishonest to advertise a laboratory post when there was no intention of building one. I had been a DVO before in Uganda and felt that to take such a post again would not help in my career, least of all at a time when posts throughout former colonies were being 'Africanized' so there would be virtually no chance of promotion. Feeling very let down,

[40] The Lamu archipelago was the cradle of the Swahili culture and language and gave rise to a number of city states — each with their own ruler or sultan — on the islands were they were well protected from marauding tribesmen on the mainland. These ancient cities declined sharply after the Portuguese intervened in their maritime trading activities in the 16th century though there was a brief renaissance in the 18th century after Omani, British and Dutch fleets challenged the Portuguese dominance of the Indian Ocean.

I sought legal advice. I was told that I could sue the Crown Agents for their misleading advertisement, but this seemed to me a rather imprudent course of action, for the Crown Agents were one of the main sources of overseas employment and I did not wish to get into their bad books as it seemed I had with FAO.

But there were other opportunities. On my way to Lamu I had spent some time in Mombasa and Malindi, where I had been told by several European residents that there was a need for a private veterinary surgeon in the area to carry out clinical work. I had had very limited experience of clinical work in the previous six years, while carrying out large-scale disease control programmes, and I was very conscious of this deficiency. However, I had come to like the coast region of Kenya. For well over two thousand years men from many points of the compass had come to trade for ivory, slaves, gum copal and timber. The Phoenicians were perhaps the first but they were followed by traders from Arabia, the Yemen, Oman, India and even China. These were followed by the Portuguese, British and many others, and over the years an open-minded amalgam of people had settled at the coast and were living, in most cases harmoniously, with each other and not in polarized ghettos as in Nairobi.

So I set about opening a veterinary clinic in Mombasa. The city of Mombasa is on an island, separated from the mainland by two deep inlets which join on the western side of the island. The old dhow harbour lies in the northern inlet, overlooked by Fort Jesus - a great stone citadel built by the Portuguese in the late 16th century. The larger Kilindini harbour, created by the British in the 1890s when they set about building the railway to the interior, is in the southern inlet and is now Kenya's main port. If it were not for the humidity, the climate might almost be described as benign, with the main rains falling from April to June and the shorter 'grass rains' towards the end of the year but, as in most parts of Africa, it isn't always so. The commercial centre is somewhat dowdy but there are many interesting mosques and domestic buildings in the vicinity of the old dhow harbour, the area known as the Old Town.

Fortunately the local branch of the Kenya Society for the Prevention of Cruelty to Animals had some premises on a headland overlooking Kilindini harbour which they were prepared to rent so I set about engaging a carpenter to make the necessary furniture. Meanwhile I got the necessary permits to work in Kenya and registered with the Kenya Veterinary Board as was legally necessary and set about purchasing the diagnostic and surgical equipment I thought would be needed.

I also looked around for a place to live and found a small cottage on the island close to the Likoni ferry. I then set about recovering Rufus, whom I had boarded in Uganda after my departure from Ethiopia.[41] The cottage was really the guest cottage of a larger house owned by an elderly Scottish couple, Mr and Mrs Nealon. At a time when I did not know many people in Mombasa they were very kind to me and often suggested I drop in for a wee dram. In return I would fix a leaking cistern or replace a burnt-out bulb for them. Then one Saturday morning disaster struck. I had been out doing the shopping and got back to the cottage when Mrs Nealon called out that she was in terrible trouble. I supposed the cistern was overflowing again and said I would be over as soon as I had put the groceries away.

---

[41] He later came in very useful as he became an (unwilling) blood donor whenever I needed blood for transfusion for another dog.

'No, come right away,' she shouted.

So I dropped what I was doing and followed her. She led me into a bedroom and there lying on the bed was her husband. I realized immediately that he was dead. I pretended to feel for a pulse and search for some reflex action, all the time wondering how I was to break the news to her. But I couldn't put the bad news off indefinitely and after a minute or so I turned to her, took her hands and told her that her husband was dead.

'Aye,' she said, 'Dr Sandifer said the same thing also.' It was as if she needed a second opinion to convince her of the awful truth.

Later her son came out from Britain to pack up the house and take his mother back to Britain. Seeing him one day in the garden I went over to offer my condolences, but they were misplaced. He told me he felt no regret over his father's death; he had been sent back to Britain for schooling when he was seven and had next seen his parents when he was twenty. Any affection he had was for the aunt who had brought him up in Britain.

It was not the first time I had had to perform the unpleasant duty of breaking such sad news. The first time had been when, as a young veterinary student, out hunting with the Brighton and Storrington Foot Beagles at Findon near Worthing. As there had been no doctor out that day the field considered I was the next best thing. I found the elderly man down on the turf with a lady bending over him attending to him. There was no pulse and no reflex activity; I presumed the lady was his wife and for a very long minute I wondered how to tell her. When I did, she asked me if I knew his name. Hunting was called off for the day and a gate was taken off its hinges to carry the body down to a main road about two miles away. Then we had to carry the gate back up the downs and re-hang it. I was feeling quite depressed about the whole episode but not so the other gate bearers, who were all in quite a jolly mood. Curious why they should be so, I asked one of the other followers to be told that the old boy had felt fit enough to go out hunting and an hour or so later he was dead and there were few better ways to go than that. As I get older I can only hope I may be so lucky.

Since then I have had to pronounce a person dead a few times; breaking the news is difficult but one that cannot be avoided. Disbelief is a common reaction.

It took several months to complete all the formalities to open a clinic in Mombasa, delayed by an intervention by the director of veterinary services, who alleged that I had been dismissed by FAO, an allegation that was absolutely untrue. It was only the involvement of the then Attorney General, Charles Njonjo, that smoothed the way. It also took time to get all the equipment and recruit the necessary staff. In that I was extraordinarily lucky, for I offered the post of assistant, what some might call a dresser, to a young man in his mid-twenties with an engaging manner and scrupulously honest, as I found over the years, from the Lamu islands whom I had first employed as a house painter. No man could have been as diligent as Kadhi Athman; nothing daunted him, neither rabid dogs nor frenzied cats, though he did draw the line at handling pigs for he was, and still is, a conventional Muslim. This, however, was not a serious drawback for, if I remember rightly, I only ever attended one pig in my time in Mombasa and that was a wart-hog piglet. When I first knew him he knew no English, but over time he picked up a smattering, not all of it in use in polite society. This caused a little embarrassment on an occasion when I was busy operating and he took a phone call from one of my more

174

difficult and demanding clients. 'F*** off' is not an expression I would use in conversation with a client, however much I might have been tempted to do so.

Eventually, in November 1971, I opened my premises. At first the workload wasn't heavy as it took time for word to get about that there was now a veterinary clinic in Mombasa and exactly where it was. Initially, most of the work involved family pets and it took longer to get the large animal side of the practice going. This I regretted as it was the area of work which most interested me.

What I had not been prepared for was the large amount of poultry work that came my way, for there were several large scale commercial producers around Mombasa. Although I did not have the sophisticated equipment of the government's diagnostic laboratories at Kabete on the outskirts of Nairobi, I did have the advantage of being able in most cases to make a diagnosis based on post-mortem findings within a few hours of a problem being noticed so that producers could institute preventive measures immediately and not wait two or three days to get an answer from Kabete, something very important where many thousands of birds are kept in close confinement.

Most of the small animal work was routine - promoting regular annual vaccination schedules and neutering two or three cats and dogs every day. However, I met with two medical conditions that I had not seen before. The first was colloquially called Nairobi bleeding disease, though it should more properly be called canine ehrlichiosis. It is yet another tick-borne disease. Dogs were usually presented with blood streaming from their nostrils and with their forelegs covered in dried blood, which can be very distressing for both the dog and its owners. Only much later did I come to think that the disease might be the cause of another common condition of dogs in which an ear flap fills with blood, a condition known as aural haematoma. Usually this is associated with an injury (a similar injury, a 'cauliflower ear' is commonly seen in men who play in the second row of a rugby scrum). In dogs the haematoma must be drained surgically otherwise the dog continues to shake its head as a reaction to the nuisance and thereby aggravates the condition. Perhaps I should have treated all the dogs with aural haematoma against ehrlichiosis, though most treatments only provide a temporary cure and not a permanent one.

The other disease of dogs which I identified at the coast was heartworm, more properly called canine filariosis.[42] The adult worms live, as their name implies, in the heart. There may be dozens of them, the size of thick spaghetti, filling both chambers on the right side of the heart, the side which pumps blood to the lungs, preventing the proper closure of the heart valves so that the heart becomes incompetent. Treatment is by serial injection of a fairly toxic arsenic compound which kills the worms; these then descend into the lungs, setting up a local inflammation and pneumonia. Fortunately the second condition is usually less serious than the first and resolves itself over a few weeks. The adult worms reproduce sexually and produce myriads of microfilariae which can be seen on a wet blood slide under a microscope swimming very vigorously. These, in turn, are ingested by an Aedes mosquito and transmitted to other susceptible dogs.[43]

One of the features of the disease which I noted was that it occurred in dogs whose homes were on mangrove-lined creeks along

[42] Human filariosis also occurs on the Kenyan coast but is caused by a different species of filarial worm, Wuchereria bancrofti, which infects the inguinal lymph nodes of the crotch thereby blocking lymph flow. It is characterized by elephantiasis of the lower legs and, in males, large swellings of the scrotum.

[43] Aedes mosquitoes also transmit the viral disease – dengue fever of humans, vulgarly known as break-bones fever though, as I have experienced, it is the joints that swell and are painful. Aedes mosquitoes are smaller than the malaria-transmitting anopheles mosquito and some of the wider mesh mosquito nets do not prevent them from getting access to a sleeping person. In WW II the allies determined to take Madagascar from the Vichy French forces holding the island. For days the East African expeditionary force dithered in their ships just over the horizon waiting for tides, moon and other factors to be favourable. They need not have worried for French military issue mosquito nets were of the wide-mesh variety and half the garrison was bed-ridden with dengue and gave up with hardly a fight.

the Kenya coast but not those on open beach fronts. One of my clients, an interested entomologist, investigated this trend and found that the mosquitoes breed in crab holes in the mangrove swamps.

Snakes were a source of injury to dogs, though I never saw or heard of a cat being injured by a snake. The commonest injury was that caused by spitting cobras, which project their venom at the eyes of their attackers. The result is an intensely painful swelling of the front of the eyes, the corneas, and the tissues surrounding the eyes. Because of the swelling of the eyelids and the associated pain it is extremely difficult to examine the cornea for any damage, though treatment is dependent on knowing whether the corneas are damaged or not. Dogs kept in houses with swimming pools were the most frequent victims because, during the dry seasons at least, snakes were drawn to swimming pools for water.[44]

At first I avoided doing any orthopaedic surgery, for I had been taught at veterinary school that it should only be carried out in purpose-built theatres with a high levels of hygiene and my premises certainly did not come up to that mark. But after I had had to put down some dogs with broken limbs following motor accidents I decided to give it a try, encouraged by an orthopaedic surgeon in Mombasa, Roland McVicker, who even offered to do the first operation if I did the anaesthesia.

The first case to offer itself was that of a small Yorkshire terrier with both bones of the foreleg - the radius and ulna - broken right across. In a Yorkie these bones are not even as big as the thigh bones of a chicken, so we had to use pins as fine as bicycle spokes to join the ends of the bones so that they would knit together and heal.

Problems soon arose. I noticed that McVicker was trying to unite the near end, what is called the proximal end, of the ulna to

---

[44] Similarly snakes are drawn to the external effluents from air conditioners and to bathrooms. I once found an 8 foot long forest cobra in a lavatory bowl in Entebbe. It took several hours to remove, retreating round the S bend every time we tried to snare it. It was eventually released in a nearby forest.

the distal end of the radius. I called his attention to this, warning him that the radius is on the medial side, the inner side, of the leg. But he ignored my warning and, as he was both older than me by a wide margin and a well-established orthopaedic surgeon, I desisted from further criticism. The end result was a dog with its paw turned 180° from its normal position, so the surgery had to be repeated. At the time I really could not understand how an experienced surgeon could be so obtuse. Only later did I realize why we had been at loggerheads. In human anatomy dissections the cadaver is laid on a table with the palms facing upwards with the thumbs on the outside. In this position the radius lies on the outside - the lateral side. But in animals the digit that corresponds with the thumb is on the inner side of the foot - the medial side, so the radius itself is medial to the ulna.

After that I did numerous orthopaedic operations with considerable success. The most interesting case was that of a young cheetah with a fractured humerus, which in humans is the bone in the upper arm. I had first seen the animal when it was only two to three weeks old, one of three tiny cubs which were found near the body of an adult female cheetah which had been snared by poachers just outside the Tsavo National Park. They had cut off all her claws to make trinkets for tourists. Two of the cubs died within a short time, but one survived. From the outset I had warned that red meat should not be fed to kittens. In cats, and particularly cats in zoos, an excess of red meat, heart or liver inhibits the absorption of calcium from the gut, a condition known as secondary nutritional hyperparathyroidism. I had first seen the condition in two serval cats, named Mandy and Christine after two famous London courtesans of the time, in the Entebbe zoo, and between them, if I remember rightly, I counted fourteen fractures. Unfortunately my advice was not followed and the surviving young cheetah was pampered with best steak and refused to eat anything else.

The inevitable happened. When it was about six months old it was brought to me acutely lame on one foreleg. On X-ray the humerus was found to be fractured. This bone is straight in humans but in most animals is more or less S-shaped so that the conventional straight pin is not suitable for fixing a fracture. A more flexible, springy pin, a Rush pin, was what I had been taught to use in such cases, but I was never satisfied on previous occasions with the degree of stabilization that the pin gave.

Another anxiety I had was that I had no idea how a cheetah would react to the usual anaesthetic drugs. Ideally I wanted to knock the animal out with a single intravenous injection before putting it on an inhalation anaesthetic, which I felt would be much safer. At the front end of an almost full-grown cheetah are some sharp teeth, a wide gape and a flattish face which cannot be muzzled. All presented problems which I would have to overcome. Then the night before I had arranged to do the surgery the owner rang me up to say she had a Swiss orthopaedic surgeon staying with her and he would like to be present during the surgery. I said that wouldn't be a problem, but as soon as I had put the phone down I realized that I had made a serious error, for now there would be a witness to my incompetence. I therefore redoubled my efforts in planning the anaesthesia and surgery for the next day.

In the event all went remarkably well; the sharp teeth were bared only slightly, the anaesthesia was a doddle, and the pin slipped in just as it should and held the two ends of the bone firmly together. Within about twenty minutes I was stitching the shoulder up to favourable expressions from the visitor of 'Sehr gut! Sehr gut!' to which I could only reply 'Danke, danke!' for my German was only just a little more accomplished than his English.

I urged the owner to try and get the cheetah to use the limb as soon as possible and suggested she put it in her swimming pool. The cheetah took to the water like a duck and a week later, when she brought it to the surgery to have the stitches taken out, it was already putting some weight on its leg - a sure sign that the bone was healing. It was then she told me her Swiss friend had told her he had never known that veterinary surgeons used such sophisticated surgical techniques and had been even more surprised to find them in use in Africa. It was all very flattering and I quickly resolved to set my fee more in line with what a human surgeon would have charged, which I knew the lady in question could well afford.

The horsey side of the business was very limited as there were probably not more than thirty horses in the vicinity of Mombasa, most of them owned by Europeans and one or two by Arabs. Lameness was the commonest affliction, usually as a result of galloping on the beach and bruising the sole on a piece of coral or a rock hidden in the sand. Treatment is by cutting away the sole of the hoof until blood is drawn, which then relieves the pressure caused by the bruise within the confined space of the hoof, minimizing the pain and so curing the lameness. Of course the horse must be rested for a few weeks until the sole regrows.

Of the infectious diseases of horses, I only saw four. African horse sickness is a midge-borne disease, so it was my practice to urge vaccination just before the rainy season began in April when midges are at their most active - not that vaccination always protects. There are nine major viral types, so vaccine manufacturers include within their vaccines those types which most infect horses in their region. At that time South African vaccines were unavailable because of sanctions against that country, so I had to make do with vaccines from Iran. Fortunately I only saw two cases despite the fact that both had recently been vaccinated. The first horse died within hours of being seen to be unwell and was dead on my arrival. Post-mortem findings strongly indicated that it was horse sickness, and when another horse in the same stables took ill the next day I was convinced. This one we managed to save by careful nursing and daily feeding by stomach tube with blended carrots and other vegetable matter, glucose and salt. African horse sickness had not been identified previously at the coast and it was assumed that the infection had come from wildlife in the Tsavo National Park some sixty miles to the west. This I found hard to believe at the time as the prevailing winds usually blow westwards off the sea and I doubted that midges could fly sixty miles against the wind, but recent reports in England of midges crossing the North Sea from the continent and infecting livestock in East Anglia with bluetongue virus has modified my belief.

Much the most common equine disease was tryps. Large areas of Kenya's south coast, much of which is wooded, were, and still are, infested with tsetse flies and I had warned one budding entrepreneur that I thought it unwise to introduce horses to the south coast. However he knew better and went ahead, and within weeks I was a regular visitor to his premises to treat one or other of the four horses he had brought in. Several months later one of my favourite clients, a butcher called 'Ginger' Bell, proudly told me he had recently bought four new horses. As soon as I saw them I knew whose horses they had been.

'How much did you pay for them?' I asked. He mentioned a price of about £100 for the lot.

'You was robbed,' I said.

'Ah, but the tack was thrown in for free' said Ginger, thus confirming his reputation for being an astute businessman.

Ginger's farm was on a treeless hillside a few miles out of Mombasa and free from tsetse fly so I proposed that we set about clearing any remaining infection in the horses. I had already determined that they were infected with *Trypansoma brucei* and the most suitable drug then available for the treatment of horses was berenil, which is injected intramuscularly. *T. brucei* however is resistant to most drugs and double dosing is advised. But berenil has a downside; it is a poison causing liver damage and repeated doses can be fatal. Try as I might I could not clear the infection from one horse so, in desperation, I administered a double dose intravenously in the hope of getting the highest blood concentration possible. The horse collapsed as if it had been pole-axed.

'You've killed it,' said Ginger.

I looked at the prostrate form and saw the horse was still breathing. 'Not yet,' I replied.

We propped it up with bales of straw as best we could and 24 hours later it regained its feet. Some days afterwards I took a blood sample in the hope of confirming that the parasites had been eliminated, but it was not to be. It was a no-win situation - the only way it seemed likely we could kill all the parasites was to kill the horse that hosted them.

Tetanus I saw only once, and that was in another of Ginger's horses. I tried to save it with a massive dose of penicillin and anti-tetanus serum, but without success. After twenty-four hours I suggested it be put down to save any more needless suffering.

Once a year Mombasa hosted an agricultural show, and when the showground was not in use several people grazed their horses there. One year, a month or so after the show, three horses there developed biliary fever, another of the many protozoal disease transmitted by ticks. Since I had not seen it at the coast before, I presumed that infected ticks had been brought in on horses from up-country which had been entered for equestrian events at the show such as polo. Similarly, I only ever saw tick fever of dogs in pets brought to the coast by holiday makers from up-country. I had seen cases of tick fever in Uganda on an almost daily basis, so I had no difficulty in its diagnosis. Biliary fever of horses and tick fever of dogs are both caused by a genus of protozoa called Babesia which are transmitted by ticks and parasitize red blood cells, causing profound anaemia. No one has yet established why these blood parasites are not commonly found at the coast, even when their tick vectors are present. The most likely theory is that Babesia do not survive in hot ambient temperatures. Some simple experiments with ticks in an incubator should prove the truth or not of the supposition.

One of the more unusual investigations I was involved in was to determine the reason for the deaths of guinea pigs being used to feed mosquitoes by an American team based near Mombasa involved with the study of mosquito behaviour - MBU.[45] The guinea pigs were being anaesthetized with pentobarbitone to make them passive while the mosquitoes fed on them. The reason for

[45] MBU is the Swahili word for a mosquito. The acronym stood for the Mosquito Biology Unit.

their deaths was soon evident: the dose of pentobarbitone administered was sufficient for a five kilogram animal whereas few guinea pigs ever attain half a kilogram.

One of the team's conclusions at the time was that mosquitoes were attracted to areas of high carbon dioxide concentrations. Carbon dioxide is heavier than air so it builds up close to the ground, which is one reason why mosquitoes so often lurk about one's ankles.

My clients came from across the whole spectrum of peoples at the coast. Comparisons are often invidious because one is not comparing like with like. Different people of different cultures have different values. In a sense the Europeans at the Kenya coast were the most homogeneous group; most were well educated and spoke English as a first or second language and shared common values based on Judeo-Christian codes. The African population, which was, of course, far the largest, was the least homogeneous, speaking a variety of languages, of different religious beliefs, different educational standards and different economic levels. The Asian population, and by that I mean people originating from the Indian sub-continent, lay somewhere in between. Yet there were some sub-groups who behaved very similarly. Politicians and *soi-disant* aristocrats, particularly of the eastern European variety, were often reluctant to pay their bills. But there were exceptions: one cabinet minister was usually on the phone within hours after I visited his ranch asking how much he owed, and within the day his cheque was in the post. He might not have known this but it always worked out to his advantage because I would have to calculate a figure quickly from the top of my head while speaking to him and he would get the benefit of any doubt. The advantage to me was that cash in the hand, like a bird in the hand, was preferable to the expectation of it. Self-styled European aristocrats were all so similar in character that after a few bad experiences I made it a rule to add 25% to their accounts to make up for the tedium of billing them month after month or having to seek court orders against them.

It was inevitable that I would meet socially with the Europeans more frequently than with the other communities, and it was seldom I could go to a party without being asked for some professional advice. I didn't mind if it was a regular client for the sake of the goodwill it engendered, but I did not feel the same way about those who plainly were trying to get something for nothing, particularly as a vet, in common with other professionals, can be held accountable for any advice he gives even if he receives no remuneration.

I once asked a medical colleague how he dealt with the nuisance and he replied that he would say in a loud voice 'Drop your trousers and I'll have a look at it' but this clearly wouldn't solve a veterinary problem. There were times I would be deliberately facetious and suggest that an infusion be made of the eye of newt and toe of frog and two teaspoons given at three hour intervals to the ailing pet. But such evasions did not discourage the more determined.

One persistent pest who regularly harassed me in the yacht club had a husband who was a bank manager. Tired of her importuning, I suggested one day that she tell her husband to bring a stack of money every time he came to the yacht club.

'Why?' she asked.

'So I can cash my cheques here' I replied.

'But the bank is open Mondays to Saturdays for business.'

'I know,' I said 'and so am I.'

There were two elements which were exclusive to the Asian community. One was what I came to call 'Asian dog disease' which affected dogs belonging to vegetarian Hindus and Sikhs. This was as a result of a specific Vitamin B_6 deficiency.[46] A single injection of vitamins and advice on feeding was usually enough to put the matter right, but the more devout refused to feed their dogs meat. Let me add that it would be wrong to say that the disease is exclusive to Asian-owned dogs, for it was taught to me in England as 'Scottish sheepdog disease' and affected sheepdogs fed exclusively on porridge.

The other element in dealing with Asians was that the veterinary profession was seen by some of them as a sort of artisanal occupation, not a learned profession, so they would send their drivers with their sick pets. Of course, the driver could provide no history, so an inordinate amount of time was spent trying to determine what the problem was. One was also frustrated by the fact that it would be a trespass to take any action without the owner's consent and aggravated by a doubt whether the unseen owner would pay up.

One case still comes to mind, that of a valuable hound belonging to a wealthy industrialist. The dog had a blood disorder which seemed to me to be a case of a hormonal imbalance affecting kidney function, though my text books made no mention of any similar condition. I wanted to refer the dog to a specialist endocrinologist in the university faculty in Nairobi but obviously could not discuss such an option with the driver. Time after time I

[46] Vitamin B6 deficiency in humans causes pellagra, an abnormal thickening of the skin, and is often associated with a diet heavily dependent on maize flour.

would phone the owner to be told by his personal assistant that he was busy or in a meeting. I suggested he called me back, but he never did. This went on not just for weeks but for months. Driven to desperation, I sent him an invoice for an outrageous amount, thinking that it would prompt him to pick up the telephone, but it did not. He just reached out for his cheque book.

Another month went by with no progress and eventually I wrote the man a letter saying that in view of his lack of care for his animal I did not wish to continue my professional relationship with him. It is the only time I have had to write such a letter. A week went by and then he phoned me at home about 10 o'clock one night saying that another of his dogs had just been run over. I reminded him that I was no longer in a professional relationship.

'But the dog is suffering' he whined.

'I expect it is' I replied 'but you allowed another dog to suffer for months and didn't feel any concern for its suffering.'

He continued to plead, but I was adamant and eventually suggested he get in his car and drive the 300 miles to Nairobi if he needed veterinary attention, for that was where the nearest alternative was.

The cattle side of the business, the side that should have been my principal interest, was not a particularly lucrative one. A number of small dairy farms stretched along the lush coastal strip, but they were owned and run, for the most part, by experienced European settlers who had sold their farms up-country at independence and retired to the coast. Away from the coast, in the hot dry hinterland, there were a number of ranches, but as these were a great distance from Mombasa, some a hundred miles and more, the value of any individual animal did not justify the cost of treating it. Where a rancher suspected tryps or other disease he treated the animal with an appropriate drug himself, and I would only be called in where there was a problem affecting the herd or part of it.

The most interesting of the ranches was the Galana ranch about 80 miles west of the coastal resort of Malindi. It was huge - one and a half million acres in all. The Galana river, along its southern boundary, was a perennial source of water, but the wooded riverine environment provided a favourable habitat for tsetse flies and was therefore unsuitable for cattle, so pipelines had been laid leading many miles away from the river to provide water for the stock. Even so the piping was only sufficient to provide water to about a third of the area while the rest - a million acres - was a private hunting ground for the lessees of the ranch.

In addition to the 20,000 or so head of cattle it held, Galana ranch was noted for its domesticated herds of oryx and eland, which were run in much the same way as the cattle were, but being native to the area were naturally resistant to many local diseases. This was just as well and I was never obliged to treat them, as previous experience with handling eland had taught me that they had very sharp horns - and oryx horns are even straighter and sharper.

Distances were so great that I was usually flown from one part of the ranch to another on my visits there. Of course, the wildlife had also learned of the availability of water along the pipelines, so it was common for elephants to come and water at the troughs while I was examining cattle within fifty yards or so of them. At first I was apprehensive, but the ranch manager urged me not to be, though I noticed the cattle gave the elephants a wide berth, which suggested that they were not totally benign.

In the dry season the scrubland away from the river was parched, so much so it looked as if a blow torch had been used to ensure that not a leaf remained, but despite this the cattle, which were all local short-horned humped zebu, remained in good condition throughout, unlike the same cattle belonging to the local pastoralists. I ascribed this to two factors: by bringing water to the animals they used no energy in a daily trek to a water source, as the pastoralists' cattle were obliged to do, and this allowed them the time throughout the day to search for any available browse or grazing in the vicinity.

There were also a number of smaller ranches on the western side of the Mombasa–Nairobi road, on the opposite side of which is part of the huge Tsavo National Park, so elephants were also encountered frequently on the ranches where they went for the water troughs as they did on the Galana ranch. One of the ranchers, Ray Mayers, with his wife, Helen, became two of my closest friends, and I spent many happy weekends on their Rukinga ranch near Voi.

Ray had a fund of stories. One of his earliest memories was of him and his brother being told stories by an elderly gentleman who, he later discovered, was Rudyard Kipling. Later he had gone up to Cambridge to read medicine but went down after only one year because he preferred Helen's company and she was in Kenya. He put his hand to gold mining without any great success and when war came he joined the forces which ousted the Italians from their colony of Somalia. He remained there after the war was over and became the district commissioner for Mogadishu.

Ray was noticeably bandy-legged, a fact which he ascribed to spending eight years on a camel. While in Mogadishu he had had to hand over El Karre to the Ethiopians because Dougie Collins refused to do so, considering it a betrayal of the Somalis, whom he liked. Nevertheless Ray and Dougie remained good friends. Afterwards Ray became the British consul in Mega, where his function was to ensure that Kenyan Borana enjoyed the same rights as Ethiopian ones.

It was Ray who drew my attention to a disease of the ears of zebu cattle which was causing serious havoc on the neighbouring ranches. I had never heard of it and it certainly did not feature in any of my textbooks. Only later did I discover that the clinical signs had first been described fifteen years earlier by a Tanzanian vet called Dr J M Jibbo, who named the disease bovine parasitic otitis. It is caused by a small nematode worm, *Rhabditis bovis*. Usually rhabditid worms live freely in the soil and are a pest for gardeners, but this species seems to have adapted, probably in very recent times, to living in the ears of cattle. The first sign of infection is a stream of foul-smelling pus running down from the affected ear. Put a drop of the pus in a test tube of water and the water shimmers with the countless worms swimming in it. The infection eats away at the walls of the ear canal, exposing all the cartilages around it, and should it perforate the ear drum and infect the inner ear, the animal loses its sense of balance and has great difficulty standing, consequently dying of starvation in a short time. The animal almost certainly loses its sense of hearing also, but that is not a question one can put to it. Among the cattle on the several ranches along the Mombasa-Nairobi road this disease was probably the most common cause of mortality, so it is surprising the disease features so little in standard text books. Although found originally in Tanganyika, the disease has now been found in the other East African countries, and as far south as Zimbabwe, and now also in Brazil. I also found it when looking for brown ear ticks in southern Sudan, but that is another story.

The year 1975 was a bad one. The long rains that usually fall from April to June were quite inadequate and when the short rains failed in October the ranchers knew they were facing big trouble. Ray acted quickly and sold a third of his herd to butchers before the bottom fell out of the market. Half his remaining herd died over the next few months. The manager of the Galana ranch also anticipated a major problem, and I was flown up to Galana, where I pregnancy-tested 400 cows and heifers over two days. Those that were not in calf were also sent to the butchers.

The Preparatory School, St George's College, Quilmes, Argentina

The author and his twin brother from the collection of Mrs Errol Trzebinski.

A Karamojong Manyatta

The Murchison Falls;
the Nile flows through a 20ft gap

A Pokot elder with wife

Any fool can be uncomfortable on safari

Two orphaned cheetah cubs

Domesticated Eland and Oryx on Galana Ranch

A Fulani boy milking a cow

A rabid dog showing
foreleg lameness

An act of animal altruism? an Eland attempting
to raise an immobilized Eland

The mobile laboratory in Southern Sudan

Juba's central business district

Dinka cattle encampment

Dinka cattle in the Pengko plains

Murle youths restraining a
calf for sampling

Loading bulls near Nanyuki for
carriage to Southern Sudan

A modern Pokot warrior

A harvest of Sorghum and Maize extending over Dodoth in Northern Karamoja

Acropole Hotel, Khartoum

Meuleh camel market near Omdurman

Pyramids at Shendi, Sudan

CHAPTER 9

Rabies on the loose

The drought of 1975 hit hard. Pastoralists such as the Maasai regard their cattle as having far greater intrinsic worth than cash in their hand and were reluctant to part with their animals to any butcher despite the drought. But they did have the freedom to move to where they thought there might still be some grazing available, a freedom denied to commercial ranchers. So over the last few months of 1975 Maasai were moving their herds from their traditional grazing grounds up-country through the tsetse fly infested Tsavo National Park towards the coast. Ominously, there were outbreaks of rabies in their wake, though it was never clear whether it was the Maasai-owned dogs that were infected or the jackals following the dying herds.

Early in 1976 one of my favourite clients, a member of the medical fraternity in Mombasa, rang me one lunchtime to say her puppy had been vomiting all morning. I had other plans for that afternoon but for her I put them aside and examined the dog. Its abdomen was tense and felt lumpy when palpated and the conjunctivae, the soft tissue around the eyeballs, were intensely congested, which I ascribed to loss of fluids because of the persistent vomiting. I suspected there might be some intestinal obstruction and felt that an exploratory laparotomy was called for; a decision with which the client concurred.

Ideally I should have put the puppy on a drip to restore the fluid loss, but there were no electrolyte solutions available in Mombasa at that time. This was a serious deficiency, but I hoped that by keeping the operation time as short as possible and operating under very light anaesthesia I might at least not make the situation any worse. So I opened the abdomen up. Nothing looked out of place and there was certainly no obstruction, the only visible abnormality being the congestion of the gut walls similar to that of the conjunctivae. Within twenty minutes the incision was closed up and the puppy taken off the anaesthetic machine.

It should have been awake within minutes but it wasn't. It wasn't awake four hours later. That night I met the owner at the theatre and had to tell her I was concerned about the dog's failure to wake up. As soon as the play was over I went to see it again. It was still asleep. Next morning it was dead. I had some explaining to do, and asked for permission to carry out a post mortem examination.

What I found surprised me. The stomach contained some pieces of bark, a few stones, a fragment of towelling and other bits of junk. An abnormal appetite is one of the lesser known characteristics of rabies and though I was fairly confident that the result would come back negative, just to cover myself I sent the puppy's head to the Kabete Veterinary Laboratories for examination of the brain for rabies.

Three days later I received in the post a laboratory report saying the result was positive. Copies of the report were also sent by the laboratory to all those who needed to know, including the provincial medical and veterinary officers, provincial and district commissioners and others. I immediately informed the owner and advised her that she and her family should be immunized against rabies and, as I had operated without gloves and my staff had handled the dog without protection, I also rang my own physician, Dr Arthur Sandford, to arrange for me and my staff to be vaccinated. Arthur was quick to point out that he would need to inform the provincial medical officer - this was a legal obligation even though the PMO should have already received a copy of the laboratory report.

A couple of hours later Arthur rang back to say there was no human vaccine in Mombasa, as rabies had never been reported in the Coast Province since the start of the colonial period, but that vaccine would be sent down from Nairobi and would be available the next day.

The vaccine then in use was a dead vaccine produced in duck eggs. It was not particularly efficient in producing an immunity, so fourteen doses had to be administered on a daily basis under the skin of the abdomen, though not into the abdomen as many people imagined.[47] Within a few days there was a reaction to the repeated doses and large and intensely irritating wheals developed at the injection sites. I have quite an expansive abdomen which could accommodate all the weals that developed, but I felt very sorry for the numerous small children whom over the coming months I had

---

[47] A few months later the Kenyan Ministry of Health introduced an inactivated diploid cell vaccine with none of the unpleasant side effects of the duck egg vaccine and much more potent so that only four injections are recommended following a bite from a rabid animal. This vaccine had first been tested on 40 Iranian peasants who had been bitten — some very seriously — by rabid wolves. At the end of one year all the immunized people were still alive except for one 80 year-old farmer who had dropped down dead while ploughing and was thus presumed not to have succumbed to rabies.

to recommend for immunization. In my case even my food began to taste of dusty poultry feathers, but I cannot be sure if this was a real reaction or just a psychological one.

Since this had reportedly been the first dog in recorded history to have rabies in the Coast Province I expected the veterinary officials to be round very soon to determine where the infected dog had acquired the infection - but nothing happened. After a couple of days I phoned a colleague of mine in the laboratory, Glyn Davies, who had been a contemporary at university, and mentioned the apparent apathy.

'It's no big deal,' was his response, 'I have been reporting rabies from the coast for the past six months.'

'So why were the PMO and other relevant officials not made aware of it?' I asked.

'It's my job to do the necessary investigations, but I am not responsible for the distribution of the lab reports' was Glyn's laconic response.

Within a few weeks there was a very sad outcome to this attempt to conceal the disease. A dog had got into a school playground in a slum area of Mombasa and bitten a number of children. They were taken to a nearby clinic, where the bites were dressed and the children treated with antibiotics. It was only later when one of them died of rabies that the reality struck. To make it worse, the names of the other bitten children had not been recorded at the clinic and there was, by that time, a great urgency to give them post-exposure treatment in the hope of averting more deaths.

Over the next half year I was seeing one or two cases of rabies every week. As it was a notifiable disease I was legally required to send the heads of suspected cases to Kabete for examination. The most commonly used diagnostic test at the time was an examination for Negri bodies, small dots within the cytoplasm of infected nerve cells in the brain. I had been taught that it was best to leave a dog to die naturally of the disease over a number of days so as to allow the Negri bodies to develop and thereby increase the confidence one could put in the test. This, sadly, increased the suffering of the affected animals.

It is generally believed that rabid dogs become frenzied and go about biting people and other animals. In fact less than half the dogs I saw showed these signs and when they did it might be for just a few seconds only. The most consistent signs were intensely congested conjunctivae, a paralysis of one or more muscles of the face and head and some degree of incoordination or lameness accompanied by a high fever, often reaching 41°C (106°F) whereas the normal temperature of a dog is about 38.5°C (101.5°F).

The most common form of facial paralysis was an inability to swallow or close the lower jaw, as a result of which saliva drooled from the mouth, signs which were even more obvious if the dog had injured its mouth in an attack on some inanimate object. On other occasions dogs with gummy eyes were brought to me because the owners thought they had conjunctivitis. It didn't take long to realize the eyelids were paralysed and the dog could not keep its eyes clean by repeated blinking. When I found a high temperature as well I knew it was no ordinary conjunctivitis.

Incoordination of movement was commonly seen, but even then the signs could be misleading. One dog was brought to me conspicuously lame in a foreleg and refusing to put the paw to the ground. There was no thorn or injury to the pad and palpation of the various joints elicited no obvious pain, but the eyes were congested and the temperature was high, which were certainly not features of an ordinary lameness.

I had a number of steel cages on the premises in which all suspect cases were confined, for I could not take the risk of letting the dogs go home, where they might subsequently bite a person or another animal. Thus I was able to observe the dogs throughout the period of their illness. Usually I kept them chained so that they could be pulled up close to the side of the cage to be injected with a sedative if they became too frenzied and to prevent them from injuring themselves further. A common sight was to see them biting at their chains or snapping at imaginary flies - an observation many other veterinarians have made.

The outbreak had been going for about two months when I got a telephone call from the local veterinary office telling me that I was not to tell people that their dogs were rabid as it was bad for tourism.

'So what shall I tell them?' I asked.

'Tell them the dog has distemper' was the response.

"They'll think I am out of my mind if I say the dog has distemper but I advise them to get themselves and their family immunized against rabies" I retorted.

The voice on the telephone had no answer to that. Of course I had to tell people when their dogs had rabies - paramount were my obligations to my clients and secondly to the community I lived in, and also on my mind at all times was my legal liability if any of my clients or their families died of rabies.

The phone call caused me great anxiety, for I had seen in

Ethiopia that the easiest way to eradicate cholera had been to deport the foreign doctors who had diagnosed it. Later I met a British doctor who had been deported from Uganda for maintaining that the disease killing people in the south-western part of that country was AIDS. I could not protect myself from arbitrary deportation, but I determined that I would keep full clinical notes on all the cases and the official laboratory reports confirming them so that if I was challenged I could justify my diagnosis.

From then on I began to suspect that I was being victimized for not keeping silent. Quite a number of the heads I sent to Kabete for examination were, on arrival, put into a deep freeze overnight or over a weekend. The ice crystals that then formed within the nerve cells so distorted them that the brains could not be used for diagnostic purposes. On other occasions when I sent two or three heads simultaneously the identification tags were said to have been mislaid, even when I had sent the heads in individual polythene bags with the labels sewn to the heads. That meant that if one head was found to be positive I had to act as if all three were positive and advise all the owners accordingly.

Since rabies had never been a problem in the past, many of my clients had not bothered to get their pets immunized. I did my best to convince them that vaccination was now essential. At the time the vaccine in use was a live vaccine which gave good protection for three years.[48] It was recommended that it be injected into the muscles of the thigh, but one of the veterinarians in the district persisted in injecting the vaccine into the neck. Over a period of months I saw four dogs thus injected, in every case exactly four months previously, which were brought to me with intense signs

[48] The Flury strain Low Egg Passage (LEP) vaccine was in common use

of irritation of the neck and which were subsequently confirmed as rabid. Horses often show signs of intense irritation at the site of a rabid dog bite and it occurred to me that there might be a connection between the site of injection and the establishment of disease. Rabies virus has an affinity for nerve tissue and the neck region is well endowed with both cranial and spinal nerves.[49] And there were other reasons for supposing that the Flury strain LEP vaccine caused rabies in this group of four dogs.[50]

The reaction of the authorities was to prohibit me from using the vaccine even though I was not the one misusing it. No other vet in Kenya, official or private, was banned from administering rabies vaccine, so I was obliged to send Rufus to another private vet in the vicinity to get him re-vaccinated. He never walked properly again and an X-ray of his hip a month later showed severe arthritis of the hip joint which I suspected at the time was caused by injection of the vaccine into the joint. By this time he was 13 years old and he died a few months later. I have had several dogs since, but none have given me as much companionship as he did.

About three months after the outbreak started the Director of Medical Research at the Ministry of Health, Dr Geoffrey Timms, came to see me. He had noted that a large amount of human anti-rabies vaccine was being issued for use in the Coast Province and as nobody had informed him of the outbreak he set out to find what was going on. The authorities at Kabete refused to give him information, saying it was a veterinary problem, not a medical one. He had a similar response from the coast veterinary authorities. So he came to see me.

---

[49] It has been shown that 80% of red foxes injected with Flury strain LEP vaccine in the neck developed rabies whereas only 20% of those injected in the rear leg did so.

[50] Fixed strain rabies virus, such as used in vaccine production, does not produce Negri bodies in the brain. None of the dogs I believed to have acquired rabies from the vaccine showed these bodies but injection of their brain tissue into suckling mice reproduced the disease.

I only knew what was happening to my clients' dogs and I had little idea of what was happening in the villages around Mombasa, although I had heard rumours of seventy people dying of *asumu* in one village in the hinterland.[51] This was very likely an exaggeration, as in the absence of any official information, rumours are frequently magnified. Whatever the number, it was a high price to pay to ensure the tourism industry did not suffer. The only other observation I could make was that it seemed as if the disease was spreading northwards from its original focus at the rate of about 20 miles a month.

The fear of rabies can cause people to behave irrationally, and I learned early on not to tell owners that I suspected rabies until I had a full history unless they started embellishing the history, or worse, concealing vital elements of it.

As if it wasn't enough to have the authorities putting pressure on me, I also had to put up with very unpleasant behaviour from some of my British clients. One English spinster of uncertain age living a solitary life dedicated to ineffectual good works went as far as writing to the provincial commissioner alleging that I was making a clamour about rabies so that I could make a lot of money by vaccinating dogs, although I was only charging the recommended fee. Her accusation I think was one of the reasons I was banned me from using the vaccine.

Then there was a Mr Smith - not, of course, his real name - a middle-aged civil servant sort of man, who rang me late one afternoon when the surgery had closed to say his Alsatian dog had bitten him when he had put down his bowl of food. This sounded ominous, so I suggested I visit his house.

[51] *Asumu* is the Swahili word used for rabies; sumu being the Swahili for poison

'That's not necessary; I'll bring him to the surgery now.'

As soon as he arrived at the surgery in his car he let the dog loose. I was watching from a distance and shouted to him to put a lead on the dog, as I was concerned that some people in the vicinity might be bitten also.

'He'll bite me again if I try.'

'Then try to get him back in the car if you can' I shouted back.

Mr Smith whistled to the dog and, fortunately, it took the cue and jumped back into the car. At least the dog was now confined, but when I went to the car to look at him he lunged at me viciously. Luckily the side window was tough enough to obstruct his attack. I made my diagnosis there and then. The problem now was to get the dog out of the car without getting hurt and the only solution obvious to me was to get a police marksman to shoot the dog, though I warned Mr Smith that it might do some damage to his car.

I went inside the surgery to put a call through to the police, which took a few minutes while I explained the problem. When I came out again I found that Mr Smith had managed to get a lead on the dog and get it out of the car, at the cost of a severely lacerated hand and arm. I surmised that if I approached the dog I might send it off in a frenzy again, so I suggested to Mr Smith that he pull the dog tight up against some nearby railings, which he managed without getting bitten again. I was then able to administer an immobilizing drug which I normally used for darting wild animals, and within seconds the dog was out to the world.

It didn't need me to tell Mr Smith what was the problem with his dog, he knew already. He also admitted that he hadn't thought it necessary to get the dog immunized. My advice to him was to see a doctor immediately to get the lacerations of his arm washed and dressed and to start the course of vaccinations without delay and then to sit down with his wife and try to telephone all the people who might have been in contact with the dog in the previous 48 hours and advise them to get vaccinated also, for dogs can shed rabies virus before showing any clinical signs.

About five days later one of my more thoughtful clients rang to ask what Mr Smith's dog had died of. I had a duty of confidentiality, so I asked if she had questioned Mr Smith.

'Yes! He said that you had reported that the dog died of heart failure.'

'I never said anything of the sort,' I replied. 'Why are you interested?'

'We were round the other night playing bridge at the Smith's house.'

'And you handled the dog?' I asked.

She said she had, so obviously she had a need to know. I explained to her what she had to do to get immunized but five days had already elapsed and, though it is very uncommon, rabies can have an incubation period as short as ten days.

Then there was a local restaurateur who rang me near midnight reporting that his Dalmatian was scratching his neck vigorously. Most dogs scratch themselves, so it had to be very vigorous to justify him calling me at that time. Of course, rabies came to mind immediately, but I didn't say so.

'Bring it to my surgery at once, if you can' I ordered.

'Don't put yourself out,' he replied, 'I have some Valium. I can give him that.'

'I want to see him now' I repeated.

On examination the dog was friendly and bolted down a bowl of meat stew I gave him, so there appeared to be no paralysis of any of the head muscles, but he had scratched his neck raw and was running a temperature. Not surprisingly the owner wondered why I had become so alarmed when he had rung me. I made clear to him that I suspected rabies, even though, as the dog was behaving so normally, it was hard to believe.

'But I have only recently had him vaccinated.'

I explained my suspicions and asked him to bring the vaccination certificate when he next visited. Meanwhile I injected the dog with a heavy dose of a sedative to stop him scratching, put him in a cage to observe him, and then suggested we all go to bed.

Next morning the dog was very unsteady on its legs, but I could not be sure if it was due to an excess of sedative or if it was another sign of rabies. I phoned the owner and explained that the clinical signs were confusing and promised to keep him informed. Another day went by and then there was no doubt. Any sedative would have certainly worn off by that time, yet the dog was very unsteady on its feet and snapping at imaginary flies. I rang the owner with the news and advised him about the need to get himself and family members immunized forthwith. Interestingly, the vaccination certificate showed that the dog had been vaccinated exactly 120 days earlier with the Flury strain vaccine, though the site of injection was not specified.

Some days later a local physician and good friend, Dr Trudy Henfrey, rang to ask what the restaurateur's dog had died of. Trudy would also have known about the duty of confidentiality and I didn't imagine she was asking out of idle curiosity so I told her.

'But why are you interested in this case?' I asked.

'He sold a Dalmatian puppy to a family with children on Saturday.'

'That's disgraceful!' I said. 'I told him on Friday night that I suspected rabies and I confirmed the diagnosis early on Sunday morning.'

I kept the puppy in isolation for a week and when it showed no signs of disease after that period I could give the family an assurance that there was no risk that they had been infected by the puppy. However, as rabies can have a very prolonged incubation period, I recommended that the puppy be put down, for if it were kept isolated in quarantine for half a year it would never bond properly with people subsequently.

Almost half the dogs I saw were puppies. I can think of several reasons for this. Puppies are known to be more susceptible to the rabies virus than adult dogs and this was exacerbated by the lack of safe vaccines to administer to puppies at that time. In addition adult dogs have a strong sense of territory and are likely to be far more protective of themselves, particularly in confrontations with strange, rabid and inco-ordinated dogs. Puppies are more trusting and will welcome strange dogs, their tails wagging happily.

The most egregious of all the dog owners was a certain Mrs Buggins. That was not her real name, and I use the past tense in the fervent hope that she can no longer make life difficult for other people. She was not a woman I had met before. She rang me one lunchtime to say her dog had a bone stuck in its throat and was unable to breathe and close to dying. I said I would see her in my surgery immediately, whereupon she asked where it was so I explained how to get there.

On arrival at the surgery, which I had reached some minutes ahead of her, I noted that she was a woman a couple of decades past her prime with a menacing look and an intimidating handbag. The little dog, a long-haired dachshund bitch, trotted after her. Immediate death did not look likely, but what was very apparent was that the little dog's lower jaw hung loosely, one of the commonest signs of rabies. I stood back for half a minute or so to see if the dog behaved strangely and then asked her to put the dog on the examination table.

'You said it had a bone stuck in its throat' I said. 'Is that why you think its jaw is hanging open?'

'I actually saw the bone' she claimed.

'I am going to ask that question again and I want you to think very carefully before answering it' I persisted. 'Do you think there is a bone in its throat or have you actually seen it?'

'I saw the bone and so did my husband.'

'And when did you first notice these signs?'

She thought for a moment. 'About eight o'clock last night.'

'So you wait seventeen hours and then ring me at lunchtime saying it is urgent and the dog is about to die?' I had begun to dislike the woman already.

'Well! It was convenient to come now. I had to drop some people off at the airport at midday and I thought I would call on you before going home.'

Rabies was already fixed firmly in my mind, but I had to take her history seriously and she was adamant that there was a bone stuck in the dog's throat. However I had no intention of examining the dog's mouth while it was conscious, not just for my sake but that of my staff, so I told her that I would examine it under anaesthesia to which she agreed.

'So you can go and get some lunch now while I forego mine, and come back in three hours' time' I said. To say I was displeased was to put it mildly, and I hoped she would take my point.

Under anaesthesia I examined the mouth. As expected, there was no bone in the throat. In fact, it was worse than expected, for the woman had mistaken the cartilages of the larynx for bones and there were livid red scratches on the surface of the larynx where she had tried to dislodge the cartilages with her finger nails. She had been so unwavering under questioning that a bone had been stuck in the throat that I used an endoscope to explore the stomach, but there was no bone in the stomach either.

Later in the afternoon Mrs Buggins returned, by which time the dog had come round from the anaesthetic. First I asked her if she had tried to get the bone out with her finger nails and she admitted she had.

'Can I ask you this' I went on, 'have you ever had your dog vaccinated against rabies?'

'No! I've never thought it necessary.'

'I am sorry to tell you this' I told her, 'but there never was a bone. What you saw, and what you tried to pull out, were the normal cartilages of the throat. In fact your dog has rabies and you should get yourself immunized as soon as possible.'

'Absolute rubbish!' she snapped back. 'Everybody knows that dogs with rabies go around biting people.'

I was beginning to get very angry. 'And just how many dogs have you seen with rabies?' I asked, trying to keep my temper under control.

'None! But it seems I know a great deal more about rabies than you do.'

'I've seen a great many more animals with rabies than you have' I said firmly. 'What marks your ignorance of rabies is that there are two forms - a furious form and a paralytic form. Your dog has the paralytic form, as you can see from the drooping jaw. Now I am going to confine your dog. You would be well advised to get yourself and family vaccinated as well as informing your friends who travelled in the car with the dog to the airport so they also can get vaccinated.'

'I'll do nothing of the sort' she said and marched off, without the dog.

Next day Mrs Buggins was back again with some mincemeat which she proposed to feed to her dear little dog by hand.

'You are going to let her starve to death' she accused me.

'Your dog is going to die of rabies, I explained that to you yesterday' I replied.

'Well! I intend to go into that cage to feed my dog.'

'No you won't. I'll have you arrested if you even try. This dog has rabies and is being detained under the Diseases of Animals Act' I bluffed.

For the first time she took note of what I said, but she still persisted in refusing to get herself, her family or house staff to be immunized. On my part I had sufficient witnesses to my repeated instructions to get them vaccinated that I was confident that if any of them contracted rabies she would be entirely answerable for that death. I could do no more.

The next day her husband turned up. He was a great deal more reasonable. 'I think you have been having a little difficulty with my wife' he suggested.

'A little difficulty' was a masterful understatement, but I thought it unwise to say so. I explained to him what I had told his wife about all the procedures for diagnosis and vaccinations that had to be undergone. At that point he confessed that he and his wife were off to England the next day, so I asked him to give me a contact number so that I could inform him of the laboratory results for he, like his wife, was still reluctant to accept that their dog was rabid.

The dog died the next day and the test results came back positive two days later, as I was confident they would. I communicated this information to the Buggins in England.

I hoped that this was the end of the matter but it wasn't. Mrs Buggins refused to pay the bill I sent her and after waiting three months I asked a lawyer to institute proceedings against her. This brought her storming to my surgery.

'I think your account is disgraceful' she began (it was, if I remember rightly, about £100). 'Would you consider reducing it? I've already had to pay doctor's fees in England of over £300.'

'And you think his fee was reasonable?' I asked.

'I had no problem with that. What's more it included the cost of vaccines.'

I don't know how I controlled my temper. 'All he did was to administer a vaccine. He took no risks and he made no diagnosis. I examined the dog under anaesthesia. I diagnosed rabies. I had to cover the expenses related to the laboratory diagnosis and I also had to pay for vaccine for my staff and myself. And you think my account is disgraceful when it is only about a third of the doctor's fees?'

'I do. And I certainly don't see why I should have to pay for the cost of your vaccines' she persisted.

'Those costs have to be covered somehow and part of those costs are reflected in my fee. And I have no intention whatever of reducing my fee in view of your very unpleasant attitude throughout' I retorted.

At that point she got out her cheque book. 'I am going to issue you two cheques. The first will be dated today for half the amount and the second for the other half will be post-dated by six months.'

I was sorely tempted to vent my spleen then and there, but was deterred by the threat of being had up by the disciplinary committee of the Royal College for 'unprofessional conduct'. Mrs Buggins, I realised, was just the kind of person to be really vindictive if I did. So I confined myself to telling her that if she thought it was reasonable to delay payment so long I might also feel it was reasonable to make myself available when it suited me and I would certainly never forgo my lunch for her again.

The outbreak of rabies petered out over about nine months as dog owners realised the need for their dogs to be vaccinated. When it was over I realised that I had a very valuable collection of notes describing the clinical signs of the disease which might warrant publication. It is necessary when writing a scientific paper to refer to papers written by others on the same subject, so I asked the librarian of the Royal College to do a literature search for all accounts of clinical rabies over the past half century. Her search came up with papers in English, French, Italian and Russian. They made it clear was that I had seen more cases than the total of cases described in these four languages over the previous fifty years.

In due course I submitted a paper entitled 'Rabies in the dog' to the *Veterinary Record*. After a month or so I had a note from Edward Boden, the editor, saying that the referees wanted me to withdraw the sentence that in my opinion the cases which were characterized initially by intense itching of the neck were caused by the Flury strain vaccine which was then in common use. I replied that I had very carefully worded the sentence that it was only my opinion but that it was such an important observation that if the referees insisted that I withdraw the offending sentence I would withdraw the whole paper and submit it to the Journal of the American Veterinary Medical Association (JAVMA). I am glad to say the referees backed down and my paper was published as I had written it.

However I was not particularly pleased when the paper was published in the Christmas week edition of the *Record* for, like many people, vets have better things to do over the Christmas and New Year period than read stodgy scientific papers and I feared it would not be noticed. My fears were unfounded. Within two months I had a telephone call from Edinburgh saying that if I was interested in a post at the Centre for Tropical Veterinary Medicine the Director, Sir Alexander Robertson, would be in Nairobi and would like to meet me there. It was an attractive proposition. I was nearing forty. I had enjoyed my life in Mombasa enormously and had made many friends. I felt I was part of a community, a frequent participant in the Little Theatre Club productions and a committee member of the yacht club and I knew that many people appreciated the efforts I had made during the rabies outbreak. But I also felt vulnerable. The constant difficulties put in my way by the veterinary authorities were one reason and problems with the immigration department were another. I might have felt more positive if the practice had been more profitable but it wasn't and I saw no way of increasing its income. All in all, the offer seemed the best way forward.

So I found a buyer for the practice and prepared to leave. The practice was in rented premises, so the total value was not great, but I used the money and the few months I had available before taking up my post in Edinburgh in putting a roof on to the 18th century ruin I had bought in Lamu some years previously and installing running water and electricity. The stone house is modest in size, only two storeys high, but it has a history, for it had been the house in which the British administration had exiled one of the last claimants to the Sultanate of Swahililand.

While I was busy with repairs I had some remarkable news. I received notice that the British Veterinary Association had awarded me the William Hunting Prize and Medal for the best paper submitted by a clinician in the previous year. Even if Mrs Buggins didn't appreciate my veterinary expertise, I was pleased that my own peers in the profession should have considered me worthy of the award.

But there was a flip side to this public notice. The World Health Organization (WHO) in Geneva, in a knee-jerk reaction, issued a notice pouring scorn on my allegation that the Flury strain LEP vaccine could on occasion cause rabies. My pride was hurt that the organization could so easily dismiss my observations without checking them properly, particularly bearing in mind what a horrible disease rabies is. Obviously I could not carry out any experiments on my clients' dogs, whereas the organization had the resources to test the vaccine for safety but seemed unwilling to do so. Four years later, I am glad to say, WHO issued another notice recommending that Flury strain LEP vaccine should only be used to immunize dogs under exceptional circumstances. I felt vindicated at last.

CHAPTER 10

Edinburgh and Nigeria

Edinburgh is a fine city with the cosmopolitan character and sophistication of a great capital but modest in size, thus making it more pleasantly habitable than other larger cities. Its northern latitude, however, makes it colder than many other parts of the kingdom, so it is ironical that the Centre for Tropical Veterinary Medicine is situated there. The CTVM, as it is more often called, is a part of the Royal (Dick) School of Veterinary Medicine within Edinburgh University. Its name might cause a sardonic smirk to those unacquainted with its history. The school had been founded by William Dick in 1823 and had been called The Dick School until it got its royal prefix, but 'The Dick' is what it is still called in common parlance.

When I had met Sir Alexander Robertson in Nairobi in February 1978, he had told me that I would be appointed to a Senior Research Fellowship and that my research project would be based at the National Veterinary Research Institute at Vom in the Plateau State of central Nigeria. I had not heard good reports of that country and it seemed Robertson had not been too impressed either, but a senior veterinary adviser, Tony Thorne, in the Overseas Development Administration (ODA) had been director of the institute prior to Independence and wanted to continue to assist it by encouraging reciprocal visits by Nigerian and British veterinarians to research centres in each others' countries. At my first meeting with Robertson, he had told me if I didn't find working conditions congenial I should say so, as he would much prefer the CTVM to be linked with EAVRO at Muguga or some other research centre close to the Kenyan capital rather than with the Vom institute.

My research project was to be a continuation of a PhD study on *Babesia* parasites carried out by Sandy Trees, a man who was later to become a distinguished academic and President of the Royal College of Veterinary Surgeons. *Babesia* are protozoal parasites, very similar in structure and life cycle to the *Theileria* parasites which had interested me previously in Entebbe and are similarly transmitted by ticks. Two principal species of *Babesia* affect cattle in Africa: *Babesia bigemina* and *Babesia bovis*, both of which can cause Red Water Fever, a disease characterized by severe anaemia and dark urine resulting from the excretion of haemoglobin released from red blood cells following their destruction by the *Babesia* parasites. While both *Babesia* species parasitize red blood cells, *Babesia bovis* also aggregate in the brain and can cause nervous disorders.

It was clear from reading his PhD thesis that Trees had had considerable difficulty in producing specific antibodies in calves to the two parasites. Almost certainly this was because the calves had already been infected with a range of organisms prior to the start of the experimental work and therefore had antibodies against numerous pathogens and were unsuitable for the production of specific ones. I therefore resolved when I got to Nigeria to try and locate calves from tick-free farms in an attempt to overcome this problem.

CHAPTER TEN

My arrival at the CTVM in September 1979 coincided with major changes in the establishment there. The director, Alexander Robertson, and the head of the parasitology section, Jack Wilde, were both about to retire, which left a partial vacuum while two new men fitted into their shoes. I was unfortunate enough to fall into this vacuum.

My major problem was getting a visa to work in Nigeria from the Nigerian High Commission office in Edinburgh. Every week I was told by the smooth, well-dressed ebony gentleman at the reception desk that my application had not been processed yet and that I should come back the following week. After a couple of months I had read and annotated every paper relevant to my own research in the centre's library and was getting restless to get to the field. The new director, Professor David Brocklesby, also got restless and said he would brook no more delay and that if a visa was not issued forthwith, he would cancel my posting to Vom and retain me in Edinburgh as a lecturer.

So, when on my next visit to the High Commission offices in Edinburgh, I was told to return the following week I informed the smooth, well-dressed gentleman that I would not be coming back again as a new position was about to be found for me in the university and the research project would be abandoned, adding that the centre's director would also be reviewing the reciprocal arrangements for Nigerian and British veterinary scientists. This had an immediate effect and within two hours the necessary visa was stamped in my passport. It was then I realized that my visa application had never passed beyond the reception desk, probably because it had not been accompanied with a backhander - 'dash' in Nigerian parlance.

CHAPTER TEN

A fortnight later I flew out to Kano. This is the major city in northern Nigeria, often called the capital of the western Sahara and predominantly Muslim. I was met at the airport by a pleasant, elderly driver from the institute who cleared my baggage through customs and then insisted on showing me around the city before driving me to Jos, the capital of Plateau State, a distance of about 260 miles, and then on to Vom, some 15 miles southwest of Jos. The most interesting feature of Kano was the ancient mud-walled part of the city. I was also intrigued to be shown the city hospital and an open space beside it where, the driver told me, people died. I was shocked that people could be so callous as to force the hospital inmates outside to die. It seemed an odd place to expire, for there were numerous holes in the ground and steaming vats. It took a little time for the penny to drop – it was where people *dyed*.

A pleasant bungalow which had recently been vacated by Sandy Trees was allocated to me on the periphery of the Vom research station. Behind the bungalow was a low rocky knoll and in front stretched a flat, parched plain, dotted with a few eucalyptus trees where there was a very modern dairy unit stocked with imported Friesian cattle. Around on the other side of the knoll were the principal laboratories and animal houses.

As a visitor I clearly could not take over facilities such as stabling and paddocks without the consent of the institute's director, but this elusive eminence was never present. If he was not attending an international conference on poultry diseases in Hong Kong, he was off to Rio de Janeiro to attend an international conference on meat hygiene or some other esoteric theme. Prudently he didn't nominate a deputy director, because his deputy might have used the temporary position to benefit himself, but it made it almost impossible to get myself established. A full hundred days passed before the director had time to see me. His first question was how much funding was available for my research and his second question was how much of that was for himself. I realized then that the stories I had heard of Nigeria's reputation for widespread corruption were all too true. I replied that my project funding was public money and I could not make any private arrangement with him without the consent of my director in Edinburgh. This proposition he immediately quashed. But there was no way he could stop me from communicating the gist of the conversation to David Brocklesby in Edinburgh, for there was a post office directly outside the station's gates.

Meanwhile, during those first hundred frustrating days I set about trying to find tick-free farms from which to buy calves in the hope that I could then use them to prepare specific antisera. My search gave me an opportunity to visit several research farms in northern Nigeria in places such as Katsina, Kano, Zaria and Kaduna, but none were even remotely tick-free.

If the government institutions were less than inspiring, I was certainly interested in the Hausa people of northern Nigeria. Their houses in the well-swept villages I passed through were circular with ochre-coloured walls covered with decorative designs. The men all wore large flowing gowns, many of them with intricate embroidery designs around the neck, and colourful embroidered caps, while the women also wore loose-fitting gowns of bright cloth with turbans or shawls to match.

In due course Brocklesby replied to my letter and informed me that in view of the problems I was facing he planned to visit Vom. As I had expected, he made no suggestion as to how much of the allocated research funds should be paid to the director. I very much looked forward to his visit. Being mindful of Robertson's reservations about the Vom institute and because of my own findings - the lack of suitable experimental animals and the director's inclination for self-enrichment - I hoped to persuade Brocklesby that the CTVM would do better to establish a link with an East African institute.

Apart from the difficulties at work, I was unimpressed by other aspects of Nigeria. The physical climate was fine, hot and dry as I was used to in Karamoja, but officials, such as the immigration officer at Kano airport or the policewoman who conducted my driving test in Jos, were arrogant and bullying. The test was somewhat surreal, for it was clear that the woman did not know how to drive, so she examined me on the Highway Code - a document that had been out of print for many years and was unavailable in all the bookshops I tried. I therefore had to fall back on what I remembered of the British version, which I had last studied seriously some twenty years previously. At the end I was told that I was the most stupid candidate to have applied for the test, but was allowed to pass. I refrained from saying it was the most stupid driving test I had ever undertaken. I suspect the measure of my thoughtlessness was my failure to part with some 'dash' to ease my way through the test. Only later did I find that a reciprocal agreement existed between Britain and Nigeria to recognize each other's licences and there had been no need for me to take the test at all.

Good manners seemed an alien concept; rudeness was a means used by civil servants and others to demonstrate their dominance over people they considered their inferiors. Apart from the deliberate rudeness there was a general lack of consideration for others. One incident I remember well. It was only my third day in the country; it was a Sunday and I had been invited out by a colleague at Vom, Barti Synge (who later went on to become head of the consultancy division of the Scottish Veterinary Service), and his wife, Elizabeth, to have lunch at a club in the vicinity. On my way I noticed the corpse of a man on the side of the road. I imagined that plenty of other drivers would have seen it also and would have reported it. My own failure to report the presence of the corpse was a cowardly thing to do but I excused myself on the grounds that I didn't know the location of the nearest police station, I didn't know the local language and I already didn't much like local officials anyway. In the evening as I drove home the corpse was still there but stark naked - all his clothes had been stolen. A similar lack of respect for corpses was not uncommon after traffic accidents and on two subsequent occasions I saw workmen shovelling the remains of corpses off the road surface after they had been driven over repeatedly by drivers anxious to get to their destinations.

Many months passed before Brocklesby found the time to visit Vom, but once there it took him no time to realize that my research project wasn't going to get anywhere very fast. I also told him bluntly that I was so frustrated that I would not sign a second contract in Vom. This made the project somewhat pointless as I could not have finished it within the first contract period even if I had been allocated stables, paddocks and other facilities which, as yet, nine months after my arrival, I had not. Brocklesby also faced a serious problem in that funding for the CTVM had been curtailed and he was looking for ways to reduce expenditure. The Vom project was an obvious candidate for the chop. So he suggested that I return to Edinburgh as a lecturer.

I wasn't overly enthusiastic, as on the few occasions when I had given public lectures I had got the impression from the faces of my audience that they were profoundly bored. Of course, it could have been that the audience was so intrigued by the profundity of my observations that they were deep in thought, but I doubted it. This differed from the times when I hade taught veterinary students on a one-to-one basis in Mombasa when they were doing the extra-mural part of their training; feedback from the universities involved suggested that the students got considerable benefit and I certainly had benefited when in practice in Mombasa by learning from students about new developments in surgical techniques in the universities.

With little to do in the absence of the facilities to undertake any research on *Babesia*, I happily agreed to assist in the darting and translocation of some animals from the Jos zoo to a game park that was being created nearby. I have little recollection of the work, but I do remember that when I had immobilized one of six eland held in a small compound two of them tried to raise it back on its feet with their horns. Here was a very obvious display of altruism by animals.

With time on my hands, I often attended the polo tournaments in Jos. Polo is now played throughout much of northern Nigeria. The well-heeled Nigerians took part in the tournaments with sizeable strings of ponies, many of them of Argentine origin, transported in air-conditioned articulated vehicles. Barti, who was not then so well-heeled, had a string of two ponies. It was at one of these tournaments that I was asked to see an expatriate-owned dog that was showing signs of rabies. Elizabeth Synge, who also was a qualified veterinarian, was originally asked, but she was in the early stages of pregnancy and I could well understand her reluctance to see the dog, not just because of the risk to herself but the possible consequences of the vaccine, if she had to be immunized, on the unborn baby.

I followed Elizabeth's instructions and found the house. It was just after six in the evening. There was nobody there except a blue-turbanned Tuareg night watchman from Niger, who told me the family had gone out to a party and wouldn't be back until late. Under questioning in French, he admitted knowing nothing about the dog's illness but did say that there were two children in the family. I was appalled by the irresponsible attitude of the owners, for if the dog had rabies the children in particular were most at risk.

The dog was loose in the garden; it looked very normal but my experience of rabies was that rabid dogs often behaved normally, especially in the early stages of the disease. Without a history and unable to ask the dog any questions or at least to get any answers, it seemed that the best thing I could do under the circumstances was to take the dog home with me to Vom and keep it under observation. This I did, and tied it with two leads to limit its mobility in my garage. About two hours later an awful howling and yelping came from the garage. I rushed to see what was happening and then the truth dawned. The dog was having an epileptic fit.

I had no telephone, so I could not ring the owners with the news, but I supposed they would contact me. So for the next four days I cared and fed the dog. Because of the owners' irresponsibility and the discourtesy of going to a party when they knew that a vet was coming to see their dog, I was determined to charge them a professional fee. They turned up late one evening and when I asked for my fee I was rebuffed on the grounds that as we were all British we should all pull together. It seemed to me to be a very one-sided arrangement and after that I refused to see dogs belonging to other expatriates, telling them that there were plenty of Nigerian vets available. Some already knew that I had considerable experience of rabies but I did not see why I should put that knowledge to their benefit or take the risks associated with rabies without getting paid. My knowledge and skills were the way I made my living, just as other professionals do.

I would have left Vom soon after Brocklesby's visit but Barti was due to go on leave and he was undertaking a long-term investigation of the productivity of Fulani cattle under traditional management in Plateau State[52] and the benefit of supplementing their diet with a protein element, namely cotton-seed cake, which was plentiful in the area. I therefore agreed to stay on during his absence to record changes in herd composition (such as births and deaths), milk yields, calf growth rates and other parameters in the several herds that he was monitoring.

In visiting these herds at first light each morning while they were still being milked I saw another side of Nigeria, a much nicer side than the one shown by officialdom. The herd owners were all Fulani, a charming people characterized by their good looks, which

[52] Plateau State in central Nigeria is one of very few highland areas of West Africa, rising to 4,000-4,500 feet elevation. It is rich in minerals, especially tin. Perhaps these two features explain the very high number of lightning strikes that occur. In the 1976 International Geophysical Year equipment was sent to measure the strikes but it was struck by lightning and rendered useless.

has led to speculation that they originated from Ethiopia, although their language, Pulaar, is certainly of West African origin. The pastoral Fulani, who are also called Fula or Fulbe, are traditionally a nomadic group, herding cattle, goats and sheep across the dry hinterlands of the sub-Saharan savannah - the vast swathe stretching from western Sudan to the Atlantic Ocean known as the Sahel. They differed from their East African pastoralist counterparts in that cattle were not enclosed in bomas at night but were individually tethered to stakes, each animal going to its own stake at dusk when it was about to be tethered. Clearly the West African herd owners had no fear of depredations by lion, which had long since been wiped out in the area, as had most of the other wildlife.

Fulani generosity was outstanding. Not only did they give up much of their time while I was measuring and recording but I seldom left their encampments, half a dozen or so domed structures roofed with millet straw, without a gift of a guinea fowl or two or a clutch of eggs. To have refused a gift would have been considered an insult but I found it embarrassing because I felt obliged to reciprocate their generosity. The easiest way to have done so would have been to treat or vaccinate their animals against the diseases enzootic to the area, but this would have distorted the purpose of the trial, which was to investigate the cattle's productivity under traditional management, not under veterinary supervision. However I did cheat a bit and treated whatever animals seemed to be sick at the time of my visits. De-worming of unthrifty calves was probably the most common treatment, but on occasion I also treated animals against tryps.

Unlike Kenya and Uganda where diseases made horse ownership

impossible and horsemanship was almost unknown until settlers imported horses, it was a great social and military asset among the peoples of the Sahel.[53] In earlier times in the great empires of Songhor, Mali and old Ghana in West Africa the dominant groups, mostly of Fulani origin, depended on cavalry to defeat their enemies and maintain control over their vassals, but horses had a short life and seldom bred in the wetter tsetse-infested areas of the savannah, so there was a constant need for replenishment from the Berbers of the Sahara and North Africa in exchange for gold and slaves from the forested Guinea coast; a trade which was somewhat disorientated when European traders and slavers started to visit the Guinea coast in the mid-fifteenth century.

Camels were introduced to North Africa from Asia only in the first centuries of the Christian era. Before that, rock paintings in the Sahara show that horse-drawn carts were used for trans-Saharan trade, which would imply that there was more water and grazing in the Sahara several millennia ago than there is now, for horses do not have the endurance of camels in arid areas.

Sadly the pastoral Fulani are now in retreat, as is happening to pastoralists elsewhere; their former rangeland is progressively being taken over for agricultural purposes by a burgeoning population, forcing them to turn to trading for a living.

---

[53] The first director of veterinary services in Kenya spent most of his first contract period in Ethiopia buying remounts for use by administrative and military officers in the new colony.

CHAPTER 11

Southern Sudan

I returned to Britain in September 1979 with the knowledge that I had already secured a post in southern Sudan, based in Juba. This had come about because I had been obliged to make an urgent visit to England two months previously for personal reasons. Unable to reach Brocklesby on the telephone from Nigeria, I rang him as soon as I reached England to inform him of my absence from my place of work. Brocklesby was well aware that I did not want to lecture at the Centre for Tropical Veterinary Medicine and, as he had been asked by an old friend of his from veterinary college days, Roy Ansell, if he knew of a suitable candidate to take up the post of diagnostician and parasitologist at the World Bank funded veterinary research laboratory in Juba which Ansell headed, he recommended me.

I met Ansell at the Carlton Club in St James's. He was a slightly-built man, silver haired and impeccably dressed. What I did not know at the time was that the impeccable exterior covered quite the most unpleasant man I have ever known. The interview, as I realised later, was unsatisfactory. It didn't help that the custom in London clubs does not allow for talking shop within their walls and the presence of the Lord Chancellor, Lord Hailsham, seated magisterially nearby with a coterie of Conservative party worthies made any discussion of terms of service difficult. I did, however, glean that I would be required to undertake a survey of livestock diseases in the Eastern and Western Equatoria provinces of Southern Sudan.

Taking blood and other biological samples from animals spread over an area somewhat bigger than the whole of the Iberian peninsula would require tens, if not hundreds, of thousands of samples to be taken for a survey to be statistically significant. It seemed to me that time would be much better spent in diagnosing disease outbreaks and using the data to map the geographical distribution of diseases and their seasonal occurrence, so as to be able to come up with appropriate disease control strategies. And there were other objections to a survey. The end consequence of many of the more serious animal diseases is death so it becomes impossible to survey for them retrospectively. To make my point, I asked Ansell how one could survey for anthrax, a disease which is invariably fatal in cattle, to which he replied 'It's not for you to reason why.' The statement sounded ominous then; little did I know how ominous it was.

Ansell had told me at the interview that there would be a delay of about three months before I could take up the post. I thus gave notice to Edinburgh University and decided to spend the intervening time getting on with repairs to the derelict house I had bought in Lamu. But three months turned to nine. This gave cause for some financial anxiety, as I was spending heavily on the house at a time when no money was coming in. However I found plenty to do in Lamu and in the evenings an interesting group collected in the bar at Petley's Inn on the Lamu waterfront for a few beers, including a distinguished historian and scholar of the Atlantic slave trade, the managing editor of the *Financial Times*, an American archaeologist excavating some of the important sites in the Lamu archipelago and other more or less erudite characters.

Eventually in May 1980 Ansell rang me saying all was ready for me to take up the post. I asked that I be sent a formal contract. When it arrived I found it very disturbing. The salary offered was half that had been mooted at the interview in the Carlton Club. Because of my parlous financial position I reluctantly agreed. And there was another menacing inclusion in the contract: I was expected to carry out all orders given to me at any time. One normally does carry out one's instructions if one wants to retain a job but I had never had it spelt out quite so explicitly.

Ansell suggested I meet him in Nairobi, where he was supervising the construction of a mobile laboratory that he had designed on the chassis of a five-ton, four-wheel-drive Bedford truck. I had had a previous experience of a mobile laboratory in Karamoja and was apprehensive, though I didn't say so - the trouble with a mobile laboratory is that every part is part of a whole and there is no flexibility; if one part fails the whole becomes useless. Even the workshop manager, who had been a sailing comrade in Mombasa, was dubious about its usefulness.

But we set off anyway, Ansell, myself and a driver. Hardly had we covered 200 miles from Nairobi before the starter motor burned out. We spent three days in Eldoret while a new one was obtained from Nairobi and installed. The second starter motor lasted another 200 miles before burning out, but this time we were stranded in the Turkana desert of north-western Kenya - a limitless expanse of stone, sand and lava with not a tree to mitigate the heat and certainly no spare part retailers or garage mechanics.

Large trucks have hydraulic brakes and if the engine cannot be started the oil pump will not operate, the oil pressure cannot be raised and the brakes cannot be released. This presented the first problem, for even if the truck was stopped on an incline overnight to assist in starting in the morning the brakes had to be released by fiddling with the brake system under the truck. Thereafter the truck had no brakes at all until the brake system had been re-fiddled. The laboratory's air conditioning then failed; this was hardly surprising, for the air conditioner was an ordinary domestic one and had not been designed to be knocked about on the rudimentary roads of the remoter parts of Kenya and Sudan.

Ansell's anger at all these failings turned on the driver, a large Ugandan named Zechariah. This was eminently unfair, for any failings were of Ansell's design and not of Zechariah's making, so I felt obliged to protect him from the abuse. This, of course, was no way to get on with my new employer. And then I made a grave mistake - in the absence of air conditioning I suggested that the laboratory might be painted white to reflect the sun and to help keep it cool within.

Eventually we made it to Juba, the administrative capital of southern Sudan. At the time it was a dusty, dilapidated town stretching two or three miles along the western bank of the Nile. Trees were few, for many had been cut down for firewood. The only part which showed any pretence of town planning was the northern end, where there were a few shops owned by tall white-turbaned Arab northerners and where the docks were situated and where from time to time a rust-covered paddle steamer, dragging three or four barges, might dock bringing wares from Kosti and Khartoum over 800 miles away in the north.

In truth, however, Juba's real commercial links were with Nairobi and Mombasa, 1200 miles to the south east, over roads of very uncertain quality. An old Bailey bridge, erected by Dutchmen a year or so earlier as an aid project, straddled the river, which was about 600 yards wide at that point. At its approach on the Juba side was a large treeless space occupied by a cemetery and a large market. Not that there was much in the market to buy. Tins of tomato paste, okra, flyblown fragments of meat and black shoe polish for the soldiery were the staples and, if one was lucky, sugar and flour (the latter more often than not enriched with sour-tasting weevils) in sacks labelled 'free gifts' from donor countries. A limited Arabic vocabulary was usually sufficient to get by in the market, the most common phrases being '*Maalesh*,' '*Ma fee*' and '*Bukra, Insh'allah*' meaning 'Sorry,' 'There's none,' and 'Tomorrow, if God wills it.'

In Juba I met with two colleagues who became valuable allies. David Dyson, a veterinary pathologist, and Roger Miles, a microbiologist, were both PhDs. It was not long before I perceived that they also were less than enchanted with Ansell. The veterinary diagnostic laboratory was part of a bigger World Bank funded project, the Project Development Unit, or PDU as it was usually called, which intended to develop agricultural infrastructure after the north-south civil war that had ended, temporarily it turned out, in 1974. The PDU was led by a Scot of dubious academic standing and a lack of leadership qualities and it is difficult to find a single word of praise for any of the project's achievements. This was the little world in which I had committed myself to work for two years.

Within days of arrival, when I would have liked to establish myself and set up the diagnostic laboratory, I was ordered by Ansell to paint the mobile laboratory white. The only white paint available in the few shops in Juba was household distemper. Ansell didn't like the matt finish, he wanted it glossy, so he ordered me to sandpaper the mobile laboratory down and paint it again. Over the next three and a half months I painted it thirteen times and sandpapered it down twelve times. I certainly wasn't allowed to forget the clause in my contract that I was expected to carry out all orders given to me at any time.

It turned out that both David and Roger had also been compelled to carry out similar menial jobs - jobs for which many poor Sudanese would have given an arm and a leg - for protracted periods. An amateur psychologist might well detect that Ansell had something of a power complex; the interview in the Carlton Club being just one indication of it. I complained to the project director about the waste of time but he feebly did nothing to redress the unpleasant situation.

A year previously Idi Amin had been forced out of Uganda by the Tanzanian army. One of his leading henchmen had escaped with his tribal followers to Nimule on the Uganda-Sudan border, looting all the cattle on the Acholi ranch - the ranch my friend, Steve, had established - and killing the admirable ranch manager, Nicanor Okema, the same man who had been of such use in Karamoja, while doing so.

Within a few months of the refugees' arrival about a quarter of the many thousands of looted cattle had died of an undiagnosed disease. David had travelled to Nimule with Ansell to investigate the cause of mortality. As David told me, he had wanted to carry out autopsies on some of the dead animals but after a quarter of an hour Ansell had ordered him to stop as he was very hot and wanted to return to Juba. So, after a round trip of 200 miles and more, all that David had to show were a few blood slides.

Numerous theilerial parasites were visible on the slides. This alone was not evidence of East Coast fever, for there are several species of *Theileria* and for a definitive identification of *Theileria parva*, the causal organism of ECF, it is necessary to identify schizonts of the parasite in lymph node biopsies.[54] ECF had only been identified once before in southern Sudan, right on its southern border with Uganda, by a Welshman, E T Rees-Evans in 1950. It's a small world for it was Rees-Evans who had taught me clinical haematology at university.

Inevitably I was drawn to finding out whether or not the cause of the massive mortality of the looted cattle was ECF. It made sense, for I knew that under Okema tick control on the Acholi ranch would have been of a high standard and so the looted cattle were likely to be susceptible to any tick-borne diseases when removed from the ranch. Eventually Ansell tired of ordering me to paint the mobile laboratory white, so I made my first safari to Nimule in it. I found the refugees camped by the Aswa river with about eight thousand surviving animals. The Aswa river at that point, about twenty miles inside Sudan, was a delightful, fast-moving river running through rocky pools on its way to join the Nile some eight

---

[54] Robert Koch, the great German bacteriologist, had first demonstrated the schizonts in cases of ECF in South Africa and they were always called Koch's Blue Bodies (KBBs) in Uganda though I was reproached at the CTVM in Edinburgh for using the term and advised to use the term schizont. Koch was the first to observe the Theileria parasite in cases of ECF but he had mistakenly believed they were Babesia parasites and it was Arnold Theiler, later to be knighted, who established Theileria as a separate genus.

miles to the west. The water was so clear that it seemed unlikely that any crocodiles could be lurking in it and the refugees confirmed that there were none, so every evening I luxuriated in its coolness. What surprised me was the total lack of people in this Garden of Eden, so I could enjoy the cool water quite naked without any embarrassment.

What I didn't succeed in doing on that safari was to identify any schizonts. The mobile laboratory had two air-cooled electric generators fixed to its chassis to power the non-functioning air conditioner and various pieces of laboratory equipment - refrigerator, centrifuges, microscope, etc. But the microscope was quite useless, for the vibrations produced by the generators made it impossible to examine cell structures in any detail.

Back in Juba I had no difficulty in identifying the schizonts of *T. parva* on a non-vibrating bench. I also discovered from an old friend from Karamoja days, an elderly white-haired unreformed gold miner called Frank Howitt, why the idyllic banks of the Aswa river were unpopulated. It was notorious for river blindness. This might well explain why local Sudanese showed no resentment to the Ugandans occupying the land. Fast-flowing, well-oxygenated rivers are ideal breeding places for *Simulium* flies, otherwise known as black flies or buffalo gnats. These flies, in their thousands, cause great annoyance and irritation to animals, including birds, on which they feed in the early mornings and evenings. Swarms of them reportedly killed over 20,000 horses, cattle, sheep and pigs along the river Danube in the 1920s. They are also vectors of several species of filarial worms, which cause irritating nodules in the skin and ligaments of man and animals, while the microfilariae shed by the adult worms invade the corneas of people living in the vicinity of affected rivers, causing a progressive keratitis eventually leading to total blindness.[55]

Having established that ECF was the cause of death of the refugee's cattle, I thought it necessary to ascertain whether the disease had now become enzootic in Sudanese herds. To do this it was necessary to sample locally-owned cattle herds and determine how widespread was the distribution of the tick vector, the brown ear tick, *Rhipicephalus appendiculatus*. In this I was frustrated by Ansell who refused to allow me to travel to Nimule again and who was adamant that there was no need to study tick distributions because, according to him, all species of ticks could transmit ECF - an indication of his ignorance of the epidemiology of the disease.

Back in 1949 an American virologist, Harry Hoogstraal, had been sent to Torit, about a hundred miles east of Juba, under the auspices of the U.S. Naval Medical Research Unit based in Cairo (NAMRU-3) to study elephant shrew malaria. Over the course of the next few years he undertook a study of the ticks of the Sudan. I don't know what conclusions he came to about elephant shrew malaria but his Volume I of 'African Ixodoidea-Ticks of the Sudan' is a massive tome of over 1100 pages and contains nearly everything one might want to know about ticks. My own copy, given to me by Hoogstraal when I had been in Ethiopia over ten years previously, is about to fall apart from constant handling.[56] Hoogstraal showed in a systematic and patient survey of ticks both of domestic animals and wildlife that whereas the brown ear tick frequently attacked cattle in the wet forested areas along the Ugandan border west of

---

[55] The Carter Foundation, set up by the former U.S. president, Jimmy Carter, has done excellent work in almost eradicating river blindness from the African continent.

[56] I had written to Hoogstraal while based in Ethiopia describing the terrible damage done to the perineal region of Borana-owned cattle by the tick *Rhipicephalus pulchellus*; sufficient I suspected to render many female animals infertile. Hoogstraal had urged me to publish this information but I had other things on my desk at the time. He was good enough then to send me his book.

the Nile, the tick was rare east of the Nile except in the mountainous areas of Eastern Equatoria Province where he found just two specimens - compared to the 1351 specimens he identified around Kajo Kaji and Yei on the west side of the river. Ominously, he found one specimen on a roan antelope at Ngangala, some 30 miles east of Juba, an area which was not forested, wet or elevated and which suggested that large parts of southern Sudan might be a suitable habitat for this tick. Sadly this has proved true and East Coast fever is now enzootic over large parts of southern Sudan and has caused considerable mortality in cattle herds.[57]

But I wasn't the only one to suffer from Ansell's capricious behaviour. David Dyson had been asked by the manager of a dairy farm established by FAO a few miles north of Juba on the east side of the river to investigate an outbreak of a disease that was affecting the cattle there. Quite correctly he diagnosed lumpy skin disease, an insect-borne virus disease of the pox family. As its name implies, the disease is characterized by hard lumps within the skin which eventually scab over. Native cattle may not show many other signs but imported exotic cattle may also become quite ill and even die. David, being a keen histopathologist, also took biopsies of the skin lesions to confirm his diagnosis. Ansell, of course, knew better and though he had not seen the affected cattle himself he wrote a letter to the Minister of Agriculture in Juba, Gama Hassan, saying that Dr Dyson was a young and inexperienced veterinarian and he, Ansell, could assure the Minister that the disease was not lumpy skin disease.

David was, not surprisingly, incensed at being disparaged in

---

[57] In later visits to Karamoja I also found that ECF had spread well beyond its previous boundaries. There could be three possibilities for this extension:

1. rainfall has increased in these areas so extending the habitat of the vector tick *Rhipicephalus appendiculatus*,

2. the physiology of the tick has adapted to enable it to survive in drier areas,

3. another tick species, possibly *R. pravus*, has become an efficient vector of the theilerial parasite.

such a way. In England he could have had recourse to the disciplinary committee of the Royal College but that option was unavailable to him in Sudan. Fortunately Glyn Davies at the Kabete Veterinary Laboratories in Kenya was a virologist so I suggested to David he send some biopsy material to Glyn for a second opinion. Within a short time a signed laboratory report on Kabete letterhead paper came back confirming his diagnosis.

Unaware of the second opinion and in order to prove to the minister that his own diagnosis was correct, Ansell decided to visit the farm with his wife, who was also a veterinary surgeon, and ordered me to accompany them. Perhaps I was becoming neurotic by that time; I was highly suspicious of their motives and fearful that I would be outnumbered by the pair of them, so I searched the Land Rover before departure and found a tyre lever hidden under Ansell's seat; this I quickly moved to where I intended to sit in the event of a physical confrontation. At the farm, Ansell made no effort to contact any of the farm staff but went directly to the paddock where the affected cattle were being grazed. All three of us then wandered about the paddock for a few minutes before Ansell said it was obvious that the animals didn't have lumpy skin disease. I objected and requested that the cattle be put in a crush so that I could examine the lesions and, in particular, to palpate them. I was overruled so we got in the Land Rover and started back to Juba. About half way back, Ansell, who was driving, stopped the vehicle. First he asked me if I had ever seen lumpy skin disease before; I said that I had.

'So you'll agree that it wasn't lumpy skin disease?'

'I don't agree,' I replied 'You didn't allow me to examine the lesions properly in a crush as I asked.'

'In that case I am ordering you to make no mention to any Sudanese official that you accompanied me to the FAO farm.'

It was extraordinary what Ansell thought he could order me to do. Even the opinion of a newly qualified veterinarian is valid, and I had been qualified for almost 18 years at that time.

It would be tedious to list all the petty insults we had to put up with. I had already complained to the project director that I wasn't being allowed to do my job properly, but cravenly he took no action. Of course, the Sudanese staff in the laboratory were not spared. Few southerners had been able to get an education during the long years of the civil war which had started in 1956, so that those staff who were recruited were selected because they had received some education as refugees in neighbouring countries, most in Uganda and some in the Congo, then called Zaire. Thus a tenuous bond was formed between myself and those who had spent their formative years in Uganda, particularly if they could speak Swahili, for my Arabic, at that time, was negligible. So I was hardly surprised when one day one of the drivers, Yusuf Omar, confided to me that they intended to murder Ansell if he insulted them once again. I said nothing, not wanting to be considered an accomplice, though inwardly thinking it was an excellent idea. The thought had even crossed my mind on a number of occasions but, fortunately for Ansell, I had reluctantly considered that his continuing existence was preferable to a term in a Sudanese jail.

Exultantly, I reported the conversation to my colleague Roger Miles. Roger was a taciturn man and his appointment in Juba was his first experience of Africa. 'Is it always like this?' he would ask regularly. Roger, too, favoured the prospect of Ansell's elimination and advised me not to tell him of the staff's intentions because it would put him on his guard. And we both agreed we could not in all sincerity offer our condolences to Mrs Ansell if he were dispatched. But it never got so far.

About the same time, an American missionary named Arensen, based at Pibor Post, close to the Ethiopian border, asked me if I would investigate the cause of death of cattle belonging to the Murle people to whom he ministered. According to him about a quarter of the twelve thousand or so cattle around Pibor had already succumbed. He also offered to fly me there at any time. Although I was keen to go, I told him that I would have to get Ansell's permission.

This was denied; as soon as Ansell heard that a plane would be made available he decided to go himself. Up to that time I had never seen Ansell do any form of veterinary work except the very peremptory hands-off and unprofessional inspection of some pimply cattle from a safe distance on the FAO farm.

So Ansell flew to Pibor, a distance of about 180 miles, stayed the night with Jon Arensen and his wife and flew back empty-handed the next day - claiming that the rain had prevented him from taking any samples. Naturally Arensen felt let down by the outcome of his expedition but I was able to temper their disappointment by telling them that Ansell was due to go to Nairobi shortly and in his absence I would be able to go to Pibor.[58]

Pibor Post lies on the Pibor river, which drains a part of the western Ethiopian escarpment and the swamps in the lowlands below. The river itself is tree-lined and shady but beyond its confines the vast treeless savannah stretches for many miles. The Murle themselves resemble the Karamojong physically with a similar

---

[58] World Bank staff and their wives found any number of pretexts for visiting Nairobi at frequent intervals.

disdain for clothing among the masculine element and were loathed by their equally naked Nuer and Dinka pastoralist neighbours for they had the reputation of being child-stealers. This was attributed, I was told, to the Murles' low breeding rate as a result of the sexually-transmitted diseases which were rife among them.

The plane flew in to Pibor Post late in the afternoon, too late to examine any sick animals. The pilot and I were put up in the mission house. He was anxious, he told me, to make an early getaway in the morning because rain was forecast and he feared that the landing strip might become too muddy for take-off. This severely limited the time available, so I was up before sunrise. The history I obtained from the Murle cattle owners suggested that tryps or fasciolosis were the most likely cause of the widespread mortality.[59] But as so often happens when one wants to investigate a disease outbreak, there was no carcase to autopsy that morning, which would have been compelling evidence of fluke infection, so I had to make do with collecting some blood slides and faecal samples.

Back in Juba I found no fluke eggs in the faecal samples, but a quarter of the twenty or so blood slides I had collected showed the presence of *Trypanosoma vivax*. Trypanosomes are only intermittently visible in the blood and the fact that a quarter of the blood slides were positive was a strong indication that *T. vivax* was the cause of mortality. This made a lot of sense epidemiologically, not only because the tree-lined river provided a suitable habitat for the tsetse vectors but because *T. vivax* can also be transmitted by other biting flies, thus allowing for the spread of the disease in the tree-less savannah plains of central southern Sudan.

So as not to be accused of acting behind Ansell's back, I wrote

---

[59] Fasciolosis is caused by a liver fluke—a flat leaf-like worm—that is spread by snails. The riverine habitat and the flooded plains beyond were an ideal breeding ground for snails.

a full report of my visit to Pibor, gave reasons for my diagnosis of T. *vivax* infection and put it on his desk to await his return. My report was returned to me with the written comment in red ink that I did not have sufficient evidence for making my diagnosis. This from a man who had had an opportunity previously to make a diagnosis but didn't do so. Again a complaint to the disciplinary committee of the Royal College would have been warranted but I felt the college might have considered any action taken in the Sudan was out of its jurisdiction.

But life was not all grim in Juba. There were quite a few expatriates in the vicinity, working with United Nations organizations and NGOs as well as private contractors such as my old friend Frank Howitt. One night a week Interfreight, a transport company operating between Mombasa and Juba, would get a film up from Nairobi and we were entertained to a film show. And at least one night a week we would meet in one house or another to play pontoon or other trivial card game - the host for the evening having to ensure that he had brewed sufficient beer to entertain the guests, for most expatriates, other than those with diplomatic privileges such as United Nations and World Bank staff, brewed their own beer and baked their own bread. Sudanese bank notes were not only filthy and greasy but the portrait of the president, General Numeiri, was frequently disfigured by having his eyes punched out as an insulting gesture. It was therefore usual to play cards using Monopoly money as a substitute and then redeeming the Monopoly money for cash at the end of an evening of cards. Thus it was a cause of considerable hilarity when one of the card players, Dennis Leete, had an uninvited visitor one night who took all his Monopoly money but left the Sudanese notes untouched.

It wasn't easy to think of exciting meals with which to entertain friends because of the paucity of foodstuffs in the market, but from time to time a fisherman would come round the houses with a Nile perch or a brace of tilapia fish to boost a menu which too often consisted of curried beef or goat. And there was another delicacy - suckling pig - bred on a government farm close by the laboratory on milk powder donated by the European Economic Community, the forerunner of the present European Union.

The vile figure of Ansell always lurked in the background, until one day he went a step too far. Maggie Dalton, the project director's confidential secretary and a card playing Monopolist, asked me to look at a letter Ansell had asked her to type for the Minister's eyes. In it he accused me of being incompetent, indolent and insubordinate. To be honest, there was some basis for the last charge, with good reason, but none for the first two. I was outraged and asked Maggie to allow me to photocopy the letter, which I then distributed to all those with an interest in what was going on in the veterinary laboratory, including the complacent project director and the Minister of Agriculture. In a covering letter to the minister I asked that he convene a meeting where I could answer the charges made against me.

I knew that if Roger, David and I combined our experiences of Ansell's management of the laboratory and its staff, he would have no leg to stand on, and I was determined to go for the jugular (to mix two metaphors). In a sense I led for the prosecution. I drew the Minister's attention to the charge of incompetence against me. I then reminded him that Ansell had written to him accusing David Dyson of being young and inexperienced and that his diagnosis of lumpy skin disease was wrong. If anybody was wrong, I said, it was Ansell and I asked David to show the minister the laboratory report from Kabete confirming his diagnosis of lumpy skin disease.

The minister looked quite unsettled, for he now realized that Ansell had lied to him on that occasion and, perhaps, on other occasions also. I then told of the fruitless visit to the FAO farm and of Ansell's order to me that I wasn't to inform any Sudanese of the visit. This, of course, reeked of racism. The minister glared at Ansell, who I could see was not just embarrassed but was actually trembling.

For the next half hour I pursued my attack relentlessly. In his letter, Ansell had set out to destroy any confidence in my professional ability and I was now determined to destroy all his credibility. In that I was successful and at the end Gama Hassan declared that Ansell would have to go. Unfortunately, the minister decided to give him three months' notice. I objected, saying that while Ansell remained in charge of the laboratory there was little chance of the subordinate staff being able to get on with any meaningful work because of his constant obstruction and denigration of staff.

Over the next few weeks some of the World Bank's supervisory staff based in Nairobi visited us to assess the situation. Ansell, like the irresolute project director, was a World Bank employee. Always well-groomed, he had undoubtedly duped them successfully and they were unwilling to acknowledge their own responsibility. He was a good vet, they thought, and merely had some character faults. David and I, who were the best judges of his veterinary competence, had to disillusion them and told them that if we had been in the United Kingdom we would certainly have referred him to the disciplinary committee of the Royal College for professional incompetence.

Some years later I discovered from another veterinary colleague that the doctorate that Ansell always boasted of was not quite what it seemed. It had been awarded for his thesis on the productivity of Friesian cattle in a tropical environment. He had made his subordinate staff in Oman do the field work and the consequent statistical analysis and then submitted the thesis as his own work.

Life and work was a great deal more pleasant after Ansell's departure. Unrestricted by his constant strictures, I was able to show that East Coast fever had spread, causing considerable mortality in Sudanese herds, which were particularly susceptible because of the very recent introduction of the disease. Norwegian Church Aid, an NGO operating out of Torit in Eastern Equatoria Province, asked me to investigate the cause of deaths in Didinga herds and made available their rest-house at Chukudum, a lovely red-brick bungalow in a grove of trees, in the Kidepo valley. The Didinga were the same people who had been refugees in Dodoth 17 years previously and I was reminded of this the first night I was staying in Chukudum when an elder approached and said he remembered me. On asking him why he should remember me, he replied that I was the person who had shot 700 of his people's cattle. This was not a good beginning but, fortunately for me, there seemed to be no rancour and I got all the cooperation I needed to examine and take samples from infected herds.

In looking for the brown ear tick I also found that other parasite of the ear canal, *Rhabditis bovis*, the nematode worm which I had seen before on the ranches along the Mombasa-Voi road. And whereas Hoogstraal had found only two specimens of the brown ear tick in that area of Eastern Equatoria, I collected over 400 in one morning around Chukudum.

I also took the opportunity to revisit Pibor Post, and as it was now the dry season I chose to travel by Land Rover. A newly remade road along the east bank of the Nile led to Bor a little over a hundred miles north of Juba, the centre of a major group of the Dinka people, all pastoralists and noted for their immense height - most men are about seven feet tall but scarcely blessed with good looks, though Dinka damsels might think differently.

From Bor I set off over flat treeless savannah country, the Pengko Plain, towards Pibor about a hundred and twenty miles eastwards, not far from the Ethiopian border. Locally these seasonally flooded grasslands are known as *toich*. Their flatness plays optical tricks, particularly if you are on your own. Because there is nothing higher on the horizon, at one moment you can believe you are at the top of the world; and then, because there is nothing lower, the next moment you can think you are at the bottom of the world.

Scattered among the *toich*, at intervals of a dozen miles or so there are slight depressions in the ground which remain filled with rainwater from the previous rainy season and provide watering points for the Dinka and Murle cattle as well as numerous wild animals, including waterbuck, white-eared kob and buffalo throughout much of the ensuing dry season.

The flatness affects the local cattle in other ways too. During the rains, as there is no gradient for water to flow down, it just accumulates where it falls - everywhere. This results, paradoxically, in cattle often losing condition in the wet season because almost all the grazing is under water. Where there are a few ridges of higher ground on which animals can gather, there are so many animals that the available grazing is insufficient. It was a matter of wonder to me that despite standing for many months in mud and water, the local cattle showed no signs of foot diseases, such as foul-in-the-foot and the softening and disintegration of the horn-covered hooves, which are so common in European breeds of cattle standing in mud and water for any length of time.

At about this time I became involved in a somewhat bizarre event. There was a constant, if small, trickle of white people passing though Juba on their way from the Cape to Cairo or reverse; some were hitchhikers, while the better-off travelled in four-wheel-drive lorries with large pigeon holes below for sleeping and bus or cinema seats above to sit in during the day. I had met some of these intrepid travellers and thought them woefully unprepared to travel through Sudan. It was a young German hitchhiker who caught my attention; he was dead at the time. He had met his end under the lorry on which he had hitched a lift from Nairobi.

Carrying hitchhikers was a useful perk for the many lorry drivers who drove this route, as they charged fifty or a hundred dollars per head. On this occasion the lorry driver and his mate decided to brew up some tea by the Aswa river bridge twenty miles or so north of Nimule while the German spread himself out in front of the lorry for a nap. After refreshing themselves, the driver and his mate got into the cab and drove away, only remembering their fare-paying passenger too late. He was quite crushed.

If it had been me, uncertain of how the Sudanese police might regard such an accident, I think I would have left the evidence behind to be consumed by hyenas, but the two Kenyans did the honourable thing and brought the body to Juba, where the small

German community arranged for its burial. Then, just minutes before the ceremony, word came that the man's parents wanted the body repatriated to Germany. They could hardly have known of the difficulties. There were no undertakers in the town, no refrigerated mortuary and temperatures only dropped below blood temperature for a few hours of the night. To compound these difficulties the only planes with holds large enough to transport a coffin were the DC9s of Sudan Airways, always referred to as Insh'allah Airlines because of the company's very erratic schedules, due, it was alleged, to its inability to pay the suppliers of jet fuel.

So the body was popped into the laboratory's cold store, in which vaccines were usually stored. About two weeks passed before a lead-lined coffin was flown in from Khartoum. To accord with international regulations and for hygiene reasons the body was then soldered into the lead coffin, ensuring it was hermetically sealed, and then taken to the airport in the few hours it took for the plane to proceed to Nairobi and back to Juba. My house overlooked the airport and as dusk fell I noted that the plane was still on the ground - another problem with fuel supplies, it turned out - but it was off late the next morning, when I suppose the airline company had found some money to pay Shell.

Roy Ansell's departure left a vacuum, but it was not at first noticed, for he had never provided any sort of leadership in his time as Chief Veterinary Research Officer. Quite the reverse, for he had frustrated every initiative we proposed. David was offered the post but asked that his salary be reviewed to bring it in line with what Ansell had been paid which, being a World Bank salary, was greatly in excess of his then current salary. This the project director refused, so when David's contract ended he left. So did Roger, leaving me and a Sudanese vet, Noel Tingwa, as the last remaining professional staff at the laboratory. Still the project director did nothing to fill the vacuum. Having been cheated, as I believed, over the matter of the salary offered to me by Ansell, I had no intention of doing his work and my own without a marked revision of my salary upwards also. This was not to be, so I set my mind to leave as soon as my own contract expired.

Behind my back the World Bank then recruited an Indian national to take over as Chief Veterinary Research Officer. He was an academic virologist but had a notable weakness in that he had never worked in Africa before and had no experience of tryps and the tick-borne diseases enzootic to the continent. It was only after he had been recruited that a World Bank official asked me to stay on to back him up because of his lack of experience. I had been irritated at being passed over and said I would only consider staying on if I was paid the same World Bank salary as the new recruit and an extra five thousand dollars per annum for the experience which the bank official admitted the recruited man lacked. My generous offer was declined.

There was one last task I had to do before my contract ended. The PDU was in the process of creating a cattle ranch at Marial Bai a few miles north of Wau on the west bank of the Bahr-el-Ghazal, a major tributary of the White Nile with its headwaters in the borderlands with the Central African Republic and the Congo. Wau is some 450 miles northwest of Juba and a major trading centre. It is also a terminus of the Sudanese Railway, which stretched in those days throughout northern Sudan, linking Nyala in Darfur to Khartoum, Port Sudan on the Red Sea and Wadi Halfa on the Egyptian border. I had had to visit the ranch on several occasions because of disease outbreaks there, most notably an outbreak of anaplasmosis, another of the numerous tick-borne diseases of cattle.[60] The outbreak had been very virulent, with deaths 8-10 hours after the first signs of disease were apparent even when I injected a tetracycline solution directly intravenously. The trouble was that in a ranching situation it may be many hours, even days, before clinical signs are observed.

There was another observation I made at the time - the foundation stock were heifers bought in from local Dinka herdsmen. In their early days the heifers had become used to being herded and they failed to settle in to a ranching situation where they were free to graze an open paddock. Instead the animals would mass around the paddock gate waiting for a herdsman to come and take them out to graze, even though there was nothing to prevent them from grazing the paddock on their own.

Of course the heifers were bought in to be mated. The ranch manager, a very competent middle-aged Australian, Joe Ritson, had arranged to buy about a dozen premier beef and dairy bulls from farms and ranches around Nanyuki on the western slopes of Mt Kenya for the purpose and I was sent to collect them.

Bulls fuelled by testosterone have a propensity to fight, so down in Nairobi I engaged a couple of carpenters to make a dozen crates in which to incarcerate them for their long journey from Mt Kenya to Marial Bai. A lorry and trailer were chartered from Interfreight and with them came a Somali driver and a turnboy of the same ilk. I also recruited Kadhi Athman, who had been my assistant in

---

[60] Anaplasmosis is caused by *Anaplasma marginale*, a rickettsial organism. The lay term for the disease is gall sickness because of the jaundiced appearance of the tissues around the eyes and the lighter skin around the muzzle, vulva and elsewhere. The disease can also be transmitted by biting flies and on inadequately sterilized equipment such as hypodermic needles.

Mombasa, and another coastal man, Ahmed Hamza, whom I knew well to assist in handling the bulls.

It took a couple of days to load the bulls on to the lorry at the various farms around Nanyuki while also loading a ton of hay and 2000 litres of water in drums on the trailer, and to obtain all the necessary papers from the veterinary authorities to export the animals. Then we set off. There were two possible routes to Juba; one through Lodwar, an option I disliked because the Turkana are notorious cattle thieves, and the other through Uganda, a country which was very unsettled at that time following the ousting of Idi Amin, with a weak government in power and a low-level civil war going on in the districts west and north of Kampala. Neither option was attractive, but the Ugandan one seemed the lesser of two evils. With such problems in mind I had managed to 'borrow' a United Nations flag in Sudan and mounted it prominently on the front of the lorry. I hoped it would bamboozle both Ugandan customs authorities and rebellious soldiery.

It took about ten hours to drive from Nanyuki to the Ugandan border at Malaba, stopping for the first night on the road somewhere near Burnt Forest on the highlands west of the Rift Valley at a height of over 9000 feet. It was bitterly cold and I hoped the bulls' hides were thicker than my own. At Malaba, on the second day, it took about six hours to clear all the paperwork for the movement of the bulls and a new Land Rover which had been consigned to me in Nairobi and which I was driving as a back-up for the lorry. It was nightfall by the time the Malaba customs had been cleared. Many miles of forest lined the sections of the road between Malaba and Kampala, sections which were notorious for hijackings, so we spent the second night in the yard of the police station in Tororo, a nearby town lying on the southern slopes of Mount Elgon, a huge volcanic mass some 14,000 feet high which forms part of the boundary between Kenya and Uganda. The police were friendly and obviously quite intrigued by the bulls we were carrying, so we spent a comfortable night in their company, sleeping beside the lorry.

By midday the next day we had reached Kampala, where even more paperwork had to be completed. Then we set off northwards through districts which I knew were very unsettled. By nightfall we had reached Kiryandongo, about a hundred miles north of Kampala. It seemed the best place to camp for the night for there was a large mission hospital in Kiryandongo brilliantly lit by electric lights all around which I hoped would enhance our own security for I had little confidence for our safety sleeping on the open road.

The fourth day we rose early and by mid-morning made Gulu, a relatively large sprawling district headquarters. Here we were detained with other lorries destined for Sudan by the police because of insecurity on the road between Gulu and Nimule on the border, but after several hours we were allowed to proceed.

Then came the most hair-raising part of the journey. Every few miles we encountered road blocks manned by soldiers of the Uganda Army.[61] Their purpose was primarily, if not entirely, to enrich themselves, and the bulls certainly engaged their more gluttonous instincts. I had taken the precaution of stacking a large number of bank notes and cigarettes in plastic bags under the bulls' crates where customs officials and other covetous individuals were unlikely to look because of the accumulations of dung and urine

---

[61] The Uganda Army had been undisciplined since the mutiny of 1964. Murder, rape and theft went unpunished and any police who dared investigate such crimes were frequently killed. Inevitably it quite devastated agricultural production for there was no purpose in producing a surplus for market for it to be looted at the nearest road block. A friend of mine turned to planting trees to mature in 20 years for sale as telephone poles. 'At least soldiers can't steal whole trees,' he told me.

there. To assuage the soldiers' greed I distributed cash and cigarettes to the Somali driver and his mate and my two coastal assistants. We were stripped of it all at the first road block. Then it was time to replenish supplies from the cache under the bull crates. This procedure was repeated several times, but then came a difficulty. Two road blocks were so closely set up that I was unable to replenish supplies secretively out of sight of one group of thieves or the next, so the latter group had nothing to steal except the bulls. I absolutely refused to hand over a bull saying, with a certain economy of truthfulness, that they belonged to the United Nations. This provoked the soldiers' anger and the African members of the team were all rifle-butted. Perhaps my lighter skin saved me, for the bruising might have been more obvious.

Not that we were out of the wood. A soldier examining my passport noticed that though it was a British one, I had been born in Argentina, so obviously I was a spy. God knows what benefit a spy would have in escorting bulls to Sudan so I explained that as my father was British I was British also but that my mother had been in Argentina at the time of my birth. Within a moment I was put up against the truck with two rifles pointed at me. I wasn't really frightened; I had no time to be. In my mind it was all play-acting and I called their bluff. It was a nasty moment, but we were allowed to proceed.

Some miles later we stopped to replenish the bribe packs and to have a quick smoke to settle our nerves. It was the wrong moment to stop, for a few minutes later an army lorry hurtled past, the soldiers in the back shouting 'We're going to kill you, mzungu.' Just as night was falling the border gate at Nimule came in sight but it was being closed when we saw it. I felt that we would be a lot more secure if we could stay over on the Sudanese side, but the border guard was adamant that the gate would not be reopened until eight o'clock the next morning. We spent a rather restless night within a yard or two of the border, fearing an attack by the Ugandan soldiers. If we were attacked, I told my helpers, we should abandon the bulls and dive under the border gate in the hope of getting protection on the Sudanese side. Luckily the soldiers must have been deterred by the proximity of the gate and we passed the night undisturbed.

The next day was a Saturday. I had just seven days before my contract ended. London beckoned, for I had been asked to attend an interview there a few days later for a possible post in Botswana. Fortunately the Sudanese border officials were easy-going and by midday we were in Juba. Here there was yet more red tape to unravel; import documents for the bulls, the lorry and the newly-obtained Land Rover had to be processed, but it could not be done until the following Monday. It seemed cruel to confine the bulls to their crates any longer so we unloaded them at the FAO farm. I was relieved to see that they all were sound and, I'm sure, they must have been pleased to have their feet on solid ground again after being rocked around on 800 miles of poor roads for five days.

I could see no purpose in escorting the bulls the next 450 miles to Marial Bai. There would be no more security or documentation problems to contend with and I felt that some of the local Sudanese staff were very capable of escorting the bulls the rest of the way. The project director thought differently. So on the Tuesday morning I set off with the bulls on a 900-mile round trip to Marial

Bai with just four days to go before I was scheduled to fly out of the country. To me it seemed a vindictive act on the part of the project director.[62] On the appalling roads of central Southern Sudan, the lorry and its trailer carrying bulls and water were only able to cover about 15 miles an hour. Over the next 17 hours we moved about 250 miles and, unable to keep my eyes open a moment longer, it was two in the morning before I called a halt. We watered the bulls and then crashed out. At six in the morning we were on the go again and it wasn't until eight that evening that we reached our destination. We had been driving 31 hours out of the previous 36 and were totally exhausted.

Early next morning we unloaded the bulls. I was apprehensive that they might have injured themselves on the last laps, for the crates began to disintegrate from all the shaking they had undergone on the dreadful roads, exposing numerous four-inch nails with which the bulls might have spiked their feet. But it was not so and I was pleased to note one of the bulls mount a nearby heifer within five minutes of being unloaded. The trip hadn't been a total waste. One Dinka herdsman did complain that I had brought bulls with very small horns, for the Dinka prize cattle with large, lyre-shaped horns.

As soon as the bulls were unloaded I set off back to Juba in the Land Rover with the two coastal men who had helped with the feeding and watering of the bulls on the long journey from Nanyuki. Without the lorry we could make better speed, but we

---

[62] I had had a very angry confrontation with him some time earlier. A young British VSO working with an agricultural project within the PDU had been diagnosed with hydatid cysts in the liver by a Sudanese doctor, Dr Hakim; a man for whom I had a lot of respect. Hakim had recommended the young man be flown to Nairobi for surgery but the project director, a man with no medical qualification whatever, had vetoed this and suggested he undergo surgery in Juba. The surgical unit in Juba had a poor hygiene record and I was aware that several cases of tetanus had followed surgery there. As the only person within the PDU with a medical background I had taken up the VSO's cause and had tried to convince the project director of the very grave danger if a cyst ruptured, for it could lead to the development of numerous daughter cysts within the abdominal cavity or even peritonitis which would very likely have been fatal in that environment. In the end I was able to get the veto reversed.

hadn't gone more than 120 miles before I diverted to avoid a section of road that had been flooded. There were several alternative routes marked by the tracks of the heavy lorries that had passed before. I took the wrong alternative but as there were no road signs I didn't know that.

I drove on and on for about six hours before coming to a wide river. It could only have been the Nile. It was then about eight o'clock at night and it took no time to reckon that I was about 180 miles off course, but time was running out and there was nothing for it but to follow the river upstream until we reached Juba.

We eventually reached Juba about two in the morning, having been on the road, if that is the correct term, for 16 hours. It was then that I found I had left my house keys back in Marial Bai. There was nothing for it but to go to the project director's house and ask if he had a master key. He wasn't exactly pleased to be woken up and said he didn't wish to talk to an Argentinian because Britain was now at war with Argentina over the Falkland Islands - a fact of which I was totally ignorant, having been tied up moving the bulls for the previous three weeks. I was too tired even to think it was funny. I had just over thirty hours to pack up before leaving Juba.

Incredibly, the project director was still capable of one more vindictive act. He then ordered me to make an inventory of all the laboratory equipment, chemical reagents, household furnishings and other items on the laboratory site. He had never instructed other senior staff on their departure to make such an inventory, least of all Ansell, whom he knew very well was regularly stealing project equipment for his own use. I objected strongly, saying I was exhausted and had a lot of personal things to attend to in my last day in Juba, but this usually indecisive man said if I didn't do so he would not allow me to board the flight to Nairobi the next day. There was nothing in my contract which would have enabled him to prohibit my departure on completion of my contract but recourse to law in Southern Sudan at that time would have been a costly and futile action, so I had no alternative but to comply. It was 11 o'clock that Friday night when I completed the inventory, though some of the numbers were pure fabrications.

Some weeks after returning to my home in Lamu I received a letter from Yusuf Omar, the driver who had told me of the intention to kill Ansell. In the letter, Yusuf wrote that I had been right in saying the laboratory would cease to function soon after my departure. In fact it had taken just five days, for the simple reason that nobody had thought to order any diesel for the generators which ran all the laboratory equipment, the air conditioners, the borehole pump and the cold room in which vaccines were stored. Once again, it seemed, the World Bank had successfully recruited yet another incompetent manager.

CHAPTER 12

Botswana

It was July 20th, 1982. Sirens screamed down the highways and byways of central London. Every ambulance, fire engine and police car was trying to get somewhere - fast. A bomb set by the IRA had exploded outside the Knightsbridge Barracks killing men and horses, and then another in Regent's Park killing yet more people. More bombs were suspected, hidden in vehicles in Piccadilly and the Mall, and even in the underground, bringing the workings of the city almost to a standstill.

The sound of the sirens did not contribute to my sense of ease as I faced my four interrogators in the Crown Agent's offices in Millbank. That very day I was being interviewed for the post of Deputy Director of Veterinary Services in Botswana, a post which primarily involved disease control.

My unsettled feeling wasn't due only to the bombings. The railwaymen had been on strike and to ensure I would be at the interview on time I had had to travel up to London by coach the previous day and stayed the night just off Harley Street in the *Domus Medica* of the Royal Society of Medicine, of which I was then a Fellow. There was at least one compensation for the inconvenience - I had been able at the last minute to get a ticket to hear José Carreras sing the part of Rodolfo in *La Bohème* at Covent Garden.

In the morning I had walked down to the National Gallery, where I spent a couple of hours trying to calm my nerves before going down Whitehall to Millbank where the interview was to take place. It was then that all hell let loose. Despite it all, I must have acquitted myself better than the other contenders (possibly because I was more used to crises, it being just two months since being put up against a truck and having two rifles aimed at me), for I was notified soon afterwards that I had got the appointment.

This, in fact, was my second interview for a job in Botswana, the first one having been immediately after returning to Britain from Juba when I had been interviewed for a post as a senior veterinary officer in Botswana. This second interview was to determine my suitability for an upgrade.

Botswana, or the Bechuanaland Protectorate as it had formerly been called, had been one of the most neglected of the British territories. Even its administrative capital, Mafikeng, had been outside the country, in the Cape Province of South Africa. So at Independence in 1966 a new purpose-built capital was built near a station called Gaborone on the Cape Town-Bulawayo railway line. The new capital was an architect-designed city with a depressing sameness about all its buildings, which were laid out in a geometrically recurrent pattern. A central mall, where vehicles were banned during daylight hours, was the predominant feature, with government offices and parliament situated a little to the west of this complex. The most impressive building was the headquarters of the Debswana Company, a joint venture between the De Beers Company and the Botswana Government, which was reputed to be as deep as it was tall and in the depths of which were kept, under very tight security, the diamonds the company mined. The only old parts in all this new development was a small railway station and a cemetery, a mile from the eastern edge of the town on the other side of the airfield, in which were buried those men who had been killed in Dr Jameson's ill-fated raid over the New Year of 1895-96 to capture the Transvaal from the Boers for Britain.

I was allocated a small bungalow near the golf club with a totally featureless garden - more a building site than a garden. Within a month I was burgled, and I used the burglary as an excuse to ask for a move to a newly-built complex of flats close to the cemetery which was somewhat more secure.

Botswana had the good fortune to have as its first president Seretse Khama, the paramount chief of the Bamangwato, the largest of the group of Setswana-speaking people who inhabit Botswana and the neighbouring Transvaal. Seretse, being a man of rank and substance already, could abstain from the corruptive influences which was characteristic of many of the other leaders of the newly independent African states. The Batswana, as the Setswana-speaking people are collectively called, also had the good fortune to have a tradition of free speech in the *kgotla*, a meeting place close to every chieftain's compound where matters of security, land tenure and other issues could be discussed by all adult men without restraint. The third element of good fortune for the country was that the great majority of its people are Setswana speakers, although there are a few minority groups, among them the Kalanga of the northeast, the Herero, refugees from the genocide perpetrated on their fellows in the German colony of South West Africa (now Namibia) early in the 20th century and the indigenous Bushmen, more properly termed the San people. Thus Botswana was blessed from its start with a system of government which had a very low level of corruption, was truly democratic and was not riven by tribal jealousies.

But Botswana was not blessed with any great wealth at the time of independence - one reason for its neglect by the colonial authorities. Most of the country, which is a little larger than France, is covered by the Kalahari Desert with rainfall of about six inches a year; only along the western edges is the rainfall sufficient for crop production. However soon after independence diamond-bearing deposits were found at Orapa on the eastern fringe of the Kalahari and a mine was opened there in 1971, followed by three more over the years.[63] These have transformed the economy of Botswana.

Jack Falconer had been the first director of veterinary services in the newly-independent and poverty-stricken country and he and Seretse Khama worked together to develop a beef industry, cattle-keeping being the traditional occupation of the Batswana. The trouble was that the country was not free from foot-and-mouth disease, which severely limited export markets. The European Economic Community (EEC), being quite the most lucrative of the export markets, was the most favoured but the EEC was in the process of eradicating FMD from Europe and had imposed stringent controls on the import of animal products from infected countries. As I came to realize later, it showed considerable foresight and courage by both men to bring FMD under control and establish an export market for Botswana beef.

By the time of my arrival in the country sixteen years later, Botswana was one of the two or three countries in Africa which

---

[63] The other diamond mines are at Letlhakane, Jwaneng and Damtshaa.

had reached a sufficiently effective degree of disease control to allow it to export beef to the European market, with a modern abattoir in Lobatse boasting better levels of hygiene than I had ever seen in Britain. In addition, a vaccine production laboratory, the Botswana Vaccine Institute (BVI), had been built on the outskirts of Gaborone capable of producing foot-and-mouth and other vaccines in liaison with the French pharmaceutical firm Merieux.

Jack Falconer had retired a few years before my arrival but had remained in the country as manager of the BVI. His place as director of veterinary services had been taken by Martin Mannothoko, a large man with a wispy beard in his late thirties, a graduate of the Nairobi veterinary school. Martin was not a Motswana but a Kalanga from north-eastern Botswana, a people related to the Ndebele of Matabeleland in western Zimbabwe. From what I could gather, though he never said it, he had been given a hard time by Falconer in his younger days and that, I think, made it hard for him to get along with the British vets, who were the most numerous of the vets in the veterinary department - though the repulsive apartheid policies just across the border in South Africa may also have contributed to his wariness towards expatriate veterinary officers. Nonetheless I had very considerable respect for the man, as did the other British vets. He was quick to make decisions and had the courage to stand up to politicians instead of acquiescing to their demands.

There were times when we disagreed, for there are often more ways than one to control a disease, but always we were able to resolve our differences. Just as Botswana was fortunate in having Seretse Khama as its first president, so it was fortunate in having

Martin as its first Motswana director of veterinary services. It was not so fortunate in its second director.

Three quarters of the country was free from FMD. Only in the northwest corner, an area known as Ngamiland containing the wildlife-rich Okavango Delta, was FMD enzootic in the buffalo population, though the buffalo themselves were symptomless carriers. For years many wildlife experts in southern Africa tried to deny that buffalo had a role in the propagation of the disease. In Zimbabwe attempts had been made to infect susceptible bovine calves by stabling them together with known infected but symptomless buffalo, but the calves had remained healthy. Even attempts to compromise the calves' immunity with injections of corticosteroids failed. But then in one such experiment the buffalo got too boisterous and they were castrated and dehorned. Immediately afterwards the calves developed signs of FMD. Thus it was hypothesized that stress on the buffalo allowed the multiplication of their virus load to such an extent that they became infectious to the calves stabled with them.

Two measures were used to contain the disease in Ngamiland. The first was to vaccinate all the cattle in the district, about three hundred thousand, twice a year with a polyvalent vaccine containing antigens to the FMD virus types known to be present in the delta.[64] The second measure, much derided by the wildlife experts, was a very solid 'buffalo fence' restricting the buffalo to within the delta but allowing access in places for cattle to get to water in the dry season.

The whole of the country was divided into disease control zones. Ngamiland was the only zone in which vaccination was

---

[64] A polyvalent vaccine is one which provides immunity to a number of strains of an infective organism whereas a monovalent vaccine provides immunity to one strain only..

practised. Adjacent to it were zones 50 to 80 miles wide in which cattle were not vaccinated. Vaccination can mask signs of disease so that vaccinated animals can act as symptomless carriers, much as the buffalo of the Okavango Delta do. The unvaccinated cattle in the zones adjacent to Ngamiland were, in fact, sentinels that would exhibit the disease if there were any escape of virus from the delta area. No beef from cattle in Ngamiland nor in the adjacent zones were eligible for the EEC market, whereas beef from cattle from all other zones was acceptable.

Other measures to prevent the virus reaching Europe were also in place. FMD virus is susceptible to low levels of acidity. Rigor mortis is a process which develops immediately after death resulting from the formation of lactic acid in the musculature and other tissues. Only in the blood-forming tissues of the bone marrow does acidification not take place. Thus the Botswana Meat Commission (BMC) only exported boneless beef to the EEC. This beef was much in demand for the making of steak and kidney pies and other food processing purposes for two reasons: it was leaner, and because the cattle had taken more years to mature on grass, their meat was more flavoursome than the beef of quick-growing steers fed on barley and other supplements in Europe.

The excised bone was made into bone meal, which was much in demand by Batswana cattle farmers as a supplement for their own animals, for the veldt of southern Africa is notably deficient in phosphorus. Young calves given bone meal make conspicuous gains in skeletal growth.

Each of the disease control zones was demarcated by fences with gates at intervals, manned by veterinary staff, to control movements of animals and livestock products from one zone to another. When one self-important ambassador complained that his car had been searched, the president replied that his car was also searched whenever he passed from one zone to another. The fact that illicit game meat was found in the ambassador's car didn't help his argument that his diplomatic immunities had been infringed.

Over a thousand men were employed to inspect the more than 2000 miles of fencing between the zones at regular intervals as well as the fences along the international borders with South Africa, Namibia and Zimbabwe and to man the transit gates. The fences certainly had a restrictive effect on the movement of the larger wild animals, especially wildebeest. I regretted this but also felt that it was worth paying that price so that the Batswana could have access to the lucrative meat markets of Europe. The revenues from beef sales went into the cattle owners' pockets, whereas the royalties from diamonds went into the Treasury. Wherever one went, conversation often centred on the future demand for cattle by the BMC and the likely price offered in the following months. Beef sales were clearly an important issue for many rural Batswana.

Infuriatingly, the game department offered little or no cooperation with the veterinary department. When the game department was asked for its opinion on the siting of a zonal fence to minimize any obstruction to wildlife movement, there was no response. When I brought to their attention the large-scale poaching of wildlife by white South African hunters for the making of biltong, the department took no action.[65] The game department, together with the owners of the various lodges in the Okavango Delta, depended on the support of the European media, of which

---

[65] Biltong is sun-dried meat, what Americans call 'jerky', now a popular snack food.

the *Financial Times* was foremost, and of European royalty to pursue an anti-veterinary department vendetta. Martin was rightly angered by these unjustified attacks and mentioned to me once that he thought the critics would only be placated if Botswana reverted back to the way it was in David Livingstone's day.

Not that Botswana had been an earthly paradise even then. In the 19th century European settlers had been allowed to establish fenced farms along the western banks of the Limpopo River, the boundary between the then Transvaal Republic and Bechuanaland, to prevent Boers from capturing the local people for slave labour (the Limpopo, by the way, is not a great grey-green greasy river as described by Rudyard Kipling but, at least in its upper reaches, a diminutive, slow-moving, forty-foot wide, muddy stream). Later, Cecil Rhodes encouraged settlers from Cape Province to put down roots in Ghanzi, in the west of the country, to prevent encroachment by Germans from their colony in South West Africa.

My work as a deputy director was very different from much of the work that I had done previously. Now I was rarely concerned with the financial aspects of running the department (a chore that had taken up many hours of each week when I had been a district veterinary officer in Uganda), for that headache fell to a second deputy director, Eddie Bradley. Eddie was a squarely-built, silver-haired Durham man with an overriding interest in food and golf and he could be loquacious on both subjects. With his wife Jean, whom he had met when both were students at the Dick in Edinburgh, they had been in Botswana for over a decade; Eddie first working in the abattoir at Lobatse as part of the meat inspectorate and Jean in the veterinary diagnostic laboratory situated at that time beside the Princess Marina hospital in central Gaborone. They soon became good friends and I was very dependent on Eddie's experience for the first few months while I settled into the job.

English usage in Botswana was fairly standard but there were some divergences to which I adjusted over time. Nobody was ever dead, they were late. This caused some confusion one morning when I called for the office messenger and was told he was late.

'Well tell him to come and see me when he comes in' I ordered.

'He can't, he's late' was the response.

'I know he's late; just tell him to come and see me when he comes in' I repeated.

'But he can't, he's late.'

It took me some minutes before I realized that we were talking at cross purposes.

No woman was ever pregnant (that was for some reason a rude word), but expectant. And there was one word in very common usage; if an object or a vehicle was damaged or out of order it was invariably 'buggerdup'.

One of my more routine office jobs was to issue movement permits for animals and their products from one zone to another and into and out of the country. Most of the international trade was with South Africa. Regrettably the then prevalent racist attitudes in that country led to many South African veterinarians issuing permits for animals to enter Botswana without any consultation with the Botswana authorities. This led to frequent calls by me to the director of veterinary services in Pretoria, Dr van der Merwe, to complain - he was, I must say, very cooperative.

The final crunch came when I had to order the destruction of fifty thousand live chickens which had been detained at one of the inter-zonal check points on their way through Botswana to the South African army in the Caprivi Strip without any import or movement permits. The people at the checkpoint must have seen this as a major windfall, but to prevent any dissemination of potential disease I ordered the burning of all the carcases. I suspect a few were burnt in a culinary manner, but at least they were no longer a disease hazard. But I had made my point and thereafter there was a regular stream of South Africans to my office requesting the required import/export and other permits.

Strict movement controls were and are a very effective means of preventing the dissemination of disease. Even game meat and trophies required movement permits, which revealed to me how much game meat was being poached by white South Africans and exported as biltong to South Africa. Poaching was a matter for the game department, but every time I rang its offices to inform them of a consignment of illegally acquired biltong, there was some excuse or another not to take action forthwith. I would procrastinate in issuing the necessary export permits but I could not do so for ever and if the poachers smelt a rat they would often make off quickly in an attempt to enter South Africa by some illicit route, of which I suspect there were many.

At the time of my arrival in Botswana there was only one other Motswana vet in the department apart from Martin. I will call him Peter Molatse, not his real name. Molatse was a senior veterinary officer in head office. Except for one Ugandan and a Zambian, all the other vets were expatriates. I was concerned about this overreliance on expatriates and tried to remedy the situation by teaming up with a lecturer in biology in the University of Botswana to find suitable candidates to send to veterinary school. We found only one young man with the necessary academic accomplishments and the desire to become a veterinarian.

There were no veterinary schools in Botswana and I favoured the school in Harare, Zimbabwe, which had an excellent reputation. Unfortunately the ministry of education then stepped in behind my back and packed the young man off to a veterinary school in Cuba. If nothing else, he would have the initial problem of having to learn Spanish.

At about the same time a newly-graduated Motswana veterinarian returned from the Soviet Union. It had taken him eight years to graduate, held back, I suspect, by language difficulties. His diploma showed he had spent considerable time in learning Marxist-Leninist dialectic, fire-fighting and some veterinary medicine and with the diploma came a licence to practise veterinary medicine in all the countries of the world except the Soviet Union. Martin didn't much care for the Soviet presumption and sent him to Harare to get a proper veterinary degree there.

Molatse was not one of the most pleasant of men. Unfortunately he made the overdependence on expatriate vets a racial issue whereas, in fact, it was simply a manpower issue. This, of course, did not make his relations with the expatriate vets easy. At a later stage I put him in charge of veterinary education and manpower requirements in order to take the pressure off this tense situation.

I had already had one altercation with Molatse, when a group of Herero exiles in Ngamiland with about six hundred cattle broke through the international cordon fence between Namibia and Botswana in an attempt to return to their traditional grazing lands in northern Namibia. The trouble was that CBPP (pleuropneumonia) was enzootic in parts of northern Namibia. The Namibian veterinary authorities did not want the cattle there and I didn't want them back if they were infected with CBPP, which had not been seen in Botswana since the end of the 19th century. However, on being assured by the director of veterinary services in Windhoek that the Herero cattle had never been closer than a hundred miles from any foci of the disease, I issued a permit for them to return to Ngamiland and, at the same time, sent a stern warning to the Herero leaders that if such an illegal movement occurred again I would order the destruction of the cattle.

At this point Molatse came to see me, full of criticism for the action I had taken. He proceeded to lecture me on the terrible consequences of CBPP, a disease he had never seen and of which I had seen all too much in my days in Karamoja. I didn't take kindly to his admonitions and told him so.

Some months after my arrival I had a letter from a university contemporary, David Wilkins, who was then Chief Veterinary Officer of the RSPCA in Britain. He had received a letter from the ladies of the Cape of Good Hope SPCA complaining of several acts of cruelty within Botswana that had come to light in the South African press. With David's letter was a copy of a letter the good ladies had written to the president of Botswana. It was couched in the hectoring terms that they might have used to their African house servants and castigated him for tolerating such cruelty in Botswana, so I was not surprised that the President had failed to respond, which was another of the ladies' complaints.

As the perpetrators of the several acts of cruelty were a South African film crew and the world-renowned South African heart surgeon Christiaan Barnard, the ladies might have done better to direct their criticisms to the South African SPCA. However I immediately contacted Derek Cullinan, a good friend and head of the Botswana CID, for more information. He then told me what he knew; it was appalling. At one point the film crew had snared a lion cub and dragged it behind a vehicle so that a clip could be filmed of a lioness stalking though the grass. Even more cruel was the shooting of a zebra in the belly leaving a trail of blood, so that another clip of a lion stalking a zebra could be filmed. But quite the cruellest act of all was to shoot a wildebeest in the pelvis, rendering it unable to move so that the son of one of the crew members could use it for target practice. On the basis of this information Derek had issued warrants for the arrest of all those involved if ever they should return to Botswana soil.

Other duties in the veterinary department's head office were not those that had been taught me in veterinary school. One of them was to answer questions that had been tabled to the minister of Agriculture in parliament. This was always done first thing in the morning so that the minister could have time to scrutinize the answer before facing parliament in the afternoon. Members of Parliament, having tabled a question, were then allowed to put a supplementary question to the Minister. The tabled question was usually over a matter of fact and was not a problem; the supplementary question, still unasked, posed the biggest hazard for it was a matter of guesswork. If asked by a member of the opposition, it was likely that the supplementary question would aim at embarrassing the minister in some way, while if it was asked by a member of the ruling party it was likely to be something that was of concern to his own constituents. Fortunately Eddie was far more *au fait* than I with the politics of the country and usually fielded the questions, but in his absence the questions would devolve on me.

Another parliamentary duty was to attend the House when it went into committee to discuss budgetary matters. On these occasions the Speaker of the House vacated the Speaker's Chair and chaired the meeting from the floor of the House, thus making proceedings more informal. Minions such as myself sat in a small room like a theatre box under the Strangers' Gallery, facing the Speaker. From time to time a messenger would bring a hand-written note from the minister asking for help if he found himself in difficulties.

I didn't much care for our minister. He was a rotund little man without any indication of humour who owned a Chinese restaurant on the outskirts of the town, which may have been the cause of his shape. To enhance his political popularity he wanted the veterinary department to provide clinical services throughout the country. There were only about a dozen vets in the country at any one time and with a population close to three million cattle spread over an area of 230,000 square miles, this would have overtaxed them considerably. The vets did what they could, but in my opinion, their primary duty was to control the spread of livestock diseases and safeguard beef sales to the EEC.

My introduction to parliament had come about when a visiting German professor of veterinary medicine had asked to meet the President, saying he had been advised to do so by the chairman of the Merieux pharmaceutical company. As the professor had only a few hours to go before catching a plane out of the country I thought it a tall order, but I phoned his private secretary to ask for an appointment. A few minutes later the secretary rang back to say the President was in the House and would meet us there.

Quett Masire, as he was then called,[66] the successor to Seretse Khama, entertained us affably to tea in the Tea Room. Then the German asked to be shown around the parliamentary building. I really thought he had gone too far in his demands on the President but Masire obliged us and showed us round the building which had two Chambers, though the second chamber, the House of Chiefs, had only a ceremonial function, before finally taking us to the Strangers' Gallery, where he sat with us while we watched the proceedings of the House below us.

Another duty I had was to scrutinize many of the consultancy reports commissioned by the government in so far as they might relate to animal health. If a report concerned secondary education my interest would centre on the teaching of biological subjects because of the paucity of Batswana veterinarians; if on a projected trans-Kalahari railway I would be concerned if any fencing adjacent to the line might interfere with wildlife or livestock movement. One of the more outlandish proposals was to build a canal from the upper reaches of the Zambezi through northern Botswana to supply water to the city of Johannesburg. Apart from the likely obstruction to animal movements, I suspected that local cattle owners might think it the longest and handiest cattle watering trough in the world and the result would be complete devastation of the very fragile plant cover in the canal's vicinity.

With all these office duties there were seldom opportunities to

---

[66] later Sir Ketumile Masire

see any animals, let alone put one's hand on one, so I was glad to get out in the field on occasion. The twice-yearly vaccinations in Ngamiland were, of course, the best breaks and I would usually take a rifle and fishing rod with me - not that I much cared to use a rifle, despite being a Crown Marksman in my school's Combined Cadet Force, for I think a live animal is much more beautiful than a dead one. Shooting for trophies never appealed to me, though shooting for the pot was a different matter.

The main town in Ngamiland is Maun. The administrative centre had previously been further north on the eastern edge of the Okavango Delta, but its citizens had been forcibly evicted after sleeping sickness had spread there and caused considerable mortality among the human population. The town was little more than a one-street dorp, but it had an airfield to cater for the many tourists who came to visit the delta and was home to a wild collection of expatriates, many of them hard-drinking, who had formed an esoteric, Masonic-like society known as the Pheasant Pluckers. Maun was also the centre of the biannual cattle vaccination campaigns. Up to thirty vaccination teams, recruited from all over the country, operated simultaneously, each one usually led by a Motswana field officer or veterinary assistant, so that most of the three hundred thousand cattle in Ngamiland were injected within three to four weeks, with a few tidying-up vaccinations afterwards carried out by the local Ngamiland-based staff.

One of the boons of the vaccination campaigns was the tons of ice brought up at regular intervals from the BMC abattoir in Lobatse to preserve the vaccine. Each team had a large sturdy cold box for vaccine storage, which when filled with ice usually lasted the best

271

part of a week before needing to be replenished. Wild melons grow in profusion on the dry savannah country that characterizes most of Botswana. In fact the profusion of melons is so great that David Livingstone watered his oxen with them when he crossed the Kalahari in 1849 on an expedition in which he became the first white man to view Lake Ngami, a lake which might better be described as an extensive shallow puddle. So chilled melon and iced South African wines were frequent accompaniments to evening meals on safari during vaccination campaigns.

On my return to Gaborone after the completion of my first vaccination campaign in May 1983, I was due to accompany Martin to Paris later in the month to attend the annual OIE Conference.[67] The OIE was created before the United Nations Organization and is as a result free from the machinations of politicians and diplomats. It is an organization of chief veterinary officers of most of the countries of the world and has as its main function the control of animal diseases and their dissemination worldwide through trade in animals and animal products such as meat, milk and hides. In the corridors, between open sessions of the conference, the chief veterinary officers of neighbouring countries are able to sort out their trans-boundary problems in an informal manner free from political interference, and I was quick to note that the representatives of Iran and Iraq, countries which were at war with each other at the time, seated together apparently amicably.

Paris, of course, has other attractions including, at the end of May, the tennis championships at Roland Garros, but what remains the highlight of my visit that year was a visit to a nightclub in the Bois de Boulogne where the *chanteuse* Juliette Greco performed.

---

[67] Office International des Epizooties, or as it is now called, in English, the World Organisation for Animal Health.

Though she was a woman of a certain age, she oozed eroticism, but not in any coarse way, and I wondered what the many ladies in the audience thought as she skilfully seduced their male escorts.

There was an absurd incident on my way to Paris. At the time there was no airport at Gaborone to take large planes, so it was necessary to get a shuttle to Johannesburg and connect there to an international airline. As so often happened, on the day I wanted to travel the shuttle was full. Jack Falconer had the same problem, so we drove to Jo'burg together. At the frontier with South Africa I was detained for about half an hour while a telephone call was made to Pretoria to determine whether the two books I had taken with me to read were dangerous in any way. One, *A History of East and Central Africa* was possibly subversive; the second, *The French Lieutenant's Woman*, possibly pornographic. The irrational apartheid policies of South Africa certainly engendered a degree of paranoia in those people who had to enforce it.

Having heard from my mother soon after returning from the vaccination campaign that my father had suffered a stroke, I flew over to England immediately after the last session of the conference to see my father and stayed a few days. His brain had been badly damaged by the stroke. I had seldom been close to my father and his inability to speak clearly increased the distance between us at a time when I wished I could have closed the gap. I feared that it would be beyond my mother's capability to nurse him after he was discharged from hospital, so I was relieved when a few weeks later he died. I think, secretly, she was too.

Soon after my return from Paris I was informed by Howard Darkin, the veterinary officer in Lobatse, that the president had moved a number of cattle from his ranch near Ghanzi in the centre of the Kalahari to a feedlot he had near Lobatse where he wanted to fatten them in anticipation of selling them to the BMC. Many of them had died soon after arrival. Howard had diagnosed the cause of death as heartwater.[68] In due course I had a call from the president's private secretary asking me to call on him. As I was somewhat informally dressed at the time in shorts and open-necked shirt I asked for half an hour to go home and change into something more formal.

When I arrived at the president's office the private secretary showed me into a small waiting room, telling me that the president was chairing a cabinet meeting. I feared that I might be waiting a long time, but within a quarter of an hour I was shown into his office.

'Have I kept you waiting long?' was his first question.

I told him that I had only been waiting a short time.

'I would have closed the meeting if only I had known' was his response.

His patent informality appealed to me. He told me of the cattle deaths and I was glad that Howard had briefed me on them. I explained to him the disease and its means of transmission and suggested that his cattle had probably been infected on arrival at Lobatse, where rainfall was higher and the environment more suitable for Amblyomma ticks, and that his animals were probably very susceptible because in the arid Kalahari they had rarely been exposed to those particular ticks, nor the causative agent of heartwater. I was also able to advise him on how to prevent such a misfortune again by immunizing the animals before they left Ghanzi.[69]

A year later, in 1984, another consignment of the president's

---

[68] Heartwater is a disease of cattle and sheep, caused by a rickettsia (*Cowdria ruminantium*) which is transmitted by ticks of the Amblyomma genus

[69] The means of immunization is by infecting the animals artificially with a culture of *Cowdria ruminantium* and treating them with a tetracycline injection as soon as there is a temperature reaction. Obviously such a procedure carries some risk as the infecting agent is not benign.

cattle from Ghanzi met the same fate. At the time he was busy campaigning in a general election. In due course, his Democratic Party won the election for the fourth consecutive time. According to people like Eddie, the results of a general election were known within a day and the new cabinet appointed a few hours later. Not so in 1984. As before, the election results were known by the evening of the day after the election, but no announcement of the new cabinet appointments was made.

A day passed and then another, and still no announcement. Rumours began to spread among the chattering classes, some of them quite wild. I knew little about the political machinations of the country but was hoping that our rotund little minister might be reshuffled or even dropped. Then late on the third day the cabinet appointments were announced. The little man had retained his post as Minister of Agriculture.

At mid-morning the next day I had a call from the president's private secretary asking me to call on him. I did as I was bid.

'It's about my cattle. I know you warned me and told me how to prevent deaths from happening again' the president opened. It was almost an apology. 'But I was so wrapped up in the election campaign I had no time for anything else.'

I said I understood and suggested how we might control the situation. At that point a woman came in with a tray of tea and biscuits for us. When she had gone I congratulated the president on his election victory but told him that the town was buzzing with rumours because of the delay in announcing cabinet appointments.

'Go on tell me, what sort of rumours?' he urged me. I told him what I had heard and included a snide remark about the rotund little minister.

He laughed. 'There's no truth in any of them. I'll tell you what really happened. My wife and I were at the polling station when it opened at 7 o'clock, as you will have seen in the newspapers. Then we drove down to Lobatse and I spent the next three days treating my sick cattle.'

'Surely you could have got your farm manager to do the necessary?'

'If you want a job well done, you do it yourself' he countered. My estimation of the man went up another notch. It was yet another indication of the importance the Batswana attach to their cattle and the good sense of the president.

There was, however, one occasion when the president and I had a slight difference. It was late one Monday afternoon when I was summoned to the cabinet room. Obviously Martin should have attended the cabinet but he was out of town. When I got there I found the whole cabinet in session accompanied by the chief of police and the head of the army. I and the lady serving tea around the table were clearly the juniors in such august company.

Evidently some crisis was afoot and it wasn't long before it was revealed. At the time there was an insurgency in western Zimbabwe among the Ndebele, which was cruelly being put down by Mugabe's government, assisted by North Korean army units. As a consequence Joshua Nkomo, the leader of the Ndebele, accompanied by many of his followers, had fled into Botswana, bringing their livestock with them, as is so often the case with refugees who have no other movable assets. Joshua Nkomo was a huge man and my first thought was that he would have flattened the boundary fence along the Shashe river, which formed the boundary with Zimbabwe at that point, as he climbed over it to reach safety. But a more important point rapidly overshadowed it. I knew that there had been some outbreaks of foot-and-mouth in western Zimbabwe, though the extent was not fully known because of the insecurity there. The possibility that the refugees' cattle might introduce the disease into Botswana was very real and would certainly compromise the country's export market to the EEC, so I voiced my concerns to the president, who was chairing the meeting. He seemed uninterested in my observations and quickly moved on to the political and security issues involved. I could see no point in his inviting me to attend the cabinet if my views were ignored, so eventually I repeated my concerns.

'Thank you, Dr Minor' the president remarked courteously, 'but I have heard your comments already.'

'I know, sir, but you seem not to have understood them.' It was a disrespectful response, but I felt confident that the tradition of free speech in *kgotla* assemblies also carried over into cabinet meetings, though certainly such confidence would have been misplaced in most other African countries.

At this point a very senior cabinet minister realized the import of my warning about the risks involved and fought my corner for me, allowing me to sit back and relax temporarily.

One product for which I was frequently issuing export permits were Karakul pelts. The fat-tailed Karakul sheep are natives of the arid steppes of central Asia and are able to forage and thrive under hard conditions. German colonists had brought them to their colony of South West Africa early in the 20th century and their husbandry had then spread to the south-western part of Botswana and adjacent parts of the northern Cape, where similar desert conditions obtained. Karakul pelts, often referred to as astrakhan, are particularly valued for the making of hats and the facings on the lapels of overcoats. As I had little idea of the industry, I decided to visit southwest Botswana, driving, because of the better roads there, through Vryburg and Kuruman in the northern Cape before turning north and crossing the Molopo river back into Botswana to meet with producers and traders.

Despite the high value of the pelts it seemed to me that neither producers nor traders made much money from the trade, as I have seldom seen such poor people in any country of Africa. Most of them were of Khoikhoi origin.[70] The highest value pelts are those with the tightest curl and are usually obtained from lambs killed immediately after birth, before the amniotic fluids have dried. An understandable consequence of this practice is that the next generation of sheep is derived from lambs born remote from the farmstead and found only days later, and these lambs and their dams are precisely those animals which do not flock together - in other words, loners - thus making their shepherding doubly difficult.

Much of the Kalahari is gently undulating country with a low plant cover and a few scrubby acacia trees wherever the sparse rainfall pools in the few wet summer months. In the eastern boundaries with Zimbabwe and the northern Transvaal, where

---

[70] The Khoikhoi, or Hottentots as early European settlers called them, were some of the earliest people of southern Africa and related to the San people (Bushmen) but whereas the San were and are hunter-gatherers, the Khoikhoi practised agriculture and herded cattle, sheep and goats. From about the 5th century both groups were pushed into the more arid areas by Bantu migrations from the north. Both groups differ in appearance from Bantu people having a yellow-brown skin and tightly-curled but sparse hair covering; they are also noted for having steatopygous buttocks (or, less delicately, fat bottoms) when food is plentiful. Khoikhoi society seriously disintegrated as a result of European encroachment and deliberate extermination programmes from the 16th century onwards and the unintentional introduction of smallpox by the immigrants.

rainfall is greater, broad-leaved *mopane* trees form thick woodland and provide welcome browsing for cattle during the dry season. But the southwest is a sand desert with wind-blown dunes. Where there is some shelter a stunted thorn tree might provide much-needed shade for gemsbok (an oryx-like animal) and other wild animals as well as sheep and people. And also for hundreds of soft ticks.[71] I learned quickly to spread a groundsheet whenever I sat under one of these trees so that I could see the hordes of ticks advancing on me and could stamp on them before they had a chance to feed.

Camels were used by the Botswana Police in this sand desert. The bulls can be aggressive and Howard Darkin was asked to castrate them. I didn't envy him. Camel castration had not been included in my surgical training, nor their restraint or anaesthesia, and I very much doubt that it was included in lectures at the Royal Veterinary College in London either. There was a story going round, apocryphal I hope, that the technique involved the use of two flattish stones. When the operator was asked if it was painful, he replied that it wasn't if he took good care to keep his thumbs out of the way.

Most of Botswana was not a suitable habitat for tsetse flies, the exception being the Okavango Delta and the tributaries to the Zambezi river in the north. The chief tsetse officer was another veterinarian, Geoff Bowles. To him fell the responsibility of organizing a programme for the eradication of the fly from the delta and preventing re-infestation along the Linyanti river from the

---

[71] Soft ticks, as their name implies, have a soft external cuticle unlike hard ticks which are more commonly seen attached to host animals for periods of several days. The soft cuticles allow them to swell as they suck blood. They feed rapidly and seldom stay on their host for more than half an hour.

Although I didn't identify them they were most probably *Ornithodoros moubata*, a tick with a propensity for feeding on people and the vector of human relapsing fever caused by the spirochaete *Borrelia duttonii*.

Zambezi (there was no way the fly could reinfest the delta across the arid Kalahari). An intricate system was devised using minimal amounts of a pyrethroid combination sprayed from aircraft flying in formation abreast, guided by GPS navigation, at about fifty feet from the ground at night in the winter months. The cold air allowed the fine spray to sink and settle gently on the tree canopy and surrounding cover. The only collateral damage that could be identified was that the pyrethroid insecticides were toxic to tilapia fish of a certain age. Thus it was arranged that only a swathe of the delta was sprayed in any one year so as to minimize any permanent damage to the fish population in it. But, of course, tsetse could also migrate back to previously sprayed areas so there was always a need to backtrack in following years and re-spray part of the last swathe so as to kill any re-infesting migrants.

I enjoyed the night patrols with Geoff. I had no real responsibilities, he did. And it got me out of the office routine. Our role on the ground was to erect a telescopic pole fixed to the rear of a Land Rover with a strobe light at the top to show the pilots where the start of the swathe was. The pilots then flew in parallel formation for a hundred miles or so, depending on the width of the delta at that point, then banked round 180° on a reciprocal track, releasing the insecticide all the while. In the time the planes flew the required transect the ground crew moved the pole and its light to the start of the next swathe. After two or three transects the planes would have to fly back to the Maun airstrip to replenish their fuel and insecticide tanks, during which time we could cook up some sausages or other victuals, reinforced with a nip or two of Scotch to keep warm in the cold night air. At about 4 am, when the last flight had been flown we would roll up in our sleeping bags and sleep.

There was always an extraordinary freshness about the mornings and, most remarkable, whereas the previous evening the tsetse flies had been a pest, there were none to worry us any more, though butterflies and other insects fluttered about, seemingly unaffected by the very low levels of the insecticide used.

There was one exception to the use of pyrethroids. Dieldrin, supplied by the Shell Company, was used to spray the tree trunks on either side of the Linyanti river, which was considered the only route by which tsetse could reinfest the delta. Unlike the pyrethroids, which have only a transient effect, dieldrin was selected because of its long-term impact, reducing the numbers of times the insecticide needed to be applied. Quantities were also reduced by limiting the application to the lower two metres of the tree trunks, as it had been ascertained that nine times out of ten tsetse flies alight on trees below that level.

Despite these precautions, the veterinary department came in for a lot of criticism by environmental groups, assisted by the world's media, for its use of dieldrin, notwithstanding the fact that the Forestry Commission in Britain used considerably more in any one year and that another neighbouring country sprayed dieldrin more randomly out of aircraft to control tsetse flies. The barrage of criticism was intensive; one day there would be a critical article in the Stockholm-based *Dagens Nyheter*, the next day a similar article in a Washington paper or a television programme on a French channel. Most of the criticism was hopelessly uninformed. Although there were no cattle along the Linyanti river to provide any source of beef, it being a game reserve, one article claimed that Botswana was exporting beef tainted with dieldrin. Beef sales plummeted as a result. Another article asserted that many people in South Africa had died from insecticide poisoning and by implication the source of the poison was Botswana, without mentioning that insecticides are frequently used for murder or as a rather unpleasant means of suicide.

Back in Gaborone I was fielding all these criticisms, which were being relayed to us from Botswanan missions abroad. At one stage it was mooted that I should go to Brussels to try and lay these accusations to rest. I was apprehensive, for I was aware that when the press has a hot story it is often so confident of its moral superiority that no amount of argument will convince it that it may be wrong. On this occasion my view was again correct.

Fortunately for me, the President's press officer decided to take a hand. I hoped that as a professional he knew which buttons to press. I briefed him on the technical issues and corrected the false stories about tainted beef and criminal use of insecticides, and a press conference was convened some days later.

An hour or so before it was to be held a reporter from a London tabloid called on me at my office asking for information. I told him that the matter was now out of my hands and that he would be advised to attend the press conference. To be helpful I also invited him to call on me in the afternoon, when I would be pleased to answer any questions he had about the selection of dieldrin for the purpose and show him the relevant maps of the area where it was being used. He never returned.

The next day his newspaper ran the headline 'Senior Veterinary Officer refuses to answer my questions.' I tracked the reporter down to his hotel room and rang him.

'It made a better story' was his excuse for the lying headline.

I was, of course, extremely angry about this misrepresentation.

'I want a retraction of the story and an apology in tomorrow's edition of your paper' I demanded. 'Or else I will arrange for you to be visited by a senior immigration officer within the hour.'

A retraction was offered. I don't know whether it was ever printed, but the damage had already been done and readers of that particular tabloid would, no doubt, be confident that dieldrin was being misused in Botswana and that the officials involved were being evasive about it.

Some months later when all the fuss was over I discovered that the whole episode had been orchestrated by the press office of an international chemical company to discredit the Shell company, on the grounds that it was supplying dangerous chemicals to third world countries - though the same company had also tendered for the supply of dieldrin but had failed to get the contract.

At about this time Martin Mannothoko asked me to represent him at a meeting of southern African chief veterinary officers and to take Molatse with me. This was an annual event where senior veterinary officers from South Africa, Namibia, Swaziland, Lesotho, Botswana and Malawi met (Zimbabwe and Zambia abstained from attending for diplomatic reasons). On this occasion the meeting was held in Maseru, the capital of Lesotho. Lesotho claims to be the only country in the world in which no part lies under 3000 feet above sea level. The highlands around Maseru reminded me very much of the Ethiopian highlands, with little white-washed homesteads and numerous Australian gum trees dotting the landscape. But in midwinter it was cold; snowdrifts piled up against any obstacle and ice crusted all the little mountain streams. In this dry mountain air I was constantly getting electric shocks from static electricity whenever I touched a bath tap or a metal door knob. Gloves might have been useful, not just outdoors but indoors as well, but I didn't have any. Maseru itself was an undistinguished little town at that time, though it was distinguished by the number of shabby cinemas along its main street showing blue movies to South African tourists deprived of such dubious pleasures in their home country.

Before flying to Maseru I informed Molatse that I would require him to speak on training and manpower requirements, while I would handle matters relating to the disease status of the country. I was shocked when at Gaborone airport he asked me for details of how many Batswana were then attending veterinary schools and when they could be expected to graduate. Over a year had passed since he had been put in charge of veterinary education and manpower requirements and, though generous in his criticism of others, he had done nothing about briefing himself on the situation. But worse was to come.

One of Molatse's less pleasant characteristics was that, despite his inexperience, he always sought the limelight at public meetings. At the session of the conference when each senior officer gave a resumé of the disease situation in their respective countries I claimed that as a result of widespread vaccinations against anthrax the disease had not been seen in Botswana in the previous ten years. Molatse immediately contradicted me in public and claimed that he knew of several outbreaks of anthrax in the country.

This was extremely embarrassing. Who were the senior veterinary officers to believe? I reasserted that anthrax had not been seen in the country for ten years and that my statement was backed up by the annual reports of the director and the diagnostic laboratory. Once again Molatse contradicted me, claiming that he had made the diagnosis himself and confirmed it microscopically. Anthrax is one of the easier diseases to diagnose so it was unlikely that he had made a misdiagnosis if, of course, he had examined any microscope slides. I was certain he was lying in an attempt to bolster a reputation for clinical and diagnostic expertise and/or to throw in doubt my own expertise, but the audience did not know that.

Outside the conference session I turned on Molatse angrily. Anthrax, I reminded him, was a notifiable disease, that is a disease that must be reported by law. His failure to report his alleged diagnosis of anthrax officially to the veterinary department was in fact a crime for which I could charge him on my return to Gaborone. Worse, I said, was that all the beef export certificates from the Lobatse abattoir certified that the beef was derived from anthrax-free areas. He had now informed an international conference that the export certificates were worthless and his comments would be reported in the minutes of the meeting and get an even wider airing.

At this he showed a degree of contrition, saying he had not realized the consequences of his interruptions, but by this time it was too late to go back into session and correct the situation. Quite the greatest damage done that day was to call in question the probity of the veterinary department, for it was on such trust that

Botswana's beef exports to the EEC countries depended.

Martin had ambitions to climb the bureaucratic ladder and he had all the qualities required for higher office. The trouble was to find a suitable replacement. He promoted my own candidature by writing a quite remarkable, but somewhat unjustified, testimonial to my personal and professional virtues. This brought the permanent secretary of the ministry, David Findlay, to my office one day for a private chat. David was a tall, somewhat shy, good-looking, chain-smoking Scot who had been Seretse Khama's private secretary and taken out Botswana citizenship and remained behind in the civil service after Seretse's death. David observed, firstly, that by Martin's standards I was quite the brightest jewel in the civil service, to which I replied that it had taken him a very long time to discover just how outstanding I was. Of course I was kidding. Both of us realized that Martin's purpose was to find a suitable director to replace him and was willing to perjure himself for that purpose. It certainly suggested that he didn't think Molatse was a suitable replacement, but there was no choice. As David noted, once the post of director of veterinary services was Africanized it would have been seen as a retrograde step politically for an expatriate to be appointed director subsequently.

I had already come to the same conclusion. I had had experience of a capricious boss in Sudan and I had no wish to repeat the experience. Molatse, to me, seemed an irresponsible braggart who might easily bring the credibility of the Botswana veterinary department into disrepute at the first international meeting he attended and I had no wish to be associated with that.

By good fortune, by the time David came to see me I had already lined up a well-paid job in Saudi Arabia. In some ways I was sorry to have to go, for I liked the country, but I realized after the Maseru incident that Molatse was so headstrong I would not be able to restrain him. Botswana had one of the most effective veterinary services in the continent under Falconer and Mannothoko and one which had done much to raise the incomes of many Batswana. Molatse, I feared, would undo all their good work.

CHAPTER 13

Consultancy work

I had been recruited to open a veterinary clinic in Seihat, a small town of modest shops and houses populated by Shia Muslims, near an ancient oasis of date palms and narrow canals called Al Qatif on the east coast of Saudi Arabia. The venture was funded by a wealthy Saudi businessman with a sentimental liking for animals. But sentimentality is not a good basis for a business. The Saudis didn't want to pay for veterinary services (it was impossible to sue them in court; a westerner's evidence is invalid because he cannot take an oath on the Koran) and the expatriate community was so transient that few westerners kept animals.

Saudi Arabia is not an enticing country to work in, though the high salaries offered are an attraction. An overwhelming religiously-bigoted puritan ethic has been imposed on the country, though most people's natural inclinations are not exactly puritanical. There is as a consequence a marked sense of hypocrisy in public and private matters. This hypocrisy is most tiresome when the locals assume that they are morally superior to westerners from countries with more liberal and tolerant traditions. However, their assumption of moral superiority is somewhat contradicted by the very large number of Saudi men on the daily Thai Airline flights to Bangkok.

The clinic was a large prefabricated building on the outskirts of Seihat, close to a major highway linking the gulf cities of Dhahran and Jubail. Unfortunately no architect nor even a veterinarian had been consulted in its design and it had a number of serious deficiencies. It did have an essential Saudi feature - separate waiting rooms for male and female clients. In the clinic I was assisted by a British veterinary surgeon, Steve Wright, three Filipino veterinarians and a locally-trained one whose real purpose was to translate for those of us with a dismal ability to speak Arabic.

The first difficulty I had to overcome, even before doing any clinical work, was the prohibition on the sale of anaesthetic drugs on the grounds that they might be acquired by people for recreational purposes contrary to Koranic injunctions. Sniffing of glue and many other solvents was, I had noted, ubiquitous among bored teenage youths in the streets of the towns, for there was no prohibition on the sale of such mind-bending substances. So it seemed ludicrous that professional veterinarians could not buy anaesthetics.

This compelled me to make two trips to Riyadh to see the director of veterinary services there in the hope of getting his authority to import veterinary anaesthetics. He was a man in his thirties who had been trained in Germany and was therefore fully conversant with modern drugs and the need for anaesthetics during surgical procedures. It was only when I pointed out to him that the Kingdom would seem backward if veterinary surgery was impossible that he relented and gave me the necessary authority to import anaesthetics.

Working in Saudi Arabia was a thankless task. If the animal recovered God was praised; if it didn't the vet was blamed. But despite the difficulties I had some interesting experiences in the year that I spent in Seihat. A visit to a Bedouin encampment one Friday evening was one of the more interesting. It coincided with the 1986 return of Halley's Comet, which, though invisible in the brightly-lit cities of the gulf coast, could be clearly seen out in the desert.

Most of the desert was sand and rock, but where rain had fallen some vegetation might grow - mainly tufted grasses among which the Bedouin showed me a sage-like plant and tiny wild onions. These people ranged though the deserts of Qatar and eastern Saudi in search of grazing for their camels and sheep, but now, in the age of the motor vehicle and six-lane highways, the animals were often transported from one site to another in the back of a pick-up. Many of the older Saudis, though now urbanized, had not forgotten their Bedouin roots and I was entertained in a tent in the desert sitting on rugs drinking coffee with a small portable Honda generator hammering away in the background powering a fan and a television set. Unlike their urban sisters, who were always chaperoned by a male relative and totally covered whenever they went out, the Bedouin women went about milking their camels with no head covering and their arms and shoulders exposed.

Hawking was a common sport in eastern Saudi Arabia. Although I was very conversant with poultry diseases, I had had no previous experience of hawks, so I regarded them as a sort of chicken with wicked beaks and sharp talons. Fortunately a good book on raptor diseases became available at that time, edited by an old friend, John Cooper, in association with Andrew Greenwood. With it in hand, my success in treating hawks slowly improved. Quite the most common complaint was bumblefoot, a name which is more amusing than the ailment.

Bumblefoot is a condition of many birds, including domestic fowls. An abscess forms in the soft underside of the foot after being punctured by a thorn or other sharp object. Pus in birds has a dry cheesy nature and even when the abscess bursts the pus does not drain out, so the bird remains very lame. It is therefore necessary to empty the abscess surgically and apply a dressing to the raw tissues underlying it. Chronic bumblefoot in hawks often prevents them from hunting, which may lead to malnutrition and death. The trouble is that hawks are a great deal more aggressive than chickens, so their treatment is much more difficult.

Religious restrictions at that time prevented the neutering of any animals, which meant that all the male horses brought to the clinic were entire. Stallions can be unpredictable and are therefore potentially very dangerous. As a student I remember seeing a thoroughbred stallion that had killed two grooms and whose sire had killed three. Consequently I learned never to examine a stallion in a box where I might be cornered but always out in the open where I had a chance of being able to avoid the horse's teeth and hooves. In Saudi the risks were even greater, for the owners and grooms were notably lacking in nerve and the moment even a muscle jerked, they were very likely to drop the bridle or twitch that was being used to restrain the animal, leaving me on my own holding a foot that could send me flying. Fortunately I had played rugby as a youth and had learned to fall and roll away without being seriously hurt.

One of the more frequent ailments of horses I saw is what is known as Monday morning disease, a condition which affected dray horses stabled in western cities and fed on concentrates such as oats. When worked on Monday morning after a weekend's rest, some would develop intense pain, particularly in their hind quarters, sweat copiously and produce very dark urine, making them totally unfit for work. The simplistic explanation for the condition at the time was that reserves of glycogen accumulated in the horses' muscle tissues when resting and when the horses were worked again the glycogen converted to lactic acid in the musculature, resulting in painful cramps, the destruction of muscle tissue and the release of myoglobin from the damaged tissues which then filtered into the urine. More complex theories now exist, but as dray horses are things of the past in Europe, few modern text books even mention the condition.

In Saudi Arabia it was not a thing of the past. It was a condition I saw repeatedly in horses used for recreational purposes after the end of the Ramadan fast and the festival of Idd-ul-Fittr. The fasting period lasts a lunar month, much longer than a weekend, and during the month few owners exercised their horses. Perhaps the horses should also have been fasted intermittently.

The feast of Idd-ul-Adha commemorates the legendary command by God to Abraham to sacrifice his son Isaac (called Ismail in the Muslim tradition) in a test of Abraham's faith.[72] Each year, all Muslim households around the world who can possibly afford it will sacrifice a ram (or failing that, a billy goat) to celebrate the event. In Saudi Arabia fat-tailed sheep from as far away as Syria and Jordan were preferred, but supply could not meet demand and hundreds of thousands of sheep were imported live from Australia and elsewhere.

At the port of Dammam, close by Seihat, I saw some hideous

[72] Genesis, 22, vv 1-14

things. A consignment of 7000 sheep, all fully fleeced, were unloaded and put in a totally inadequate pen with shade covering for less than a quarter of them and a water trough ten foot in length served by a half-inch water tap. The trough never filled, for the strongest rams sucked the water directly from the tap while the rest were dying, a dozen or so every hour. The temperature in the sun was over 120°F.[73]

The butcher, which seems an inadequate term to describe the consignee, wanted me to inject them with an antibiotic, seemingly yet another example of the incredible faith put into an injection. I refused to treat the animals and told him that he needed to get a canvas awning up immediately to give the animals shade and to spray them with water throughout the daylight hours in an attempt to reduce their body temperature. He refused to do as I suggested and as I would not do what he wanted, he refused to pay. The only consolation I could hope for, and it was a consolation paid for by terrible animal suffering, was that he might make a huge financial loss on the transaction.

Another group of animals, a dozen imported black-coated Aberdeen Angus steers, suffered similarly. They had no shade at all, but at least they had an adequate water supply. They stood with their heads in the trough with a constant stream of urine flowing from their pizzles in an attempt to moderate their body temperatures. My advice to get an awning over them and spray them with water was similarly ignored.

The alternative name of the country, Sordid Arabia, seemed very apt when witnessing such heartless cruelty. The financial viability of the clinic appeared quite hopeless. I realized that I could

[73] i.e. 50°C

go gracefully or be sacked. I chose the former option. It wasn't a difficult decision. I had found great contentment in my house in Lamu, the first home I could truly call my own, and I wanted to enjoy more time there. I therefore decided to try my hand at consultancy work.

The Food and Agriculture Organization of the United Nations based in Rome (FAO) was on to me before I had even packed my things. In September 1986 I was asked to head a mission to make recommendations for the restoration of animal health services in Uganda. I had never been on a mission before so I wasn't too keen on being the head for I lacked the experience necessary, but it was a foot in the door. And I liked the idea of going back to Uganda where I had started my career over twenty years earlier.

However in the intervening decades, Uganda had suffered a period of misrule and civil war lasting over 15 years. The economy was in ruins and the infrastructure in tatters. A visit to the Animal Health Research Centre in Entebbe revealed a group of buildings in the last stage of dilapidation and a completely demoralized staff. The Uganda shilling was all but worthless.

Although much of the mission's work was with the Bank of Uganda, it was a bank employee on my first day in Kampala who showed me where I could change my dollars on the black market at an exchange rate ten times more favourable for me than the official rate. This made much sense, because at black market rates breakfast in my hotel cost four dollars, whereas at the official rate it would have cost forty dollars, a price which would have been exorbitant for a breakfast that consisted of a slice of pawpaw, two pieces of toast and a cup of instant coffee. But at black market rates which for all purposes other than official ones was the going rate, senior officials in government such as permanent secretaries earned the equivalent of $2.50 a month, veterinary officers $1.80 a month and the young man who cleaned my hotel room a dollar a month.[74]

Inevitably all of them supplemented their incomes with extra-mural activities, government officers using such facilities as government vehicles for their business activities - a practice which led to widespread dishonesty in the public service and which still persists, though the Uganda economy is now flourishing. As one international civil servant remarked to me at the time, 'Government employees pretend to work and the government pretends to pay them.'

Another consequence of the worthlessness of the currency was its bulk. On one occasion I had had to make an official transaction at Barclays Bank, one of the leading banks in Kampala. I noted that everybody in the queue around me had baskets or cartons with them, which made me somewhat apprehensive. I only needed to change $150 into Uganda currency and I could not help wondering if I had brought sufficient containers; fortunately the banknotes just fitted into my airline pilot's bag. Back in my hotel room I weighed them; they totalled 13 kilos.

In the dire situation Uganda was then in, two objectives of the FAO mission were uppermost. One was to promote some income-generating animal production activities and the other was to encourage government veterinarians to leave government service and set up in private practice in order to provide the improvement to veterinary services necessary to support the production activities.

Of the several options available, support of the dairy industry

---

[74] At then existing exchange rates the equivalent of approximately £1.25, 90p and 50p respectively.

appeared the most promising. The high rainfall to the north and west of the Lake Victoria basin provide an ideal environment for the production of milk from cows grazing the lush grass with minimal use of feed concentrates. I remembered the enthusiasm of many dairy farmers when I had been attached to the Kabaka's government two decades earlier. There was a ready market for milk in urban areas such as Kampala; what was needed was the infrastructure to collect the milk, process it and then market it. A milk-processing plant had been built in the industrial area of Kampala but it had been looted and was barely functional.

Fortunately the mission contained two experts on dairy production and with their expertise and funding from the United Nations Development Fund, the processing plant was eventually restored. Since then the dairy industry in Uganda has gone from strength to strength and I feel a sense of pride whenever I see milk from Uganda for sale in shops in Lamu.

My own focus in the mission was to promote the privatization of animal health services. I was sceptical that it would work because, almost certainly, all the government veterinarians were already supplementing their meagre government incomes with private work and I didn't think they would willingly forfeit a part of their income and the benefits that went with government employment for the uncertainties of full-time private veterinary practice. Despite my reservations, a poll I conducted among over three hundred Ugandan vets showed that almost half approved of going into private practice (whereas few were interested in research). Unfortunately the vets who were interested in private practice had an overblown idea of the income that might be earned. When I had been in private practice in Mombasa I had learned that farm work, though interesting, wasn't particularly remunerative despite the fact that Kenyan farmers were certainly considerably wealthier than their Ugandan counterparts.

Ways had to be found to finance the establishment of private practices. Vets would need some sort of mechanized transport. I suggested motorcycles; they thought they should have Land Rovers. They would also need drugs and diagnostic equipment such as microscopes and centrifuges as well as surgical equipment, furniture and a host of other things. At best, each private vet would need a capital of $10,000 to start up business; if they insisted on Land Rovers they would need at least $30,000.

Because of the terrible depreciation of the Uganda currency, interest rates on bank loans hovered between 30% and 40% and, as few vets could provide any collateral, interest rates could even be higher. The high interest rates, in my opinion, were likely to cripple any embryonic venture, yet despite my words of warning the Ugandan veterinarians seemed determined to start their businesses with a high level of debt.

On this and later visits to Uganda I found, more so than in any other country I worked in, a belief that donors would fund every venture without any contribution from the government or private individuals. There is risk in every new venture and it is desirable, for without risk there is no stimulus to make the venture work. With nothing to lose, there is a strong likelihood that beneficiaries might take a casual attitude towards any funds allocated to them and use them for other purposes - the purchase of alcoholic beverages being one.

Moreover there are moral arguments against giving benefits to a small section of society, not least the one of equity, and I could see no reason to give money to a relatively well educated elite in preference to poor uneducated peasants with only the resources for subsistence farming. When later I suggested that several vets could form partnerships so as to raise the necessary capital, as is commonly done among professional colleagues in other countries, the president of the Uganda Veterinary Association told me the vets didn't trust each other sufficiently to enter into partnerships. It was a terrible indictment of the profession in Uganda. If they didn't trust each other, it gave me no cause to trust them either. The privatization of veterinary services subsequently lagged well behind similar programmes in the other East African countries.

Over the next fifteen or so years I provided consultancy services in several countries in Africa and one in India, a country with a long history and one where three generations of my Hickey forebears had lived. Consultancy work is not particularly enjoyable. Much of the time is spent confined to nondescript hotel rooms collating figures and reading through masses of papers (some of them intended to deceive) and trying to make sense of them. I was hardly ever in any place long enough to make friends or to become familiar with any livestock owners and rarely did I see any animals.

In my previous career I had had little need for economists despite an apparent excess of them in all aspects of the aid industry. I now realized that they were, indeed, necessary and I went about studying some basic economics to make me fit for consultancy work.

Economists define their field as the dismal science. Dismal it certainly is, but to call it a science is excessively flattering. The sciences attempt to characterize natural laws; economists seek to describe the irrational behaviour and, sometimes, the exuberantly irrational behaviour of people. Natural laws are consistent; people's behaviour is not. At times I felt I was no more than a fraud prevention officer and an accountant would have been able to do the job better than I could. As a person with a deep interest in veterinary science I found these other roles very frustrating, but at least I found contentment in my frequent returns to my home in Lamu in between consultancies.

The agricultural policies in some of the countries I worked in defied belief. Often the currencies were overvalued as they were in Uganda. This allowed the elite to purchase Mercedes cars and other imported luxuries cheaply, but conversely gave the farmer selling an export commodity such as tea, coffee or cotton a poor return when converted back into local currency.

Zambia had particularly irrational economic policies. Because it largely depended on copper as an export product, most of the population were urban, in contrast with other African countries where the majority was rural. In an attempt to please the urban majority, the government set the price of maize well below the cost of production. As a result farmers then turned to feeding their maize to pigs and poultry because the price of pig and poultry products was not so restricted, while black marketeers bought the cheap maize in bulk and sold it over the border in Zimbabwe and the Congo at true market prices and made a quick *kwacha*. The government then tried to thwart such rational entrepreneurs by bringing in legislation prohibiting the feeding of maize to animals and limiting the amount of maize meal sold at any one time to a kilo.

At the time I was in Zambia caretaking a project for FAO, funded by DANIDA, to determine the benefits both in terms of health and productivity, if any, of controlling ticks on indigenous cattle compared to cattle without tick control. I became aware of the ludicrous maize marketing policies when I noticed huge queues of women in Lusaka each day waiting for a kilo of maize meal to feed their families. It was said that women spent an average of six hours a day in queues. Clearly the government was oblivious to the opportunity costs of such a waste of time every day.[75]

While I was in Lusaka I met up unexpectedly with a former colleague, Michael Walshe, a silver-haired Irishman. Although seriously handicapped by deafness Michael had a great fund of stories and a wide knowledge of the works of Mark Twain. He was based in Washington with the World Bank and was an expert on livestock production.

I had first met him on a previous assignment in Tanzania. At that time we differed: he thought that poor nutrition was the biggest constraint to livestock production in Africa, whereas I maintained that disease was. I managed to change his opinion when I took him to see a small dairy farm on the outskirts of Dar-es-Salaam. When the normal tick control measures were suspended for about ten days following heavy rains, a third of the herd had died of East Coast fever. In Zambia I thought to play the devil's advocate when I took Michael to the Lusaka Agricultural Show and steered him towards the stand of the National Milling Corporation of Zambia, a government parastatal organization. As soon as I had introduced Michael as an expert from Washington, the young man who had greeted us suggested that he call one of

---

[75] The opportunity cost is the loss of potential income the women might have earned if they could have undertaken some income generating activity during the time they stood in the queues.

the corporation's directors from the hospitality lounge at the back of the stand. With wickedness aforethought I asked if the corporation produced any pig rations.

'Certainly' said the director, showing us a meal heavily littered with rich orange-yellow maize flakes.

'And poultry rations?' I asked.

Again we were shown a meal rich in maize.

'But I thought the use of maize in animal rations was illegal' I remonstrated.

'It is' agreed the director, 'but one can't make a profit out of maize unless one feeds it to animals.'

Out of the director's hearing, Michael remarked to me, 'President Kaunda would like two and two to add up to five, but they never will.'

While the ill-designed economic interventions of some governments were a factor in the impoverishment of their poorer citizens, many of the various agencies involved in the Aid industry were not blameless. As was described in a previous chapter, the World Bank often recruited remarkably incompetent people to implement their projects. Another failing of the Bank was to try to establish common institutional changes in the countries in which it operated, as if one size fitted all. When I was doing a consultancy in Tanzania I had been compelled by the Bank (which was funding my consultancy) to make proposals in line with the institutional changes the Bank was recommending. I was appalled by them; they seemed more suitable for a mainly crop-producing country, whereas Tanzania, being a predominantly dry country, had a bigger livestock industry. Over time I discovered that the institutional changes had been drawn up with Malawi in mind and the same expert had then amended the Malawi text to cover Tanzania - after spending all of five days in the country, two of which were a Saturday and a Sunday. Unsurprisingly, the expert had had no time to consult with the senior civil servants who were meant to implement the policy changes. Like me they were appalled and though I did not stay in Tanzania long enough to discover if the changes were ever made, I suspected they were not because of the hostility they understandably aroused.

Another change the Bank proposed was to divorce the research sections of veterinary departments from the field operating sections and to create two separate institutions. I suspect that this change was proposed by Bank staff with PhDs and a bias towards research and academia. I have no animosity towards research - there would be no progress without it - but this action left the veterinary departments of countries such as Tanzania and Sudan without any diagnostic facilities. It didn't help that in Tanzania there was little love lost between the director of veterinary services and the head of the research laboratories and, consequently, no cooperation between them.

Wherever I went in Tanzania, I asked what were the principal livestock diseases of the area, to which the reply was invariably tryps and tick-borne diseases. Yet only one of the one hundred district veterinary offices in Tanzania had the laboratory resources to confirm such diagnoses microscopically. It seemed to me, and I repeated it often, that such unproven diagnostic assumptions were a poor basis for an effective national disease control policy.

The European Commission was another of the international

organizations deeply involved in the Aid business. It abdicated any responsibility for the performance of the projects it funded by putting them out to tender to various contractors based within the European Union (or Economic Community as it was called earlier).[76] It was left to the recipient countries to assess the tenders. Corruption is not something that can easily be proved but it was obvious even to me, and supported by a colleague's observations, that on occasion some contractors were offering bribes to secure contracts. Management of any given project was in the hands of a national of the recipient country, whereas the external consultant was merely designated as a Technical Assistant (TA). Although the TA was responsible for financial control of European Commission funds he (or she) had no authority or control of policy or staff. Payment of fees to the TA depended on the Commission's delegation receiving regular notice from the recipient government that it was satisfied with the TA's performance.

This, of course, left the TA wide open to be blackmailed. In The Gambia, where I was posted as a TA between 1990 and 1992, the minister and other senior ministry officials considered that the project's vehicles were for their personal use. When I protested, I was told that if I maintained my objections an adverse report of my performance would be submitted to the Commission's delegation. I immediately made this attempt at blackmail known to the delegation's staff in the capital, Banjul, but got no support. I got round this problem by removing the rotor arms from the distributors of all the vehicles not in use. Thus whenever a driver came from the ministry demanding the use of a vehicle, I would, apparently willingly, give the driver the keys with the caveat that

---

[76] When I asked one EU ambassador how country performance was assessed in Brussels, he replied that it was assessed by the amount of money that was disbursed.

if he could get the Land Rover to start, which I had been unable to do, he could certainly have it. Of course, without a distributor arm there was no chance of the engine firing, though there was a risk that the driver might exhaust the battery with his attempts.

But perhaps the most egregious of all attempts to persuade me to disburse European Commission funds beneficially for a few of the élite was at a meeting chaired by a very senior official of the Ministry of Agriculture in Uganda. There I was told, not asked, that the funds allocated for an animal disease control programme that I controlled were for the ministry's officials to 'eat', since money from a World Bank-funded project was no longer available after that project's termination. The project had, in fact, been woefully mismanaged. I demurred, repeating that the funds were for disease control.

'You don't seem to understand' said the official.

'I do understand what the funds are designated for. It is you who doesn't understand' I replied.

Tediously, he carried on haranguing me. In the end I had to remind him that there was a contract between the Commission in Brussels and his government.

'Then you can change the contract' the official said.

'I can't do that' I replied. 'It was signed by a European Commissioner and your ambassador in Brussels. Only they can renegotiate a contract and I doubt very much that the European Commission would be willing to do so.'

What irked me most that I was accompanied by an official from Brussels. During the interchange he gave me no overt support, although he had both diplomatic immunity and a Brussels-based pension to look forward to, neither of which were available to me. All he said as we left the meeting was, 'I now understand some of your difficulties.'

In the same vein and only a year or two later a considerable loss was discovered in monies supplied to the Uganda government by the Global Fund, a multilateral agency for dealing with HIV, tuberculosis and malaria. In all, about 70% went missing. It was a great step forward, but a rare one, when four people, including a former head of economic monitoring in the President's office, were convicted and given prison sentences for the theft.

Too often I wondered if the aid agencies existed primarily for the benefit of their employees or for the benefit of the needy. The World Food Program (WFP), an agency of the United Nations, comes to mind. In August1999 on a working trip to Karamoja I was twice driven off the road by a convoy of vehicles conspicuously flying the United Nations flag as if that gave them the right to hog the whole road. I was sufficiently annoyed by the arrogance of the drivers to set out to discover what organization they worked for and what was its purpose. It was the WFP, which was organizing the distribution of food to the Karamojong; this at a time when I had never seen such a good crop of maize and sorghum stretching as far as the eye could see and just at the point of being harvested. Inevitably the farmers would be the great losers for with so much free food available they would not be able to sell their surpluses.[77]

---

[77] In the early 1990s, a time of bloody conflagration and associated famine in Somalia, it was common knowledge within shipping circles in Mombasa that Somali warlords were demanding a quarter of all foodstuffs to be given them as the price for getting their consent to land food in their fiefdoms. Ships discharged their cargoes of food in bulk in Mombasa from where it was air-lifted to a multitude of landing strips in Somalia controlled by the warlords. Some ships never discharged their cargo in Mombasa and the ships went on to sell their cargoes to other markets in Asia and Europe. It would not be unreasonable to assume that the money generated went towards paying the warlords' militias and arming them and that the warlords were not in the least anxious for the termination of hostilities which generated so much money for them.

Another example of Aid undermining local enterprise was told me by a Briton working for the Lutheran World Federation (LWF). By remarkable coincidence he was living in the same house I had occupied 35 years previously when I had first been posted to Moroto in Karamoja - he was curious to know what the numerous wall brackets were used for and I explained to him that in those days there had been no electricity in the town and the brackets were for paraffin lamps. In his self-deprecating story he told of how his organization had established a free service to repair water pumps in the villages around Karamoja. The Karamojong, always opportunists, started taking pipes and other fittings for their own use, knowing they would be replaced for free. Eventually, frustrated by constant thefts, my informant imposed a charge for repairs to village pumps, to be paid in advance. Immediately all demands for the service stopped. Two to three months later he was stopped by a local in the Moroto market who told him that he, the local, was glad that a charge had been imposed as his own business of repairing water pumps was now looking up again.

I made several visits to Karamoja in the late 1990s. In many ways it was pleasant to be back again and flattering that two people remembered me after an interval of thirty years and more. The country was much the same as it had been, but the warriors were now armed with automatic weapons and not spears as they had been previously. This had come about after the fall of Idi Amin and his army in 1979. The army had treated the Karamojong viciously and taken sport in killing them. Little wonder that after the army's collapse at the hands of the Tanzanian army that the Karamojong had stormed the army barracks in Moroto and taken more than

60,000 automatic rifles and other assorted weapons. The ubiquity of these weapons made for a far greater degree of insecurity than there had been in earlier years and institutions such as the formal auction markets and the quarantine at Iriri had collapsed, contributing to a decline in the health status of the national herd. Dress had also changed. Only a few old men remained naked, while the rest were trousered and the traditional black shukas had been exchanged for red tartan ones. The women seemed little changed in dress except that their old goatskin skirts were now made of cotton material.

Not all the consultancies I undertook were confrontational or unpleasant. I remember with pleasure two consultancies I undertook in Sudan. The first was to Khartoum, a place where I had never been. Sudan has not had a good press for several years but I found its people hospitable, tolerant and with a good sense of humour, even though a fairly rigorous interpretation of Koranic law is in place in the northern part of the country. I had been recruited by a British consultancy firm to put forward proposals for further funding of the rinderpest eradication programme that had been under way in that country and throughout most of Africa for almost two decades, with considerable financial support from the European Union and other agencies.[78] If anything, the hospitality was excessive; meetings often started with a veritable meal, taking an hour or so of valuable time. The furnishings of the offices of senior officials I found idiosyncratic; whereas a director would have one television set in his office, a first secretary or higher had two.

Khartoum is a fascinating city astride the Blue Nile at its confluence with the White Nile. A high bridge over the White

---

[78] This was part of the Global Rinderpest Eradication Programme which has been a great success. The official declaration of the world-wide eradication of rinderpest was declared in May 2011.

Nile joins it to Omdurman, a Saharan city consisting largely of single-storey, mud-brick houses. If it were not for the intense heat I would have enjoyed walking round Khartoum more, for I never felt any apprehension about being mugged even when walking about in the late evenings when it was somewhat cooler. But the heat is a dry desert heat, so dry that if I washed a pair of socks they were dry in an hour and a half. This meant that I was seldom discomfited by a wet, sweaty shirt sticking to my skin.

I stayed in the Acropole Hotel, a quarter mile back from the south bank of the Blue Nile. The hotel, run by two Greek brothers, is certainly not the most luxurious, but it is one of the most friendly hotels I have stayed in anywhere.

As a result of the wealth generated by the exploitation of huge oil reserves in the last couple of decades, Khartoum is fast developing into a city of giant office blocks and hotels and multi-lane highways and has earned itself the soubriquet 'the Dubai of Africa'. By contrast other towns I visited such as El Obeid, in the western province of Kordofan, and Atbara in the north near the 5th Cataract appeared little changed since the time when General Kitchener and Winston Churchill had marched through late in the 19th century. These differences were also reflected in the division of resources to the central veterinary offices in Khartoum, which were abundantly stocked with vehicles, computers, air conditioners and the rest, and provincial offices which lacked even the most basic equipment. I could not help feeling that these differences contributed towards the resentment felt by the provinces towards the centre and are a cause of the several divisive movements in the Sudan, most notably the attempt by the south to gain autonomy and ultimately independence.

In the allocation of so many resources to the centre I suspected that, under pressure from the Sudanese project manager, the TA had been complicit (as I had been under pressure when a TA elsewhere) but it was not the purpose of my consultancy to evaluate the past performance of the programme but to ensure funding for its extension and the final eradication of rinderpest from the country - an outcome which was achieved within three years, a very commendable achievement in that huge country with its serious political and security problems.

Although it wasn't a part of my consultancy, very soon after my arrival in Khartoum I was co-opted onto a committee to take measures to deal with an outbreak of avian influenza caused by the H_5N_1 strain of the virus which had affected a number of poultry farms north of Khartoum and was thought to have emanated from an Egyptian hatchery. The H_5N_1 strain was causing considerable anxiety world-wide at the time because of the high mortality among poultry workers exposed to it. Although confined to those in direct contact with birds, the overriding concern was that the strain might mutate to enable person-to-person transmission and lead to a pandemic as terrible as the 1919 Spanish 'flu pandemic.

The committee had the good fortune to be assisted by Dr Bill White from Plum Island in the USA.[79] My own knowledge of the disease, relative to his, was negligible. What was of interest was that despite the extreme virulence of the strain, it was not readily transmissible except by direct contact, so that in a case where two flocks were kept in one poultry house, separated only by a six-foot wall, over 90% of the birds in one flock were dead within two days whereas there were no deaths in the second flock in the adjacent

---

[79] The Animal Diseases Center on Plum Island, just off the north east corner of Long Island in New York State, is a federal institute specializing in the exotic (i.e. non–American) diseases of animals..

section. Influenza viruses are transmitted on tiny droplets exhaled, or more frequently coughed out, by an infected animal or person. I suspect that in the very hot and dry conditions prevailing in the Sudan the droplets evaporate almost instantly, leaving no vehicle to carry the virus particles to a fresh victim.[80]

My second visit to Sudan was in 2007 when I was recruited by *Vétérinaires sans Frontières - Belgium* (VSF-B) to assess the performance of a rinderpest eradication programme in Southern Sudan which had been undertaken by a number of NGOs including VSF-B and funded by the European Commission. I had had an unhappy time there under Ansell 25 years previously but, despite the tremendous difficulties resulting from a prolonged civil war, I found great pleasure in the enthusiasm and optimism that prevailed in Juba just two years after the cessation of hostilities.

For 11 years Bryony Jones, a diminutive British vet, had worked in Southern Sudan promoting a series of rinderpest eradication activities. This was known as the OIE Pathway to rinderpest eradication. The first phase was to get a blanket vaccination cover of all the cattle in the area, numbering about seven and a half million - a vast undertaking in itself. When no more disease was reported or diagnosed, a country could then declare itself 'provisionally free from disease'. At that point the country had to stop all vaccinations to prove that it was really free, for there was a possibility that some cattle that had evaded vaccinations or been illegally imported from a neighbouring country or wildlife carriers might start new outbreaks. This required a widespread group of individuals capable of identifying the disease and a good reporting system - what in a country not embroiled in a civil war would be called a veterinary department.

To complement these activities, blood samples had to be

---

[80] a similar observation had been made in the transmissibility of foot-and-mouth virus in the hot and dry conditions of Botswana where in addition to the aridity the intense ultraviolet radiation during daylight hours would also have contributed to inactivating the virus particles

collected on a random basis throughout the area and tested for rinderpest antibody to allow for what statisticians consider with 95% confidence an absence of infection. But of course all vaccinated cattle had rinderpest antibodies, so only young animals born after the ending of vaccination were suitable for sampling. Altogether over 16,000 samples from cattle and a few from wildlife sources were collected. Three of the sera were found to be positive and these animals were subsequently traced and retested, along with fifty other animals from the herds in which they were kept. None proved positive when tested for the second time. With all this evidence, the Sudan had sufficient grounds to appeal to the OIE to be declared 'free from rinderpest infection' - the final stage of the rinderpest eradication programme.

I was immensely impressed by what Bryony Jones had achieved in collaboration with her Sudanese counterparts, sometimes under circumstances of considerable danger in rebel-held territory and often having to walk great distances in areas where the rebels did not control the roads. Even two years after the ending of the conflict I had had to fly between the various towns on my itinerary to avoid land mines on the roads.

When the consultancy was all over I wrote to the British High Commission in Nairobi suggesting that Bryony might be a suitable candidate for an honour. It was the first time I had ever presumed to make such a suggestion. I got no reply. As I found out later from a more experienced person, she should have had a public relations firm behind her to blow her trumpet.

CHAPTER 14

Foot and mouth strikes Britain

In late February 2001 a herd of pigs in Northumberland fed on swill from various restaurants south of Newcastle developed foot-and-mouth disease. A few days later a number of sheep from a farm downwind of the piggery were consigned to Longtown market in Cumbria, the most north-westerly of English counties. Cattle and sheep bought at the market, of which there were several thousand, were then transported not just to local farms but to farms in southwest Scotland, Devon, Gloucestershire and Wales. Too late it was discovered that they were infected with foot-and-mouth disease.

It was a disaster. Within days, the Minister of Agriculture made a statement in the House of Commons about the outbreak and the measures that were proposed for its control. He regretted the fact that there were few veterinary surgeons with experience of the disease. Back in Lamu I heard his statement on the BBC World Service. I was confident that I was one of those few.

I had first seen the disease on the Estancia *El Refugio* in Argentina when I was twelve years old and had then seen it once or twice a year when I worked in Uganda. In Botswana I had been responsible for its control, despite the fact that in the three years there I never saw a case (though false alarms occurred sporadically when suspicions were aroused, particularly in the dry season, when cattle would browse on prickly vegetation and injure their mouths). I immediately faxed my CV to the ministry's headquarters in London, applying for a post of temporary veterinary inspector (TVI).[81]

Six weeks went by and I had no response to my application. Once again I heard the minister on the BBC lamenting the scarcity of veterinary surgeons with knowledge of FMD. I wondered what had happened to my application and contacted an old colleague from Botswana days, Roger Windsor, who was then on the Council of the Royal College of Veterinary Surgeons. The chief veterinary officer, Jim Scudamore, was also on the Council as an *ex officio* member and as Roger had also known him in Kenya, where both had worked on CBPP, he had a word with him about my application. I was asked to send a second application, with a CV highlighting my experience of FMD, direct to him.

Ten weeks after submitting my first offer to assist in the control measures, I received a telephone call one Sunday afternoon from the ministry's offices in Page Street, London. Sunday afternoon is never the best time to make any arrangements and at the time I was in somnolent mood after a well-lubricated lunch. Nevertheless I thought I could make the necessary arrangements on the Monday morning and suggested the caller ring me again on Monday afternoon when I would be able to tell her what travel plans I had in mind.

'Will MAFF pay for the cost of the flights?' I asked.

'No, those costs must be borne by yourself. We only pay for travel costs in the United Kingdom,' was the reply.

In all my other consultancy work travel costs and travel time were considered part of the consultancy but MAFF obviously had

---

[81] The ministry was then called the Ministry of Agriculture, Fisheries and Food (MAFF). For political considerations it was later called the Department of the Environment, Food and Rural Affairs (DEFRA) which implies little interest by the department in how the food reaches supermarket shelves. Temporary veterinary inspector (TVI) was the title given to a veterinarian recruited on a short-term basis during the FMD emergency

a different set of rules. Its parsimony was just one of the reasons why it was unable to recruit the necessary number of vets from within Britain.

Before ringing off I asked the caller what her name was.

'Jenny' she replied, in what is now considered sufficient identification, despite the fact that there are thousands of women of that name. It also gives such briefly-named individuals a degree of anonymity and freedom from responsibility for their statements - as anyone dealing with a bank is aware.

On the Monday afternoon she rang again. This time I thought she said she was called Genevieve. I told her that I had arranged to fly to London on the Thursday night and asked what I should do then. 'Just come to our office in Page Street and ask for me' was her reply.

That seemed simple enough, and I reported to Page Street on the Friday morning, tired and somewhat bedraggled, having travelled for a little over 24 hours from Lamu without any opportunity to wash or change.

'I've been told to ask for Jenny' I told the uniformed security officer at the entrance. He looked at me doubtfully. 'She is attached to the foot-and-mouth disease office here.' He started to look through an office directory. 'She might be called Genevieve' I added helpfully.

'Oh, you mean Jenny Reeve,' he said.

'It could be' said I. 'She rang me in Kenya and I thought she said her name was Genevieve.'

He continued to scrutinize the office directory methodically. 'There's nobody here called Jenny Reeve' he said eventually.

I was becoming somewhat exasperated. 'Look,' I said, 'I'm here at the request of somebody called Jenny to assist in the foot-and-mouth outbreak. She works somewhere in this office block, so why don't you call the relevant office and ask for her?'

'Do you know her extension number?' he asked.

'No, I don't. She rang me. I didn't ring her.'

'Then I can't help you, sir' said he.

'Are you suggesting that I should just fly back to Kenya because you can't locate her?' I asked.

'Yes sir.'

My voice rose a few decibels. 'I've just flown 4000 miles from Kenya last night and you haven't the initiative to find a person whom I know is within these walls not more than 400 feet from this desk!'

There were murmurs from the queue forming behind me, most of them in my favour. Under this pressure, the official rang the foot-and-mouth section and discovered that I was expected, as I had said I was. However Jenny didn't have much to say for herself and I later discovered that the information she gave me was incorrect.

Sadly, during the three months I worked in Cumbria I encountered the same lack of initiative and avoidance of personal responsibility throughout the ministry. This was something totally alien to me. In most of my time in Africa I was usually the only trained person on the spot when a disease outbreak was discovered. Mobile phones and other means of instant communication were unavailable. The vet on the spot was the one to make a decision and act on it. I remembered fondly David Morris's words of advice, 'Always make a decision, even if it is the wrong one.'

I arrived in Carlisle the next morning and found my way to the

Wallfoot Hotel, a very friendly hostelry some six miles out of town and close to Hadrian's Wall, hosted by Fraser and Sarah Allison. It became my base for the next few months; a pleasant haven from an unpleasant job.

The first two days I spent with another new arrival, a burly Australian veterinarian whose name now escapes me. Together we were instructed in the different aspects of disease control and the legal requirements involved. These included disinfection requirements on the farm and for oneself and one's vehicle and the procedures to be undertaken when FMD was discovered. It was a lot to digest in just two days.

Many people have asked why vaccination was not used to bring the disease under control. An outbreak in the Netherlands, an extension of the British outbreak, was successfully controlled by ring vaccination around the primary site of disease, but in Britain, where the disease had extended to southern Scotland, Wales, Devon, Yorkshire, Kent and parts beyond, it would have required a very extensive ring to contain the disease; so extensive that the area within the ring might well have been greater than the area outside it. The only real alternative would have been blanket vaccination of the whole country.

The policy of the European Union was, and still is, to ensure that Europe is free from FMD infection. This was achieved by a pathway similar to the one described in the previous chapter for the elimination of the rinderpest virus from the Sudan and from Africa as a whole. Britain, being an island, had achieved this status long before continental Europe, except for occasional outbreaks following the importation of infected meat from South America and escapes of FMD virus from vaccine production institutes in France.[82] These outbreaks had been contained before FMD vaccines had been available by the time-honoured means of identification and slaughter of infected animals and their contacts.

A blanket vaccination campaign was considered and eventually rejected. Previous economic analyses of outbreaks in Britain had shown that a slaughter policy was a cheaper option than twice-yearly vaccination procedures using expensive polyvalent vaccines.[83] A vaccination programme would have brought the outbreak under control somewhat more quickly and cost far less in animal lives. The reverse side of the coin would have been that a blanket vaccination policy would have led to the complete cessation of the export of FMD-susceptible animals and their products to the European mainland, North America and other countries that were disease-free, as well as considerable restrictions on trade within Great Britain. Some time would have had to elapse before the veterinary authorities could declare the country to be 'provisionally free from disease.' From then on the country would have had to undergo all the steps laid out by the World Organisation for Animal Health (OIE) in the pathway to 'freedom from infection' status - a process that might have taken several years to achieve even if all went well, and many years if sporadic outbreaks continued despite vaccinations, during which time all trade in animals and their products both internally and externally would have been severely restricted.

Bearing these limitations to trade in mind and despite the widespread extent of the disease, I suspect the economists within MAFF decided that the slaughter policy was still a cheaper option,

---

[82] Denmark too had suffered numerous outbreaks of FMD in its piggeries following virus escapes from vaccine production units in the former East Germany. More recently an outbreak in Surrey was traced to an escape of virus from the World Reference Centre for FMD at Pirbright — as a result of an inadequate budget for the maintenance of the facilities.

[83] On 2005 the National Audit Office estimated the cost of the outbreak to taxpayers as more than £5 billion while other losses, mainly to the agricultural and leisure sectors, as about £2 billion.

even though the general public considered it to be deeply distasteful.

To put the slaughter policy into effect two kinds of premises were initially singled out for slaughter. The first were the infected premises where FMD was diagnosed - IPs for short. The second were direct contacts, the farms where animals were held in fields adjacent to an IP or which had brought in animals from other farms or markets where disease was later confirmed - DCs for short.

The government, facing an imminent general election, was aware of the public distaste for the slaughter policy. However it was keen to get the outbreak under control quickly. The Chief Veterinary Officer's advice was ignored and policy was put in the hands of the government's Chief Scientist, a former professor of physics at Cambridge. He and a professor of mathematical modelling from Oxford proceeded to carry out what Roger Windsor described as the world's largest uncontrolled animal experiment on disease eradication without so much as a Home Office licence.

They introduced a third category - contiguous premises, or CPs for short.[84] These were premises which a faceless official in Page Street judged by reference to an Ordnance Survey map to be contiguous to an infected premise, even though a river, road or 2000-foot fell intervened between the animals on the adjacent premises. Roger Windsor told me he had coined the term 'Post Code Slaughter' for this policy at a council meeting of the Royal College. Veterinarians on the spot who adjudged that there was no risk of transmission of the disease, despite the farms having a common boundary on a map, were overruled. A few British

[84] The CP status was not legally defined. It was an ad hoc status for which there was no legal obligation to keep records. This I discovered when I had been some time in Carlisle. There was therefore no record of the number of farms that were depopulated or the number of animals slaughtered under this category. Six million animals (cattle, sheep and pigs) is the minimum estimate for the number of animals slaughtered under this category, some believe ten million. Subsequent epidemiological studies showed that the slaughter of all these animals in no way contributed towards hastening the control of the disease. Perhaps the opposite; for too many scarce resources were diverted to killing out so many contiguous premises from the main purpose of eradication which was to remove all infected animals and animals incubating the disease as quickly as possible from IPs

veterinarians were so appalled by the needless slaughter that they resigned their appointments as TVIs, putting a further load on those who remained in the field.

Farms within five kilometres of an outbreak were surveyed every two days for a fortnight after the outbreak had been confirmed and less frequently subsequently. Many farmers were suspicious of the vets' regular visits; they rightly regarded them as the most likely vectors of FMD because of their numerous visits to other farms in the outbreak area. My colleagues and I were well aware of this hostility and took the utmost precautions to disinfect ourselves, our clothing and our vehicles between visits - a process that took up to forty minutes every time. I am glad to say that in retrospect no vet was implicated in carrying disease from one farm to another. Milk tankers, however, often were.

Hostility was more marked towards the foreign, non-English speaking vets who had been recruited, thus increasing even further the load on the English-speakers from Britain, Ireland, the United States and Australia to survey the farms in the outbreak area. Unwelcome on the farms, the Spaniards, for instance, spent most of each day playing poker. Meanwhile the MAFF veterinarians worked their usual hours from Monday to Friday safely seated behind their computer monitors. What was particularly galling were the regular outbursts from the senior government veterinary officer in the region, the veterinary manager, that TVIs were being paid more than he was (though he made no mention of his pension or other benefits) and he would dismiss any of us instantly if we were derelict in our duties.

The average age of a farmer in England at that time was 57.

Many, of course, were much older. The ministry regularly boasted that farmers could get all the information they needed from the internet, forgetting that many older farmers were not computer literate. Conspiracy theories abounded. One theory was that Brussels had ordered the British government to reduce the size of its sheep flock, the largest in Europe. Mr Blair, so the conspiracy theory went, realizing the electoral disadvantage of destroying millions of sheep, arranged for FMD to be introduced, so enabling disease to be used as an excuse for reducing the numbers. Military helicopters flying over the Cumbrian countryside were believed to be dropping infected material into fields and moorlands. This theory was reinforced by a rumour that the government had brought huge quantities of railway sleepers from Canada the previous autumn to fuel the funeral pyres. Another theory, far more plausible, was that some slaughtermen were enhancing their earnings by spreading the disease deliberately to ensure further work.

Tenant farmers were the most disadvantaged. Many rented fields separate from their main holdings but with the movement restrictions then imposed were unable to move their animals to them for grazing. What was more, these separate fields extended the farm boundaries very considerably and made them contiguous to numerous other premises, unlike farmers with one single holding. Other livestock owners had serious cash flow problems and banks were reluctant to extend them credit facilities because of the risks involved.

Dairy farmers were least worried, as they could continue to sell their milk and collect a monthly cheque from the dairy. Most affected were traders who bought and sold livestock for fattening on small holdings. With markets closed they were unable to market their animals, and without credit they were also unable to buy in foodstuffs to feed them. Fields got overgrazed and were badly fouled with dung, aggravating the worm problem.

Most of my work was on farms centred around the little town of Brough on the road over the Pennines linking Penrith and Scotch Corner. Over time I was able to overcome the suspicion that the farmers felt for veterinary inspectors and I remember many of them with considerable affection. They were all living under very great tension. Their social life was severely restricted as each farmer isolated himself as much as possible from his neighbours. Two brothers, really splendid characters, told me they had seen too much of me but hadn't seen their mother since the start of the outbreak. They spent part of each day sitting out on a hillside with a pair of binoculars scanning the valley before them and noting which fields had no animals in them, fearing that this was an indication that the disease was approaching their farm.

There were, of course, lighter moments. I regularly had to inspect a Vietnamese pot-bellied pig kept as a pet. All the procedures of disinfection had to be completed before and after each visit. One problem was how to examine its mouth. I quickly learned that an apple was a great help - I held the apple over its head and as it looked up at the apple with its mouth wide open in the expectation of getting it I was able to look inside the mouth for any signs of lesions there. Of course, the pig always got the apple in the end as a reward for its forbearance.

'Hygiene! Hygiene!' was drilled into us monotonously by the veterinary manager at morning briefings in Carlisle. The idea was to instil into farmers the need for disinfection of all vehicles and persons at their farm gate. The trouble was that many of the traders had no cash to pay for stirrup pumps and disinfectants, nor had they any great incentive to improve their hygiene, for some of them would have welcomed the compensation available if the disease had struck their holdings.

At one briefing I suggested that every farmer should be given a basic hygiene kit and then prosecuted if he didn't use it properly. 'Good idea,' said the veterinary manager. A week went by and nothing was done, so I put the suggestion to the veterinary manager again.

'We think Brussels wouldn't approve of it' was his response. 'It would be considered a form of subsidy.'

It was another fine British example of passing the buck and taking no initiative locally. One of my colleagues from Botswana days, Tony Holmes, told me how at a briefing by Jim Scudamore before my arrival in Carlisle, he had noted a similar vacillation and had thought to himself that had he been as dilatory in Botswana and failed to take an initiative he would have expected some harsh words from me.

Fortunately the worst of the outbreak had been reached before I arrived in Carlisle in late May. The days of the great funeral pyres stretching right across the horizon that featured on television and in the press were over. Vast swathes of Cumbria had been totally depopulated of cattle and sheep, but new outbreaks kept occurring on the fringes every other day, so there was no room for complacency.

Two months passed before I saw my first case of FMD in sheep. They belonged to a very likeable old boy in Kirkby Stephen, a widower, eighty if a day, who lived alone with his sheepdog in a small house which appeared not to have seen a coat of paint since the year dot. He kept two flocks of sheep, one in a meadow close to the town centre and the other on a hillside about a mile out of town. Daily he inspected his sheep, walking with the dog from one flock to another. Regularly I warned him that his hygiene was unacceptable and equally regularly he took no notice of my warnings. He lived his way and he wasn't going to change it.

Then one day I noted on the briefing board in Carlisle that a neighbouring farm had been diagnosed with FMD and thought to myself that the old boy was unlikely to be spared with his disregard for hygiene. In the briefing room I met a robust Australian vet – her name was Lydia Matheson, if my diary notes are to be trusted - who told me that she was about to return to Australia and had not yet seen the disease, so I suggested she accompany me to see the old man. I am glad I did, for she was much more experienced in handling sheep than I.

We decided to look at the hill flock first. It was a wet, windy afternoon. A derelict barn stood in the middle of the stone-walled field and the old boy with his dog collected up all the sheep and penned them into the barn. Within five minutes Lydia had found a sheep with very early lesions of foot-and-mouth, not more than a day old, on its dental pad. She called me over and I was as convinced as she was that it was really FMD. All the stuffing went out of the old man when I told him; he looked quite devastated and I felt a great pang of pity for him, suspecting that with the destruction of his flocks the main purpose of his life would be taken from him.

While my colleague continued inspecting the remaining sheep I phoned Carlisle on my mobile and reported the new outbreak. I was told that I should report the outbreak to Page Street in London. For the life of me I could not think why I had to do this. It seemed so much easier for a person sitting comfortably in front of a monitor screen out of the wind and rain to call Page Street from Carlisle.

At this point bureaucracy became overwhelming. There was a special disease pack that had to be completed. If I remember rightly it consisted of twenty-six pages that had to be filled in. The sheep filled the barn and outside there wasn't even a wall close by to write on, and the rain continued relentlessly. Every ten minutes or so my mobile rang with fresh instructions from Page Street or Carlisle to collect tissues from the mouths of all diseased sheep followed by further instructions to collect fifty blood samples.

Mercifully at that point the battery of the mobile ran out, so I could continue uninterrupted with my colleague to inspect the sheep and isolate the diseased ones. One thing stuck in my mind - even the diseased sheep looked alert and bright, unlike cattle with FMD, who usually look quite miserable, with heads drooping and saliva dribbling from their mouths.

After about an hour a valuer arrived to put a value on the flock before slaughter. I was supposed to supervise him - a time and motion expert might well ask how one is to inspect sheep, collect an assortment of samples, complete twenty-six pages of bureaucratic bumf and supervise the valuation simultaneously. I was certainly very glad to have Lydia to assist me.

Another hour passed and a car arrived from Carlisle with a fresh battery for my mobile but no offer of assistance. From then on the mobile rang incessantly just to add to my other preoccupations. I had just about had enough of the phone calls when I had one from

Page Street asking me to describe the lesions. By this time I had seen at least a dozen sheep with mouth lesions so there was little difficulty in describing them.

'Then I can confirm it is foot-and-mouth disease,' said the anonymous voice.

'Really?' I said. 'It's me who is confirming it is foot-and-mouth disease.'

'No, we make the diagnosis here in Page Street.'

'Oh! Does the Royal College know of it?' I asked. 'You are 300 miles from this holding and you can make a diagnosis and I am on the spot and can't?'

'Are you making an issue of it?' asked the anonymous voice.

'Yes, I am!' It is a matter of professional etiquette and discipline, as the anonymous voice should have known, that a vet who has not seen a case cannot contradict the diagnosis of a vet who has. It was the very same point that had brought David Dyson and myself in conflict with Roy Ansell in Southern Sudan almost twenty years previously.

'Well, let's drop the matter' said the anonymous voice. I had made my point, and saw no reason to continue the argument, particularly with so much else to be done.

Then the slaughtermen arrived, a rough bunch if ever there was one. The valuer had done his work and I had corroborated the valuation document as a true record. Before he went I asked him to take the old boy home, for he clearly knew him well. Not only was the farmer totally dispirited but soaking wet, so I was getting more and more anxious about his welfare. The slaughtermen did their work in short time and by a little after seven in the evening all the work had been finished.

The evenings stretch until close to ten at night in midsummer in northern England. I thought it very likely that the old boy's town flock would also be affected and it seemed to me highly desirable that we eliminate any infection as soon as possible so as to reduce the chances of transmission. So straight from the hillside we moved to the town flock. Fortunately by this time the rain had stopped. Within minutes Lydia had found another sheep with mouth lesions. Several more were found soon after. Happily all the bureaucrats had long left their offices, leaving me undisturbed by any more mobile phone calls so that by a little after ten that evening the hundred or more sheep in the town meadow had also been valued, slaughtered and carted away for burial in a land-fill site.

Early next morning I had to label all the samples Lydia and I had collected the previous day and pack them ready for transporting to the World Reference Centre for FMD at Pirbright. The other Australian vet who had been with me in the initial training session when I had arrived in Carlisle was in the laboratory, also labelling samples he had collected the previous day. Halfway through, he broke down in tears, overwhelmed by the unpleasantness of the job he had just done. This was somewhat surprising to me, for his official duties in Australia were those of a meat inspector in abattoirs there - places designed for mass slaughter. But this outburst of emotion by a big, burly Australian was understandable and, I think, most other TVIs had similar feelings. The people behind the computer screens were, of course, screened from the horrors we TVIs so often faced.

August opened. A day passed without a new Infected Premise being marked up on the situations board in the briefing room. Then two days passed. Then three. The worst was over. The outbreak at last was being contained, a little over five months after it started.

I and a number of others felt it was time to pack our bags. The veterinary manager at this stage admitted that when all the TVIs had gone, there would be no one left in Carlisle who would know what clinical foot-and-mouth looked like. It was a remarkable admission and I could not help but wonder to myself if the anonymous caller from Page Street was also one who had no clinical experience of FMD but could presume to inform me that he had diagnosed foot-and-mouth disease based on the knowledge he had acquired from looking at pictures of lesions in a handbook of FMD.

EPILOGUE

Almost fifty-five years passed before I went back to Argentina, the country of my birth. I had wanted to go much sooner, but for many years I would have been arrested as a deserter because I had not done military service there as I should have done, for I had, and still have, dual nationality. However, after the Falklands War and the disgrace of the Argentine generals, an amnesty was given to all previous deserters. So in 2006 I decided to fly down to Buenos Aires via Cape Town.

Having made the arrangements I informed my twin brother in Greece by email of my intentions, only to find that he had made plans to visit at the same time. Some might think that is proof of some psychic association between twin brothers. I don't believe in the paranormal. In my mind it is much more likely that with identical genetic profiles and very similar education and experiences, at least until early manhood, our thought processes run very much in parallel. During our working lives neither of us had had cause or opportunity to visit Argentina, so only in our retirement did we get around to making arrangements to do so. Sensibly we arranged to go before old age overtook us and, not unnaturally, we chose to visit in the spring and not in midwinter or midsummer - and so our plans coincided.

Philip and I went together to look up two of our childhood homes in Quilmes, east of Buenos Aires on the southern banks of the River Plate. I was saddened to see that the hitching rail for horses had been removed from the front of one of our old homes. The house had gone too, replaced by two bungalows, but it was the disappearance of the hitching rail that made clear the passing of a whole era. What both of us also noticed was that not only the houses but distances and heights were only two thirds or less than the size we remembered them. It made me suspect that we judge size relative to our own body size, for when we were twelve we were only about two thirds of our present height.

I, of course, wanted to see a commercial beef estancia in operation, something in which Philip had little interest, so for much of the time we went our separate ways. I had quite a few contacts around Buenos Aires, but none knew of any such working estancias, only the tourist ones - what North Americans call 'dude ranches'. I travelled about two and a half thousand miles mainly by coach, for the railway network which the British had built up over a century earlier was moribund except in the environs of Buenos Aires and Rosario. From Mendoza, the centre of a growing wine industry and an attractive city (though frequently shattered by earthquakes in the past), I crossed the Andes over the Uspallata Pass, well over the snow line, to Valparaiso on the Chilean Pacific Coast. In those travels over the pampas it became clear why I was not able to see a commercial estancia - few exist any more. In fact I saw many more horses than cattle on my travels.

Throughout the late 19th century and the first half of the 20th century and beyond, Argentina had been a major source of meat and grain for Britain and other European countries. But industrial agricultural methods developed in Europe since the Second World

War have made Europe largely self sufficient. Moreover foot-and-mouth disease was widespread in Argentina - I first saw it as a boy at El Refugio -and this had been the nail in the coffin for beef exports to Europe. Now the pampas are covered by endless miles of cereals and soya beans and 80% of the shipping leaving the River Plate goes to China.

In my career as a vet, almost entirely in Africa, I had been primarily concerned with the control and, where possible, eradication of infectious livestock diseases. To my great satisfaction Africa and the entire world was declared free from rinderpest by the OIE and the Food & Agriculture Organization in May 2011. One of the worst of Africa's animal diseases is now contagious bovine pleuropneumonia, which is widespread throughout the continent. Where corruption has become commonplace, quarantine and movement restrictions are almost useless. The T_1 broth culture vaccine which I had found to be so effective in controlling the disease in Karamoja was found to be inadequate many years later when used in a freeze-dried form in controlling an outbreak of CBPP in Ngamiland in northwest Botswana.

Since much of the motivation and financing for the control of the major animal diseases comes through various aid programmes it is a matter of great regret, more akin to disgust, that superannuated politicians and *passé* pop stars have taken the lead to campaign for aid to sub-Saharan countries, though they have minimal - if any -knowledge of the social and political environments.[85] They do, however, know how to attract media attention after many years of hogging it. So, in the hope of future canonization after less than stellar performances in their previous

---

[85] There is a campaign going to 'make poverty history.' Many westerners define poverty by their own standards and the standards of a consumer society. However many people in Africa define wealth by the numbers of cattle, wives and children they have and by these criteria many people in the western world are a great deal more impoverished.

careers, they hang around the periphery of every major summit and plead for more money. Aid has become an industry in which many thousands have made their careers, whether within United Nations organizations or non-governmental organizations (NGOs), in this more secular age the new missionary societies delivering salvation to the heathen to whom they minister. Apart from those few with the integrity to admit that their functions might be harmful to the local economies, the majority, seduced by high salaries and numerous perks, continue to assert that ever more cash is required.

All other industries and businesses have to generate money for their survival, but not the aid industry. There are many facets to the potential harm aid can bring. Donating free food undermines the ability of local farmers to sell their crops. Aid brings dependency. This dependency can deteriorate further, leading to pessimism and a belief that all personal initiatives are likely to fail, so no new ones are undertaken. Never before in the history of mankind have whole societies been dependent on the charity of others for their own survival. It makes a mockery of Darwinian theory. Plant and animal populations have become extinct in the past because of their failure to adapt; humans, however, with their considerable intellectual capability are the species most capable of adaptation. But, bolstered by continued aid programmes, governments do not make the sensible political and economic decisions necessary for the survival and prosperity of their citizens - though they are very capable of ensuring their own.

What is more, aid rewards incompetence. This was brought home to me by David Findlay, my permanent secretary in Botswana, who had just returned from a World Bank-funded meeting in Lusaka where he had failed to get any backing for development projects in Botswana. 'I learned one thing' he told me. 'If you run a prudent economy, the World Bank gives you nothing. If you screw up your economy you can have everything you ask for.' And to make matters worse, the same superannuated politicians and faded pop stars aspiring for canonization then campaign for debt relief, ensuring continued irresponsibility in the use of development funds.

Nowadays the world is concerned about global warming, carbon emissions and greenhouse gases. Domestic livestock are blamed for methane production as if this was a new phenomenon. Before man's domestication of livestock the plains of North America were covered with bison, the savannahs of Africa with antelope and the pampas, plains and steppes of South America, Asia and Europe by other grazing animals, mostly ruminants and camelids. They had similar digestive systems and were just as capable of emitting methane, so its production is not a new phenomenon contributing to present-day global warming. Although seldom admitted because of political considerations the two principal factors contributing to increased carbon dioxide production are an ever-growing human population and, with the increasing prosperity of a greater number of people, a greater use of energy in all its forms.

Neither politicians nor pop stars are best equipped to resolve the population problem and I would suggest that economists and biologists could do a better job. Every population, be it plant or animal, requires certain essential resources. In plants they are sunlight, soil nutrients and water. Animal requirements are a little more complex, human requirements even more so.

Looking at the problem as a biologist it is obvious that the human population of Ethiopia, for example, now exceeds its resource base and needs permanent food aid for its survival, though the more ingenious Ethiopians have found their way to Rome, New York and elsewhere. Yes, they do contribute to the Ethiopian economy with their remittances back home, but their ingenuity might contribute even more if they were to remain at home. Just maintaining the Ethiopian population with food aid and even encouraging its expansion ensures that a crisis will erupt some time in the near future with horrendous consequences to the Ethiopians themselves and, if it degenerates to war, to neighbouring peoples as well.

Some radical solutions have to be found. Might I suggest a search be made for chemical contraceptives rendering men and women infertile for a year? Only adults willing to undergo such treatment would be eligible for food aid during that year. Of course eligible candidates would have to be identified in some way, possibly with a microchip (though consideration would have to be given to women already pregnant). If food aid is required for only one year there would be a temporary cessation of reproduction, but where food aid is continuous there would be a marked population reduction over time which would allow the community to readjust itself to its food resource base again. It would also give time for the various Aid agencies to come to their senses and try to restore the agricultural potential of the land. Pro-life campaigners would certainly object but they are mostly people leading comfortable lives and ignorant of the terrible consequences of famine. It would certainly be worthwhile to ask those people in famine camps, women in particular, whether they would appreciate such spacing in their reproductive lives; I think planners might be surprised by the response they got.

Maintaining the status quo is not an option because there is no status quo to maintain; yet it seems the primary objective of many relief organizations. I still retain a deep affection for Karamoja and its people. They are generally regarded as illiterate semi-nomadic pastoralists, despite the fact that several hundred are university graduates (including, at one time, the Registrar of the High Court of Botswana).

The first British attempt to administer Karamoja was in the early 1920s with the primary intention of halting Ethiopian slave raids into the district. An estimate of the cattle and human populations at about that time were 180,000 and 60,000 respectively. A definitive livestock census undertaken in 1963 showed a cattle population of 603,000 and 500,000 shoats (sheep and goats). At the time the human population was estimated to be about 180,000. In other words there were about three bovines for each person. Though the numbers of both populations had increased because of greater security and better disease control, the ratio of cattle to people did not alter in the intervening forty years.

Except for ceremonial purposes the Karamojong, like virtually all African pastoralists, rarely slaughter their cattle - they are much too valuable for that - but they do consume their milk and blood. Their other staple foods are sorghum and millet flour which require a period of about 70 days rain during the wet season for a good harvest. But when the rains fail or do not persist for long enough the pastoralists' herds and flocks are their guarantee of survival. On my last visit to Karamoja I was told that the population of both cattle and people had reached a million, that is the ratio had reached parity and not three to one as previously, so the people's guarantee of survival in a drought year has been very seriously diminished.

Unhappily the numbers are very dubious. There has been no cattle census since 1963; the present numbers have been calculated by adding 2.5% annually to the previous sum. If this fallacious method of estimation were true the world would be overrun with cattle! It is much more likely that the cattle population is dependent on the grazing availability and there is no reason to believe that there is more grazing available in Karamoja now than in 1963. Assuming the present cattle population is little changed from figures collected in 1963, the ratio would now be closer to three bovines for five people and not three to one as it was in earlier years. It is clear that it is now essential in Karamoja to diversify into other areas of economic activity besides livestock keeping. With an increasingly literate society, this is possible.

Tourism and mineral extraction suggest themselves immediately but for investment in these areas security has to be much improved and this is a responsibility of the Ugandan government which, despite having an army many times larger and better equipped with helicopter gun ships, armoured personnel carriers and other military toys than at the time of independence, it has failed to provide. It is hardly surprising that the military are not deployed in Karamoja, since the pickings there are meagre compared to those in the Congo. Regrettably, what Karamojong graduates there are take up salaried employment in national and local government or NGOs where the risks are minimal but which are unproductive in comparison with private enterprise.

I do not agree with those people who disparage colonization

and with it colonialism. The first colonists were of African origin. Had it not been so, *Homo sapiens* would have remained an isolated group of primates in an African environment (and it wasn't only *Homo sapiens* that migrated out of Africa for earlier hominids had preceded them). It was Africans who first colonized Asia and Europe and their descendants who colonized Australia and the Americas. Nobody I am aware of decries the Roman colonization of Britain or the Norman Conquest. They are historical facts and it is quite impossible to put the clock back. I have little doubt that those early colonists were as proud and culturally arrogant as their later successors.

With migration and colonization came new skills and the dissemination of new foodstuffs such as maize, potatoes, cassava, bananas and many other items. With the development of better ship-building techniques and navigational aids in the 15th century, the speed of migration and colonization became more rapid. But it was merely an extension of a process that had started about 50,000 years earlier and resulted in the remarkable expansion of the human species. Of course, there were some losers; Neanderthals, probably, being the first to lose out. But there are losers in all living systems, as visitors to any national park will see every day of the week.

My days as a veterinary surgeon are virtually over. If I were a young man again I doubt that I would be tempted to become one. The role of the veterinary surgeon has been diminished, as the British Prime Minister's dependence on a physicist to advise him on foot-and-mouth disease control in preference to a veterinary surgeon clearly demonstrated. Farm animal work is arduous and poorly paid relative to other professions. Not surprisingly, most veterinarians, attracted in their youth by numerous sentimental television programmes involving dogs, cats and furry animals, now gravitate towards small animal practice, which is more lucrative. It is not that I did not enjoy small animal practice, particularly the often rewarding surgical aspects of it. But for me the most obvious goals of the veterinary profession in society are the guarantee of wholesome and plentiful food, the control and eradication of the zoonotic diseases affecting man and animals, and the mitigation of animal suffering. In Britain the government sees the countryside as a theme park for tourists to visit, with food production being a secondary concern. This was shown most dramatically when the Prime Minister visited Cumbria during the foot-and-mouth outbreak: Mr Blair spent a morning watching a pair of ospreys nesting in the Lake District (great for photo opportunities) and forty minutes talking to farmers and their leaders in Penrith afterwards.

Badgers are viewed as cuddly little animals, although anyone who has handled one knows they are not that. Without any doubt they are reservoirs and carriers of bovine tuberculosis, yet they are protected while more than twenty thousand cattle are culled every year having been diagnosed as infected with the disease. And this is a disease which I know to my cost also affects humans. In Britain there is as yet no rational and effective policy for the eradication of bovine tuberculosis and no agreement between the English, Welsh and Scottish administrations on how best to deal with this dreadful scourge.

We are daily reminded by the media of the dangers of global warming. The possibility of tropical vector-borne diseases spreading to temperate zones is becoming more imminent; in fact one of them, bluetongue, has already struck in Britain having also caused considerable mortality in the Netherlands and other north European countries. The British Government's reaction to the threat has been to restrict funding to the Centre for Tropical Veterinary Medicine in Edinburgh, all but emasculating it.

On the other hand I don't think I would have enjoyed life as much if I had been anything else but a veterinary surgeon.

SOURCES

Baer, George M. ed. (1975) *The Natural History of Rabies, Vol. I & II*, Academic Press, New York.

Bere, R.M. (1962) *The Wild Mammals of Uganda*, Longmans, London.

Blood, D.C. & Henderson, J.A. (1974) *Veterinary Medicine*, Baillière Tindall, London.

Brown, Monty. (1989)*Where Giants Trod*, Quiller Press,

Bruner, D.W. & Gillespie, J.H. (1971) *Hagan's Infectious Diseases of Domestic Animals 6thEd*, Cornell University Press, Ithaca.

Burton, Sir Richard (1856) *First Steps in East Africa*, London.

Cooper, J.E & Greenwood, A.G. ed. (1981) *Recent Advances in the study of Raptor Diseases*, Chiron Publications, Keighley, W. Yorkshire.

Fraser, David. (2000) *Frederick the Great*, Penguin Books, London.

Greenfield, Richard. (1965) *Ethiopia, A new political history*, Pall Mall Press, London.

SOURCES

Henning, M.W. (1956) *Animal Diseases in South Africa*, Central News Agency, South Africa

Hickman, John. (1964) *Veterinary Orthopaedics*, Oliver & Boyd, Edinburgh and London

Hoogstraal, Harry. (1956) *African Ixodoidea, Vol I, Ticks of the Sudan*, Research Report

Irvin, A.D., Cunningham, M.P. & Young, A.S. ed. (1981) *Advances in the Control of Thileriosis*, Martinus Nijhof of The Hague.

Jeal, Tim. (2007) *Stanley*, Faber & Faber, London.

Matthysse, John G. & Colbo, Murray H. (1987) *The Ixodid Ticks of Uganda*, Entomological Society of America, College Park, Md.

Novelli, Bruno (1988), *Aspects of Karimojong Ethnosociology*, Museum Combonianum, Verona

Oliver, R. & Fage, J.D. (1962) *A Short History of Africa*, Penguin Books Ltd, Harmondsworth, Middlesex.

Pakenham, Thomas. (1991) *The Scramble for Africa*, George Weidenfeld & Nicolson, U.K.

Pazzaglia, Augusto (1982) *The Karimojong, Some Aspects*, EMI, Bologna.

SOURCES

Soulsby, E.J.L. (1968) *Helminths, Arthropods and Protozoa of Domesticated Animals, 6th Ed*, Baillière Tindall & Cassel, London.

Thomas, Elizabeth Marshall. (1965) *Warrior Herdsmen*, Alfred A. Knopf, Inc. U.S.A.

Turnbull, Colin M. (1972) *The Mountain People*, Simon and Schuster, New York.

Walker, J.B., Mehlitz, D. & Jones, G.E. (1978) *Notes on the Ticks of Botswana*, GTZ, Eschborn, Germany

GLOSSARY

acaricide	En	A chemical used for the control of ticks
antibody	En	A substance circulating in the blood or other body tissues exerting a restrictive or destructive effect on foreign proteins, including those of bacteria, viruses, toxins, etc.
antigen	En	A substance, usually a molecule, which stimulates the formation of antibodies
askari	Sw	Soldier, policeman, guard
baraza	Sw	A public meeting; also a meeting place
boma	Sw	Any kind of structure for defensive purposes, usually related to a cattle enclosure or administrative headquarters
crush	En	A narrow defile of wood or steel to restrain cattle for vaccination or other purposes.
Ekapolon	Ak	A government appointed chief in charge of a Karamoja county
Katikiro	Lu	The Chief Minister of the government of Buganda
kuni	Sw	firewood
manyatta	Sw	A small settlement of living quarters and livestock pens surrounded by a common defensive stockade of brushwood
mashua	Sw	A small fishing dhow

GLOSSARY

mzungu	Sw	White person; pl. wazungu
nahoda	Sw	Boat captain
shamba	Sw	plantation, garden, plot of cultivated gound
shifta	?	Raiders with political and/or criminal objectives
uniport	En	An aluminium hut made in sections that are bolted together

Ak akarimojong
En English
Lu Luganda
Sw Swahili

INDEX

C

E

F

G

H

K

L

N

Q

R

S

T

U

Made in the USA
Middletown, DE
11 April 2018